Contents

FOOD SERVICE OPERATIONS

Other Hotel and Catering Texts available from the Publisher

People and the Hotel and Catering Industry—Andrew Lockwood and Peter Jones

Principles of Hotel and Catering Law—Alan Pannett

The Hotel Receptionist, Second Edition—Grace and Jane Paige

Book-keeping and Accounts for Hotel and Catering Studies—Grace and Jane Paige

Commodities for Caterers—E. H. Lingard and J. Sizer

Catering Costs and Control, Second Edition—Grace Paige

Food Service Operations

PETER JONES, BA, CERT. ED., MHCIMA
*Lecturer in Food and Beverage Service Systems,
Brighton Polytechnic*

HOLT, RINEHART AND WINSTON
LONDON · NEW YORK · SYDNEY · TORONTO

Holt, Rinehart and Winston Ltd: 1 St Anne's Road,
Eastbourne, East Sussex BN21 3UN

British Library Cataloguing in Publication Data

Jones, Peter L.M.
  Food service operations.
  1. Food service management
  I. Title
  647'.95'068   TX943

ISBN 0–03–910408–7

Typeset by Phoenix Photosetting, Chatham
Printed in Great Britain by Mackays of Chatham Ltd

Last digit is print number: 9 8 7 6 5 4

Acknowledgements

Acknowledgements go to the following organizations for their help and assistance:

Edward Arnold (Publishers); The Automatic Vending Association of Britain; Barrie & Jenkins; Brewers Society; Berkshire Department of Education; Blackie and Son; British Airways; British Home Stores; British Railways Board; Caterer & Hotelkeeper; Charterhouse School; Catering and Hotel Management; Cornell H.RA. Quarterly; Department of Health and Social Security; The Design Council; Dickens Inn; Education; Europa Hotel; Fast Food; Ferranti; Gardner Merchant; Glass Manufacturers' Federation; Grand Metropolitan Hotels; Grandmet Catering Services; Grant & Cork (Sheffield); Happy Eater; Heinemann; Holt, Rinehart and Winston; Hotel and Catering Review; HMSO; Hotel, Catering and Institutional Management Association; Hotel and Catering Industry Training Board; Hotel Piccadilly; Huckleberry's; IPC Business Press; International Textbook; Kaul Prever Harle Simoes; Lodging Hospitality; Luncheon Voucher Catering Educational Research Institute; MacLaren; McGraw-Hill; Management Today; Mintel Publications; Modern Railways; Northwood Publications; The Open University Press; Regethermic UK; Ring & Brymer; Routledge; Royal Doulton Tableware; Royal Surrey Hospital; Staff & Welfare Caterer; Somerset Education Authority; Times Newspapers; Travellers Fare; Trusthouse Forte; Walsgrave Hospital; Wiggens Teape (UK); Wimpy International; Wiley; Winterhalter Gastronom; Worplesdon Place Hotel; University of Surrey; and to any other company, publication or organization who has contributed to the writing of this book in any way.

Sincere thanks also go to the following people without whom this book would not have been possible:

Doug Allen; Chris Bone; Mr B. T. Bowers; Jon Gillespie; A. E. Jones; Liz Jones; Mr David Lacey; Simon Lake; Mr P. McDougall; Wendy Lockwood; Liz Page; Trevor Perrott; Graham Russel; Guy M. Stevenson; Captain G. W. Stonehouse; Harry Sutherland; Clive Viner; and Graham Brice, for his long-distance encouragement.

For Catherine, Stella, Liz and Katie Jones

Preface

THIS book assumes that the reader will be familiar with the most common forms of food service used in the industry and have some prior knowledge of food and drink. It is designed for students following 707/2, BTEC, Higher BTEC and HCIMA courses and for those working in the catering industry whose eventual aim is restaurant or cafeteria management or some other management/supervisory position in food service operations.

The first part of the book is concerned with the different sectors of the industry. It provides a comprehensive breakdown of the industry, illustrating the alternative systems of food and drink provision to a wide-ranging clientele, an outline of personnel and staffing requirements within each sector, and evaluates the role of each sector within the catering industry and the British economy in general.

The food service industry in the UK is divided into eight sectors, namely hotel food service, restaurants, public-house catering, fast-food units, industrial catering, institutional catering, transport feeding and outside catering. This division is not arbitrary but an attempt to examine particular aspects of food service, and in many respects it is a classification that many caterers would accept as being identifiable in the industry. But the great danger with such a classification is that it will be accepted without question. The diversity of the industry inevitably means that there are some operations which cannot easily be classified into one sector or another, for example, public-house catering, takeaways and the role of automatic vending. At the same time, the distinction between one sector and another is blurred when the same firm operates units in more than one sector. Other queries might be: are restaurants in airport terminals in the popular sector or transport catering? Can a steak bar be classified as a fast-food operation? What sector includes banqueting? And so on.

In answer to these questions (for the purpose of this book) the industry's classification is meant to illustrate the *essential* feature of providing food and drink under particular circumstances. Each chapter has a subtitle which is the theme of the chapter. It attempts to put into a single sentence the features or problems of that sector which differentiates it from any other. For instance, the chapter on transport catering is subtitled 'The art of feeding people on the move', so that all restaurants and cafeterias at airports, on motorways or at railway stations are excluded, since the customer is not 'moving' in these circumstances and is being served using systems discussed elsewhere in the book. Thus transport catering is concerned with in-flight catering, railway catering and catering at sea. The reader is therefore advised to remember the subtitle of the chapter when reading through it, as it should provide the basis for what is discussed thereafter.

More specifically, the supervisory principles and skills demanded by each sector are identified in this first part of the book, as I believe that individuals who wish to pursue a career in food service must consider carefully their strengths and weaknesses and work in that sector of the industry to which they are most suited. I hope that the reader will be made fully aware of the fact that there is no such thing as a 'typical' food service outlet and that equally there is no certain answer to the problem of how to make a unit successful. The diversity of the industry is extraordinary and success depends heavily upon understanding and implementing the *essential* operational features or 'system' of a particular style of service. Even so, a great deal still depends upon the flair of the person in charge and on luck. The purpose of this book is to help the reader to develop the knowledge, skill and flair required to be successful and thereby minimizes the effect that chance and fortune may have on operational success.

The second part of the book is directed towards this purpose, since it introduces the reader in particular to those aspects of the operation that the successful operator must consider, irrespective of whichever sector he or she is working in, but essentially 'front of house operations'. It deals, therefore, with questions such as why people choose to eat out, how to attract customers, how to arrange restaurant and function seating, what equipment is required for different types of operation, how to select and train staff, how to control stock and handle cash or credit cards and what legal and statutory obligations impinge upon the food service operator.

Since the underlying theme of the book is the application of supervisory principles in food service operations, I have included in each chapter tasks and activities that are designed to illustrate or involve the reader in one or more of the functions of *planning, organizing, directing, co-ordinating* and *controlling*. These activities are reinforced with case studies illustrating the application of systems, techniques and ideas in the industry itself. The reader is reminded that a case study shows how *one* operator or firm approached a particular activity and these studies do not necessarily show the only nor even the best approach to that activity. Each chapter is also outlined in the form of objectives so that readers can clearly see what knowledge and concepts they should have acquired after reading the chapter and questions at the end of each chapter are designed to test this understanding.

Finally, a word about the career opportunities in the food service industry. This immediately involves problems of nomenclature, since depending on which sector of the industry the reader may wish to work in, different job titles are used for persons in responsible positions. Furthermore, it is possible that although one's career begins in a supervisory capacity, the eventual career development will be as a manager. There is also a tendency in the industry to call an employee a manager when in fact the person is really only a supervisor. For example, in hotels the restaurant manager is more often than not a supervisory position, likewise assistant management posts in many other sectors involve the application of supervisory skills rather than those of management. Having said that, the catering industry probably more than any other industry has no clearly defined demarcation between its white-collar and blue-collar workers and it is still possible for someone to start at the bottom of the ladder and work their way to the top. It is for this reason that the book may be read by people without college qualifications, who hope to go on to more senior positions. College leavers will find that despite following a course of study for two or three years, they will be expected to begin their career, if not at an operative level, most certainly at the level of a trainee or assistant supervisor/manager. Both types of reader must recognize that the industry regards *experience* as the most essential requirement for its supervisory or management personnel.

PART ONE
SECTORS OF THE FOOD SERVICE INDUSTRY

1 The Food Service Industry

The undertaking of the supply (whether for profit or not) of food or drink

OBJECTIVES: to define the food service industry . . . to outline the development of the industry in the UK . . . to identify the component sectors of the food service industry . . . to describe the contribution of the food service industry to the economy of Britain.

1.1 INTRODUCTION

In order to discuss the food service industry in some depth, it is first necessary to define the industry. However, to the best of my knowledge nobody has yet attempted to do so in the UK, primarily because food service is seen as a part of the hotel and catering industry as a whole. This assumption was perfectly reasonable 40 years ago, when with a few exceptions, the main establishments serving meals were hotels, liners and inns. However, since 1945, the entire complexion of hotelkeeping and catering has changed with the development of institutional and industrial catering, the growth of the 'popular' catering sector and in recent years, the boom in fast food. Thus there is now a very real need to separate the provision of accommodation from the provision of food and drink in order to appraise and evaluate the food service industry in its own right.

1.2 WHAT IS FOOD SERVICE?

The simple definition of food service is the provision of food and drink ready for consumption away from the home. This, however, fails to differentiate the food service industry from the retailing industry—a distinction that is becoming increasingly difficult to identify in view of the growth in takeaway 'restaurants' and fast-food outlets. Professor S. Medlik (in *Profile of the Hotel and Catering Industry* (1978) London: Heinemann) recognized this problem and defined a catering establishment in these terms:

1. The goods sold are usually consumed on the premises.
2. The buyer is able to determine the quantity of the goods purchased in a retail shop, but in a catering unit the caterer determines quantity, i.e., portion size.
3. The caterer also determines quality as in most cases the customer orders the meal without seeing it before the order is placed.
4. The caterer is a processor of materials as well as a retailer of goods.
5. In general, the caterer holds less stock and there is a shorter time between receipt of raw materials to point of sale than most retailers.

This brings us on to the question as to the distinction between food service and food production. In this respect too, the distinction that was clearly identifiable in Escoffier's time is no longer so obvious today. In many operations such as cafeterias, fast-food and tray-serve systems, the same staff are responsible for preparing and serving the food. There is likewise a growing trend of allowing the customer into the kitchen by designing open-plan operations. In many ways, the development of food-production techniques and systems has probably had more impact on the way in which people are served than have new ideas about food service systems.

1.3 FOOD PRODUCTION SYSTEMS

In order to clarify this point before we begin to examine each sector in depth, it is necessary to identify and describe the four major food production systems. Four systems can be identified (see Fig. 1.1).

Conventional or traditional

The customer's food is prepared on the same site as it is to be eaten, using mainly raw or semi-prepared products, such as pre-portioned meat, frozen vegetables and so on. This system is to be found typically in the hotel and restaurant sectors of the industry.

Commissary

This system has food prepared in a central kitchen, probably using conventional methods; service, however, takes place on several different sites. This system may be used in the industrial or institutional sector and is of particular significance in outside catering.

Ready-prepared food service system

This is the cook–chill or cook–freeze system whereby foods are prepared in bulk to be served at a later time, either on the same site or in several different locations. It is the

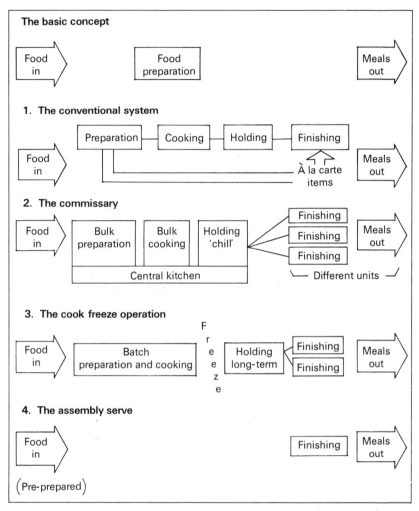

Figure 1.1 *Food production systems.*

system adopted by in-flight airline caterers, but may also be used in the industrial or institutional sectors.

Assembly serve

In this instance foods are purchased pre-prepared from the food-processing industry and reconstituted in the premises. Such foods are typically frozen or of the boil-in-the-bag type. This system is successfully used in the fast-food industry, although almost any other sector of the industry could adopt such a system.

This analysis is implicitly based on the development of food production systems over the last 40 years and although certain sectors of the industry can quite clearly be identified with one particular system, there is no reason why this should be so. It may well be that economic restraints and technological advances will result in *all* sectors of the industry moving away from the more conventional systems towards less labour-intensive systems. There is no reason to suppose that hotels and restaurants might not adopt assembly-serve production methods. Indeed, if such methods were sophisticated enough, the customer could be quite unaware of how the food has been prepared, for the establishment could continue to *serve* the food in their traditional manner.

While recognizing that in discussing food service one cannot ignore food production, the prime concern of this book is not how the food is prepared but how it is served.

1.4 TYPES OF FOOD SERVICE

To clarify this point as to what part of the catering operation can be described as 'food service', look at Fig. 1.2 which represents the food service 'system'. It outlines those activities involved in operating a restaurant and although it is still a very generalized picture, it neatly illustrates those factors that are the prime concern of this book. For want of a better expression, they are 'front-of-house' activities or the activities that arise from *establishing contact between the customer and the product.*

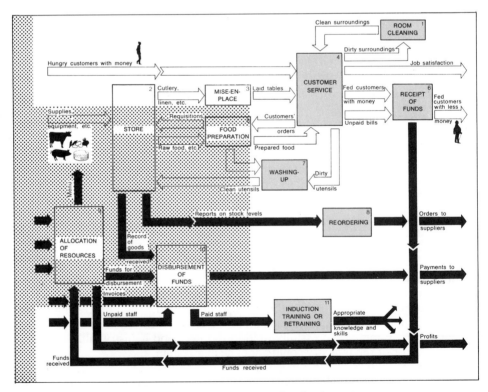

Figure 1.2 *Food service system (reproduced with permission).*

This brings us to another important question—how is food served to the customer? Dennis Lillicrap (in *Food and Beverage Service* (1971) London: Edward Arnold) identifies nine styles or types of service. *Gueridon*, the preparation and service of food from a trolley placed next to the customer's table. *Full silver*, the service of foods presented on flats by staff using service implements, e.g. spoon and fork. *Plate/silver*, some food is plated (usually the meat) and some items are silver served (the vegetables). *Plate*, all food is presented and served on the plate. *Family*, dishes are placed on the table on hotplates for customers to serve themselves. *Counter (or cafeteria)*, the customer selects his own food by passing along a counter display. *Snack bar*, the service of light meals and refreshments from behind a counter. *French*, a style of service similar to family, also using a gueridon. *Russian*, a service style based around the service of large joints from a sideboard.

Of these, the last two—French and Russian styles—are hardly used at all in the industry today. Likewise, cafeteria service developed during the 1970s with several variations designed to increase throughput such as free-flow, scramble and carousel systems. In addition, we must also consider *buffet service*, the presentation and service of food from behind a buffet table; *tray systems*, meals are assembled on trays and transported in containers to the consumer; *trolley service*, food and drink is served from a trolley to the customer; *automatic vending*, food and drinks are served to the customer by a machine.

1.5 CLASSIFICATION OF RESTAURANT TYPES

In the same way that food-production systems can be broadly identified with sectors of the industry, so food service styles can be broadly categorized with certain types of operation. For instance, gueridon service is found in top-class restaurants, tray systems are employed in hospitals, counter service in department stores and so on. It is of course incorrect to assume that food service only takes place in a 'restaurant', since a survey of food service sectors must include hospital wards, student refectories, takeaway food shops and trolleys. Nonetheless, it is important to attempt to classify different types of restaurant operations in order to fully understand the industry. The following sections examine the various ways in which this classification may be made.

Based on the service style

While this is fairly easy to identify and is relevant to the caterer, it fails to include many significant factors that are equally relevant to understanding the operation—notably the style of menu, the price charged for the product, staffing requirements, size and scale of the operation, and so on.

The Spectrum

This analysis, carried out in the USA, is meant to include some of these significant factors. It assumes that the three most important variables are menu, service style and price. Its purpose is to define restaurant categories in today's hybrid market so that in theory, there should be room for at least one of each type of restaurant, since they each appeal to a different market segment. Eleven types of restaurant are defined:

take away
snack stand
limited menu, low price, self-service
limited menu, low moderate price, self-service
limited menu, moderate price, service
full menu, low moderate price, service
full menu, low moderate price, self-service
full menu, moderate price, service
full menu, moderate high price, service
luxury menu, high price, continental (gueridon) service
social caterer

Task 1.1

For each of the eleven categories give one or two examples found in the UK. The major problem with this classification is that although it could be applied to the UK, as yet no data have been compiled here on this basis.

In the USA the Spectrum study yielded some interesting information. Over 55 per cent of sales were in operations with a full menu, so that speciality restaurants (like McDonald's) are tending in the USA to extend their menus to provide greater appeal. Second, over 60 per cent of sales are made in operations that provide service as opposed to self-service. This contradicts slightly the third point, that nearly 70 per cent of the market is through low- or moderately low-priced outlets.

THE IMPACT OF US IDEAS

This does not refer to the introduction of US 'cuisine' (hamburgers, fried chicken or exotic ice creams) which is related to the main and more important trend, but to the significant influence over the last 20 years of US ideas and techniques on the British food service industry. These ideas and techniques are not only applicable to US foodstuffs—for example, fast-food techniques have revolutionized the traditional British fish and chip shop. Neither is there necessarily anything wrong with this trend; after all, the foundations of the catering industry were laid down on ideas imported from France.

The extent of US influence is, however, quite staggering:

the Ganymede tray system for food service in hospitals was developed in the USA;
the development of the popular catering sector of the industry was significantly influenced by three British operations based on US ideas—Kentucky Pancake Houses, Wimpy bars and Golden Egg restaurants;
the nationwide chains of roadside restaurants (notably Little Chef and Happy Eater) were developed from a US prototype;

the largest growing sector of the industry, fast food, is based firmly on US practices;

coffee shops and grill rooms in hotels originated in the USA; and so on.

What is important about this trend, however, is not so much what has happened in the past, but what is likely to happen in the future if it continues.

There are four types of operation found in the USA that are not yet very common in Britain. They are:

1. *Home-delivery meals*—this type of operation is a development from the takeaway, but instead of customers having to visit the shop in person, all they need to do is telephone their order and the meal will be delivered to their home. At the moment the only similar operations in this country are the meals-on-wheels service provided by local authorities and the delivery of meals to offices by outside caterers.

2. *Drive-ins*—these have been slow to develop in the UK partly due to its different climate and car size. Nonetheless, Rank opened the first roadside 'drive-up' fast-food facility on the A1 near Darlington in 1981.

3. *Electronic cafeteria*—this is a completely automated restaurant where customers are sold chilled or frozen meals which are reheated in microwave ovens. This too is seen in some institutions in this country, notably in hospitals which provide reheat facilities for chilled meals for night-shift workers.

4. *Robot serve*—a recent report in an American journal records that a fully automated counter-service restaurant was opened in 1980 by Burgerworld in Ontario. Customers sit at a U-shaped counter and order their meal from a console on the counter top. The prepared meal is sent up on a lift and an automated arm transfers the tray to the correct position on the counter. These robot arms have coloured flashing lights which are interchangeable so that the customer does not become bored by seeing the same 'waiter' serve every day!

A Restaurant Typology

Also developed in the USA, this attempts to analyse restaurant types using completely different criteria, namely the sophistication of the system and the system's innovativeness. The classification is shown in Fig. 1.3.

Task 1.2

Redraw Fig. 1.3 so as to exclude those restaurants that are typical of the USA and include restaurants found in the UK. For instance, replace 'shopping-mall restaurant' with 'department-store cafeteria'.

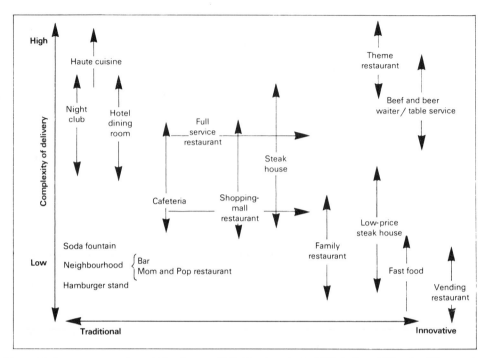

Figure 1.3 *A restaurant typology. (After Powers, T. F. 'Food service in 1985', in* Cornell Hotel and Restaurant Administration).

Wages Council definition

For the purpose of establishing a minimum statutory wage, the Catering Wages Council has defined a 'licensed restaurant' as follows: 'any place which is used either regularly or occasionally, as, or for the purposes of, a restaurant, dining room, café or similar place at which it is lawful to sell intoxicating liquor for consumption on the premises.' In effect, therefore, this definition is based upon the licensing requirements of catering establishments in this country and takes no account of any other operational feature. It also defines 'catering contracting businesses', 'industrial or staff canteen undertakings', and 'central catering establishments'. These definitions too are of interest but of little use as they break down the industry only by the criterion of employment levels in those sectors as defined by the Council.

Standard Industrial Classification

The SIC was begun in 1948 in an attempt to provide uniform statistical records of industrial growth and activity. It defines the hotel and catering industry, under the 1968 classification, as 'Establishments (whether or not licensed for the sale of intoxicating liquors) providing meals, light refreshments, drink or accommodation.' The classification is shown in Table 1.1.

There are, however, problems with the SIC approach, notably in the area of industrial catering. The classification only includes those operations undertaken by specialist

Table 1.1 *Structure of the hotel and catering industry.*

SIC activity	Section	Number of units 1975	Employees 1980
6611	Eating places providing food for consumption on the premises	35 000 (11 000 licensed)	172 000
6612	Takeaway food shops	10 000 (fish and chip shops)	
6620	Public houses and bars	62–73 000	257 000
6630	Night clubs and licensed clubs	30 000 plus	114 000
6640	Canteens and messes 1. Contractors 2. Others	5000 (200 organizations)	64 000
6650	Hotel trade	34 000 (500 000 bedrooms)	233 000
6670	Other tourism and short-stay accommodation 1. Camping and caravans 2. Holiday camps 3. Other	 1 million plus beds 150 000 plus beds n/a	

Source: Medlik, S. & D. W. Airey (1978) *Profile of the Hotel and Catering Industry*, London: Heinemann.

catering contractors; and the turnover and employment of staff in units operated by business firms is measured under the main activity of the firm. For instance, both BP and ICI run their own catering operations, but this would not be included under SIC activity 6640. For this reason, it is useful to have another source of information concerning the industry.

NEDC reports

The National Economic Development Committee for the hotel and catering industry is now defunct, but at the time that it was running, it classified catering establishments as follows.

Takeaways: units providing cooked meals for consumption off the premises, e.g. Chinese takeaways, fish and chip shops, etc. *Public houses and pub restaurants*: establishments with a full on-licence. *Store restaurants*: operations providing food and refreshment in the large retail department stores, such as Debenhams, British Home Stores, or Army and Navy. *Cafés and snack bars*: the popular catering sectors of the market. *Hotels and restaurants. Place of work*: the provision of food and refreshment in offices, factories and so on. *Educational and hospital*: the institutional or welfare sector.

Drawing on all these sources and, in particular, the government sources, this book breaks down the industry into the following sectors.

Hotel food service operations.
Restaurants (both speciality and popular catering).
Public-house catering.
Fast food.
Industrial catering.
Institutional catering.
Transport catering.
Outside catering.

1.6 DEVELOPMENT OF THE INDUSTRY

The impetus to the growth of hotels, and subsequently the food service industry, was provided by the railways. The profitable companies began to invest in large comfortable hotels generally located near the main railway stations, and by 1902 there were 70 major hotels owned and controlled by them. This stimulated hotel building by other companies in city centres and at seaside resorts, and the result was a transformation from relatively poor culinary standards of the old coaching inns to the highest and most sophisticated standards of cuisine. The lead was taken by Doyly Carte, who brought over Cesar Ritz, and the man whom Ritz himself described as 'certainly the best chef in the world, he surpasses all the other chefs I have ever met'—Georges Escoffier. Escoffier was responsible for creating many classical dishes, perfecting the partie system and influencing greatly the organization of kitchen practice. Eating out in such establishments was, at that time, very formal. Customers were expected to wear evening dress and women were seldom seen in public restaurants. Ritz was largely responsible for breaking down this formality and grill rooms 'emerged from the desire of American tourists to avoid the dining ceremonial each night.'*

At the other end of the scale, two companies emerged to provide eating out of a better quality for the masses—the Aerated Bread Co. and J. Lyons. Their immediate popularity was due largely to women, who could not frequent taverns or fashionable restaurants unless escorted. Although they began as tea shops, they began to serve more substantial meals and to establish national chains of restaurants around the country. What is more significant is the fact that they were far more profitable businesses than the hotels.

The development of the motor car revitalized a sector of the hospitality industry that had declined during the railway age, namely smaller hotels and inns. Many such establishments had become public houses, selling only alcoholic beverages and neglecting the provision of food or accommodation. By 1900, the public house sector had been considerably affected by government legislation during the nineteenth century, such as the Sale of Food and Drugs Act 1875 and numerous licensing Acts. The restriction on the number of licences issued had the direct result of influencing the brewers to invest in the retail trade and in effect cause the start of the tied-house system. The growing influence of large brewing companies also led to a gradual transition from the old tavern and ale house into the splendid Victorian public house. None the less, standards of public house operations were not immediately improved by the expanding brewing companies who effectively kept new entrants out and forced low profit margins upon their tenants, as a result of which beer in particular was often adulterated or diluted. So bad was this state of affairs that Earl Grey began the Public House Trust Company in 1903, which was to become Trust Houses. The Company bought up free houses and redeveloped the art of innkeeping by offering commission to the company's managers on the sale of food and accommodation but not on liquor sales. The motor car ensured that Trust Houses and other burgeoning hotel companies were to become very successful.

The First World War interrupted the development of the industry and severely limited food service in particular, due to the imposition of restrictions, regulations and towards the end of the war, rationing. The greatest impact was in the field of industrial

---

* Taylor, D. (1977) *Fortune, Fame and Folly*, London: IPC Business Press.

catering, which hitherto had been virtually non-existent. Feeding millions of service personnel and eventually the whole population compelled the Government to consider a nation's dietary requirements. This led to the Government pressing employers to recognize the importance of adequate nutrition for the workers. By the end of the war, the number of industrial canteens had increased tenfold to nearly 1000, supplying nearly a million meals a day. It is sad to reflect that immediately after the war, the industry failed to maintain these catering facilities so that it was not until the emergence of the Welfare State and the effect of another world war that industrial feeding developed more fully.

Another effect of the First World War was to raise the expectations of the population. This is not to say that *haute cuisine* was introduced to the general public: although popular catering in the ABC and Lyons style became smarter and more hygienic, it remained basically simple fare—'for the masses it was tea shops during the year and the landlady's cooking at the seaside on holiday'.* So in the 1930s a new type of catering establishment emerged in this sector. Between 1935 and 1937, nearly 100 milk bars opened up around the country and although they originally only sold milk products and ice creams, many of them moved into the main stream of popular catering.

Despite the Depression years of the 1930s, over all the inter-war years were good ones for the food service industry. After rationing ended, there was a growth amongst all except the lowest social class in the popularity of eating out. Restaurant sales were boosted by the Licensing Act of 1921, which allowed drinks to be served after 11 p.m. if accompanying meals. London, or at least, Soho, saw the growth in Chinese and Indian restaurants, so that for the first time there was an alternative to the expensive French cuisine of top-class establishments or the British fare of the popular catering units. Slowly too, the more enlightened employers were recognizing the value of canteens and their contribution to job satisfaction and productivity. Public houses built in the period were more spacious and more comfortable than ever before, while rural inns found they were increasingly popular with cyclists and motorists. An increasing number of roadside hotels began to concentrate on providing good and well-cooked food, with a reasonably good wine list. Finally, for the first time in peacetime, the Government began to concern itself with the nutritional needs of the population and the foundation of school meals was laid by the introduction in 1934 of the 'Milk in Schools Scheme'.

In many respects, the impact of the Second World War was similar to that which had ended only twenty years previously, except that business was further devastated by the destruction due to bombing, as well as the disruption caused by rationing food and requisitioning premises. Thus, whilst the luxury hotel and restaurant trade declined, there was a tremendous increase in mass feeding. Professor Medlik writes that 'probably the most important development of the war was the emergence of communal feeding on an unprecedented scale', while 'industrial catering developed beyond recognition'. But unlike after the First World War, the expansion in these sectors did not decline at the end of the Second World War. The election of a Labour Government resulted in the development of institutional catering in schools and hospitals within the framework of the Welfare State, and the sheer number of industrial and staff canteens, some 25 000 by 1945, ensured that catering for employees would continue. From this, industrial catering contractors developed during the 1950s, such as Bateman's, Sutcliffe's and Midland.

---

* Taylor, D. & D. Bush (1974) *The Golden Age of British Hotels*, London: Northwood.

The fact that people were now being catered for at work introduced many to the eating-out experience for the first time. Furthermore, the 1950s and 1960s saw a real improvement in living standards and a narrowing of the gap between the expenditure of the richest and the poorest sections of the population. At the same time, the working week gradually became shorter with a consequent increase in leisure time and holidays. The availability of cheap mass travel abroad has widened the horizons of most Britons and dietary trends show that we drink more milk and coffee and consume more poultry, eggs, vegetables and fruit than before 1939. This does not mean that everyone can afford the luxury of an extensive à la carte menu served in sophisticated surroundings.

Frank Berni recognized the need for the simpler meal experience in a pleasant atmosphere and developed the concept of a steak house, which filled a gap in the market between public houses and popular catering units. This latter sector has always had to keep pace with the changing tastes of the public and developments in the industry. Since the milk bars of the 1930s, there have been innumerable variations on the popular catering theme—Kardomah cafés, Golden Eggs, Wimpy Bars and espresso coffee shops—and the last in this long line of changing images and products is the fast-food operation. Speciality restaurants too have expanded, due to the growth of our multiracial society and membership of the EEC, so that in large cities and towns the national cuisine of many European and Far Eastern countries may be experienced. As Taylor and Bush say—'changes in the last 30 years have indeed been immense, whichever facet of catering one examines' (*The Golden Age of British Hotels*).

1.7 THE INDUSTRY TODAY

It is estimated that nearly 4.5 billion meals occur in this country every year, and it is reckoned that over 23 million people eat out in a week. One recent survey of the catering industry was conducted in 1980 by Market Intelligence (Mintel). This showed that in 1979 the catering market had a total turnover of £8 200 million (excluding institutional caterers). Although this is almost double the turnover in 1974, this increase can be accounted for by inflation and the industry as a whole has not shown any real growth over the last five years. Breaking this down into sectors, Mintel estimated turnover as in Table 1.2.

Table 1.2 *Turnover derived from food and non-alcoholic drink sales 1979.*

Establishment	£m at retail selling price
Licensed hotels	388
Holiday camps	12
Restaurants and cafés	1175
Fish and chip shops	190
Public houses	544
Canteens	330

Source: Mintel Publications.

The number of outlets in the catering industry is shown in Table 1.3.

Table 1.3 *Catering outlets (excluding institutions) 1979.*

Outlet		Per cent
Cafés, snack bars	16 000	10
Restaurants	13 600	8.5
Fish and chip shops	10 500	6.5
Other takeaways	5 000	3
Hotels	9 000	6.5
Public houses	71 000	43.5
Clubs	30 000	19
Others	5 000	3
	160 100	100

In addition to these sectors, the institutional sector has a considerable turnover as shown in Table 1.4.

Table 1.4 *Number of meals served 1979.*

Type of institution	Meals served
School meals	1 101.3 million
National Health Service (including meals on wheels)	600 million
Penal institutions	125 million

1.8 ORGANIZATIONS IN THE FOOD SERVICE INDUSTRY

In looking at the industry, we can identify a large number and variety of organizations, many of them quite small. The growth of such organizations is a result of the following factors.
1. The structure of the industry which continues to have very many small, individually owned units, in spite of the growth of large companies.
2. The industry is heterogeneous—split up into many different, identifiable sectors, each with its own specific needs.
3. Geographically, the industry is widespread, with some types of operation concentrated around population centres, although this is not essential for all types.
4. The industry is a very large employer and offers a wide range of job opportunities and employment categories.

There are broadly two types of organization: voluntary ones, and government and statutory bodies.

Voluntary organizations for individuals

Hotel, Catering and Institutional Management Association

This is the professional body for the mainstream of the industry. Its membership exceeded 20 000 in 1981 and comprised fellows, members, licentiates, students and associates. The Association sees its main priority as establishing recognition of the Association in order to influence developments in the industry and to provide better job opportunities for its members. In this respect, it provides advisory services for members, maintains a central library, publishes a monthly magazine called *Hospitality*, and employs officers specializing in employment, careers and technical aspects. The HCIMA is also closely involved in discussions concerning catering education at all levels and runs its own full-time and part-time courses leading to Association membership, which is recognized as a management qualification. Its address is 191 Trinity Road, London SW17 7HN.

Guild of Sommeliers

This is the 'Craftsman's Guild of Wine Butlers of the United Kingdom'. The Guild was inaugurated in 1953 with the primary object of promoting a wider interest in the knowledge and proper service of wine and to improve the professional status of sommelier. There are four grades of membership and all receive the Guild's monthly journal called the *Wine Butler*. The Guild's address is 5 Kings House, Kennet Wharf Lane, Upper Thames Street, London EC4V 3BA.

United Kingdom Bartenders' Guild

This is an organization for bar personnel which in many ways resembles the Guild of Sommeliers. It too wishes to promote the excellence of its profession by sponsoring events, publishing material and so on. Its address is 70 Brewer Street, London W1R 3PJ.

Other bodies exist such as the Licensed Victuallers' Association, the Hospital Caterers' Association and the Catering Managers' Association which promote social events mainly on a local basis and encourage professional practice.

Voluntary organizations by sector

British Hotels, Restaurants and Caterers' Association

This is a typical trade association—a 'voluntary, non-profit-making body formed by independent firms to protect and advance their common interests.' In order to do this, it has a strong Parliamentary lobby, discusses legislation affecting the industry with Government Departments, offers advice on recruitment and training of staff, and provides information services to its members through publications or from its specialists. Its address is 13 Cork Street, London W1X 2BH.

Brewers' Society

This too is a trade association involved in sponsoring scientific research into brewing, improving trading relations, discussing with Government changes in licensing law, which resulted from the Monopolies Commission report, and liaising with other national and international brewing organizations. Of particular interest is the

Society's annual reports on trends in the sale and consumption of alcoholic beverages in the UK.

Government and statutory bodies

Hotel and Catering Industry Training Board

The Industrial Training Act 1964 intended to ensure a trained workforce, secure an improvement in the quality and efficiency of industrial training and share the cost of training more evenly among firms. To this purpose, Industrial Training Boards were set up, including (in 1966) the HCITB. It is now funded by a levy of the 1500 or so largest employers, as defined by the size of their payroll. Those employers who systematically meet their own training needs are exempt from the levy, while the money over is spent as specific grants to encourage training in particular areas or as key grants to the smaller, non-leviable employers. It operates mainly by training on-the-job instructors within the firms themselves, by providing regional training centres to undertake specific training of personnel and by offering advice and aid through their staff of training advisors.

Following the Employment and Training Act 1973, the Manpower Services Commission was set up in order to 'assist people to select, train for, attain and retain suitable employment and to assist employers to obtain suitable employees.' The MSC was made responsible for the ITBs. Since then, the Conservative Government has questioned the role of the MSC and closed many of the ITBs. It seems likely, however, that the HCITB will continue to play a part for some years to come and meet some of the high priorities it set in 1979. These priorities included:

Offering a range of courses for women which will prepare them for employment in those areas in which they have been traditionally under-represented.

Improving awareness and understanding of job opportunities in the industry.

Running development programmes for training specialists in the industry.

Promoting the diagnostic approach to supervisory training.

Making available the new range of specific skills training and encouraging colleges and employers to run qualifying courses.

British Tourist Authority

Although predominantly concerned with the development and promotion of tourism in Britain, the British Tourist Authority has had an impact on food service through the regional Tourist Boards and campaigns such as the Taste of England. Probably the greatest impact has been the opportunity that the Boards have offered to independent hoteliers and restaurateurs to publicize and advertise their establishments. Some caterers and hoteliers, however, regard the Board's spending of funds as too 'up-market' and their operation as too bureaucratic. This partly arises from the funding of the Boards which is predominantly from the Department of Trade and Industry—for instance, in 1978–1979 the English Tourist Board received £5 014 000 from the Department. The industry also reacted with hostility to the recommendation of the English Tourist Board that hotels and restaurants should be registered and graded under an official scheme.

Catering Wages Councils

In the 1940s, the Government sought to help workers in low-paid industries by setting up Wages Councils which would stipulate and enforce minimum wage levels and conditions of service. The Catering Wages Act 1943 led to the setting up of Catering Wages Boards which eventually became the Wages Council following the Wages Councils Act 1959. Although less broadly based than the original Boards, the Wages Councils now concerned with the catering industry are:
1.   Licensed non-residential.
2.   Licensed residential and licensed restaurant.
3.   Unlicensed place of refreshment.
The Councils have been criticized over a long period of time both by employers and employees. Certainly the statutory minimum remunerations that they have set are lower than the wage levels of many other industries, and indeed lower than what many larger companies in fact pay. At the same time, the Council's surveys show that nearly 20 per cent of catering establishments are actually paying *less* than the statutory minimum.

1.9 FUTURE OF THE INDUSTRY

The catering industry has always been a risky venture for the entrepreneur and today, even in public sector catering, the outlook is bleak. The economic recession has reinforced the industry's trend to remain static, even though the proportion of household expenditure on meals bought away from home has increased (see Table 1.5). This suggests that the average family may be eating out more often but that it is slowly changing its eating habits by moving away from traditional, speciality restaurants towards

Table 1.5 *Meals bought away from home as a percentage of all consumer expenditure per family per week.*

Year	Per cent
1975	3.4
1976	3.4
1977	3.6
1978	3.7
1979	3.8

Source: *Family Expenditure Survey,* London: HMSO.

snack-type meals in pubs or fast-food restaurants. The most buoyant sector appears to be fast food, although as we shall see, it too has seen some companies pull out of the market. Takeaway outlets too appear to be in a healthy position, helped by the fact that takeaway food is exempt from VAT. The Mintel 1980 survey* estimated that both these areas will experience an annual growth of between 5 per cent and 10 per

---

* *Market Intelligence Report: Catering* (1980) London: Mintel.

cent in real terms over the next few years, with the growth gradually slowing down as the market becomes saturated with outlets. This growth is resulting in a decline in other sectors—notably fish and chip shops which have been unable to compete with the more modern takeaways. In the 1970s, nearly 20 per cent of the 12 000 such outlets closed down. Likewise hotels and restaurants are experiencing a decline, the former due to falling demand for accommodation (particularly in London) and the latter due to the impact of fast food. The Mintel 1980 survey said that the restaurant chains will fare better than independent operators. This is reflected in the trend for breweries to standardize their restaurant operations by introducing national or regional themes to their pubs, rather than allowing their tenants to develop their own food service operations.

2 Food Service Operations in Hotels

The art of making a facility for residential guests into a profitable food service operation

---

OBJECTIVES: to describe the organization of food and beverage operations in hotels . . . to outline the alternative styles of hotel restaurants . . . to identify the operational features of gueridon, silver, plate and buffet service styles . . . to understand the operation of room service in hotels . . . to understand the planning and operation of functions and banquets.

A hotel is a factory producing goods as surely as tinned pears come off a conveyor belt, but it is a special sort of product, vanishing like the fairies when dawn breaks and the room was not let, the restaurant table empty, the bar stool unoccupied.

Taylor, D. & D. Bush (1974) *The Golden Age of British Hotels*, London: Northwood

2.1 INTRODUCTION

As we have seen in the last chapter, good cooking was brought to Britain by the great chefs and hoteliers who came from the Continent to work in the grand hotels of Britain. For a long time the only place where one could eat in style was in a hotel and during their heyday these hotel restaurants were very successful, although not necessarily very profitable. Hotel restaurants were usually the loss leader designed to entice the clients to book bedrooms. Restaurants acted as positive attractions and in assessing profit and loss many genuine costs were ignored or forgotten in hotels. But with the increase in the growth of speciality restaurants, the narrowing of the gap between rich and poor and the increase in travel for business rather than for pleasure, hotels have increasingly become a facility for accommodation rather than for dining in. The image of many hotel restaurants was old-fashioned and uninspiring by the 1960s, and the early 1970s saw a conscious effort by hoteliers to improve this image, typified

the unit is serving. This will ensure that the essential operational features of the coffee shop or floor service, for example, are recognized and maintained. After all, a hotel does not need to have three or four different types of restaurant, if all its clients' needs are the same.

2.4 RESTAURANT OPERATIONS

Gueridon

This style of service was developed during the Edwardian era and is symptomatic of the Edwardians' gastronomic indulgence. A gueridon is a table or trolley placed beside the customer's table at which the waiter prepares, fillets, carves and sometimes cooks the dishes to be served. This style of service is flamboyant and emphasizes the personal attention and service that a customer receives. It is also associated with menu dishes that are of the highest quality, and very expensive, being based on classical French cuisine. For this reason, gueridon service is restricted to restaurants catering for a market that is prepared to pay the high prices that must be charged to cover operating costs. High costs are due to several factors: (1) the service is labour intensive requiring a *chef de rang* and *commis de rang* to serve an average 10 to 12 customers; (2) staff must be trained extensively and paid a salary commensurate with their high level of technical skill; (3) fewer customers can be seated in a restaurant operating gueridon service than other styles of service due to the need for space to move trolleys around the room; and (4) this style of service requires relatively greater capital expenditure in equipment than other styles of service, which due to the expectation of clientele is usually in silver plate.

Silver service

This is the 'standard' style of service found in very many hotels and restaurants. Food is presented on flats or in dishes to the customer and then served by the waiting staff onto the plate. It is remarkable that it has remained common for so long, but it is interesting to note that the evolution of *nouvelle cuisine* has resulted in plate and family service being introduced in its stead. Silver service originated because food is traditionally served on silver flats to enhance the appearance and maintain the temperature of the food and it provides the customer with a degree of 'service'. It is becoming out-dated because the economic necessity of using stainless steel instead of silver has removed one of the main attractions of '*silver*' service'. If food can be presented attractively on the plate from the kitchen then the need for service equipment, dishes and flats is reduced, along with capital investment and operating costs. Also, silver-service waiting staff require a level of skill and consequent training that simpler food service methods eliminate.

Plate-service restaurants

Typically, plate service is found in the coffee shop—an American concept introduced into hotels during the 1960s. The operation is usually open from early morning until

SIDEBOARDS

Many styles of food service operation require the use of a sideboard or service stand. The food service supervisor must check that these are laid up correctly at the beginning of the service period to ensure that the waiting staff may operate smoothly without hold-ups. Most operators have a standard way of laying up the sideboard because:

1. it is easy for the supervisor or the staff to identify if any item is missing:
2. staff become familiar with the layout which speeds up mise-en-place and sideboard operation;
3. any member of staff can go to any sideboard and easily locate an item without needing to search for it;
4. the layout of the sideboard should minimize the amount of bending and lifting of equipment during service; and
5. the standard set-up should satisfy the hygiene requirements.

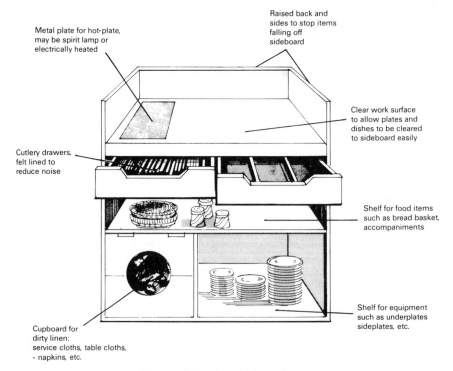

Figure 2.3 *Standard sideboard layout.*

late at night serving breakfast, morning coffee, lunch, afternoon tea and supper. In some cases there are different menus for each of these meal periods but more often than not one menu is in use throughout the day. The service style is table service or plate service, with all dishes portioned and plated in the kitchen. This development occurred in order to: (1) reduce the operating costs of conventional silver service restaurants by introducing plate service, which increases the number of customers served per member of staff by up to 60 per cent, eliminates the capital investment in service equipment and reduces the floor space per customer by up to one-third; (2) provide a meal and beverage facility that serves throughout the working day to guests travelling from abroad who may arrive from different time zones and require full meals at unusual times: (3) modernize the image of hotel restaurants by introducing a more contemporary and relaxed atmosphere, and meeting the growing demand for snack meals rather than traditional three- or four-course meals; and (4) to meet the growing demands of the American tourist market and the youth market.

Case study 2.1   Post House, Reading

Many of the Post House chain of hotels have both a traditional restaurant and a coffee-shop operation (often called the Buttery). The approach of Trusthouse Forte to the management of these units illustrates the different role that the two types of restaurant perform in the modern hotel. At the Reading Post House, there is the Icarus restaurant and the Romany Coffee Shop.

Icarus restaurant	Romany Coffee Shop
Number of covers	
80, usually operated on the basis of one waiter to a station of 20.	80, usually operated on the basis of three stations.
Opening times	
12.30 p.m. to 2.30 p.m. for lunch, 7.00 p.m. to 10.30 p.m. for dinner.	7.30 a.m. to 10.30 p.m., i.e. open all day.
Covers served per day	
Breakfast nil Lunch 70 Dinner 100	Breakfast 160 Lunch 80 Dinner 150
Style of service	
Silver service, with some flambé dishes prepared at table.	Plate service
Average amount spent per customer	
Not available	£3.60 on food and 50 pence on drink.
Number of staff	
Restaurant manager and/or head waiter, four waiters, wine waiter and cashier.	Buttery supervisor, cashier and three waiting staff (at main meal times).
Staff working hours	
Mainly split shifts on a five-day week.	Straight shifts, either 7.00 a.m. to 4.00 p.m. or 3.00 p.m. to 11.00 p.m., also on a five-day week.
Labour market	
Predominantly male waiting staff with previous experience in silver-service restaurants and recruited from a fairly wide catchment area.	Predominantly female staff, with little or no experience, who are trained on-the-job, and recruited locally.

TO START

Appetisers

Prawn Cocktail £1.65
Freshly Squeezed Orange Juice 95p
Half a Melon in Season £1.50
with stem ginger
Coarse Country Pate 95p
in an individual terrine

From the Soup Kettle

Minestrone 75p   Tomato Soup 75p
with freshly grated parmesan   laced with cream

SNACKS

Sandwiches

Open Prawn and Egg £1.95
served on wholemeal bread
Glazed Welsh Rarebit £1.75
with crispy bacon

Farmhouse Platter £2.95

two fried eggs with two rashers of smoked
back bacon, fried mushrooms, sausage,
grilled tomato and fried bread

Pasta & Omelettes

Lasagne £2.80
Spinach pasta layered with meat sauce, and
glazed with cheese sauce
A SELECTION OF THREE EGG OMELETTES
served with french fries
Prawn £2.50
Cheese and Ham £2.50
Plain £1.95

Hamburgers

– with special relish tray
Cheese and Bacon Burger £2.85
6oz pure beefburger with molten cheese
on a toasted sesame bun
topped with two back
rashers of smoked bacon.
Served with
french fries

Burger Stack £2.85
6oz pure beefburger, double stacked on a toasted
sesame bun with bacon and onion. Served with
french fries
Delicious with our special mixed salad 95p

MAIN DISHES

Cold Salad Platters

Florida Salad £2.75
Fresh orange and grapefruit segments set with
cottage cheese on a bed of
crisp lettuce with apple

Chicken Elizabeth £3.50
Breast of chicken masked with a creamed curry
mayonnaise, topped with toasted almonds, and
served with a bowl of mixed salad.

Fried English Calf's Liver
with Bacon £3.95
served with french fries

Grilled Gammon with
Spiced Fresh Pineapple £4.65
10 oz uncooked weight,
served with french fries

Grilled Whole Plaice £3.95
(1lb uncooked weight) with tartare sauce, lemon
and french fries

Deep Fried Scampi and Scallops £4.85
(10oz uncooked weight) served with tartare
sauce, lemon and french fries

Sirloin Steak £4.85
(7 oz uncooked weight) prime steak grilled,
served with french fries

SIDE ORDERS

Our Special Mixed Salad 95p
Dressings:
Lemon,
Blue Cheese,
Thousand Island,
Vinaigrette
French Fries 45p
Grilled Mushrooms 55p
Buttered Peas 45p

Coffee Shop Steak Platter

Grilled Sirloin Steak £6.95
(10oz uncooked weight)
French fries, special mixed salad
Sherry Trifle
or the Cheeseboard

ICE CREAM · SWEETS & PASTRIES

Ice Cream Specials

Three Flavour Ice Cream Boat 75p
Fresh Pineapple Dipper £1.25
tutti frutti and vanilla ice cream with
sliced fresh pineapple masked
with crushed raspberries and
topped with fresh cream
and nut brittle
Banana Split £1.15
banana with strawberry
and vanilla ice creams
with chocolate sauce
topped with
whipped cream
and hazelnuts

Sweets and Pastries

Blackcurrant Cheesecake 75p
Sherry Trifle 75p
Double Time
Chocolate Gateau £1.15
Frangipane Apple Flan 75p
with whipped cream
Fresh Fruit Salad 95p

CHEESEBOARD

85p
Mature English Cheddar, Country Stilton,
Camembert served with Bath Olivers

Figure 2.4 *Trusthouse Forte coffee-shop menu.*

Menu compilation

Left to the discretion of the chef and the management team of the unit and approved by the district manager. The menu will change approximately every three months and will tend to reflect local and regional themes.

The coffee shop menu is standard for all such operations throughout the Trusthouse Forte group. It is compiled, priced, designed and printed centrally.

Sales and marketing

There are no major differences in the media used or investment in sales and marketing for either of the units. Whether a promotion or advertising campaign is aimed at increasing sales in the restaurant or coffee shop will depend upon the circumstances and the market segment at which it is aimed. The hotel has used local radio, local weekly and evening papers, leaflets, and so on to effect sales, and regularly promotes speciality evenings, food festivals and children's menus.

Task 2.1

Outline the effect that using plate service in the coffee shop has had upon the operation and staffing structure of that unit when compared with the silver-service restaurant.

Figure 2.5 *Icarus restaurant menu.*

Carvery

A carvery-style operation is not a new idea, restaurants were operated in this way in the early part of this century. The basic concept is that roast joints form the basis of the menu. These are carved in the room and customers serve themselves from the carvery counter, selecting whichever meat and vegetables or salad they choose. The name 'Carvery' is in fact the registered brand-name of restaurants operated in this way by the Joe Lyons organization and other firms have had to find other names to describe their operations, such as 'The Chef's Table'.

The typical carvery menu comprises a three-course table d'hôte menu, with a selection of five or six starters, three or four roast meats and possibly one or two alternative main courses, and a selection of sweets. Waiting staff take the customer's order and are responsible for serving the first and third course, and coffee if required, while the customer is served at the carvery counter by a 'trancheur' or 'carver', who is usually dressed in chef's whites. The counter may be a straight line or bow-shaped and consists of boards for carving, hot cupboards or overhead heat lamps and bains-marie for vegetables. Sauces and accompaniments may either be served at the table by waiting staff or customers may help themselves at the carvery counter. The advantages of this style of operation are:

1. The presentation and carving of meats and food items in the restaurant is a promotional tool and enhances sales.
2. Many carvery operations allow customers to select as much as they wish for an all-inclusive price which promotes a sense of value for money in the customer.
3. The menu requires a smaller kitchen area and fewer kitchen staff to prepare the dishes, as little or no cooking to order is done during the service period.
4. Since there is an element of self-service, fewer waiting staff are required for a carvery than in a traditionally organized restaurant.

For the carvery supervisor or manager, there are specific potential problem areas:

1. The policy of allowing the customers to help themselves to as much as they wish makes control and pricing very difficult. Many such operations have abandoned this policy by either stating on the menu the portion size or using portable carving trolleys with the trancheur serving customers at the table, rather like gueridon service.
2. Since joints are pre-cooked, close control of the appearance and palatability must be exercised, and unused meats must be reused in rechauffé dishes or in cold meat salads to reduce waste.

Case study 2.2   Regent Palace Hotel carvery

The carvery at the Regent Palace Hotel in London is typical of many carvery operations and certainly those operated by Trusthouse Forte hotels since there is a standard menu throughout the group (see Fig. 2.6). Thus at the Regent Palace, since all their foodstuffs are purchased through Trusthouse Forte Supplies, the joints that they serve on their carvery will be of the same specification and quality as those served elsewhere. However, the catering manager selects and serves the choice of vegetables and salads that accompany the roast, and also determines the items to be found on the sweet trolley. The menu is priced at £7.75 which is the standard price for carveries in

Figure 2.6 *Trusthouse Forte carvery menu.*

London and the unit operates on about 55 per cent gross profit. This is lower than the average gross profit percentage for the hotel of about 65 per cent, but is accounted for by the carvery's policy of allowing customers to help themselves to as much as they like.

The unit is open every day from 12.00 to 2.30 p.m. and 5.15 to 9.00 p.m. This is not typical but reflects the type of custom that the carvery attracts; at lunchtime, trade is fairly regular and is predominantly business people, whereas in the evening, custom is derived from residents, pre-theatre diners and business people, and it is particularly busy at weekends. There are 112 covers in total, operated by eight waiting staff with their own stations, each serving 14 covers. The unit is managed by a senior supervisor, who reports directly to the deputy catering manager, and she is assisted by two or three assistant supervisors. In view of the set price for the meal, nearly every customer spends approximately the same; the lunchtime average spent is around £9 and it is slightly less in the evening. In an average week the unit serves over 1600 covers, so that the weekly turnover is between £11 500 and £13 800.

Apart from their restaurant (or restaurants), many hotels also provide room service, lounge service and banqueting facilities.

2.5 LOUNGE AND ROOM SERVICE

Lounge service

This type of service is now only provided in four- and five-star hotels or in those hotels where there is no coffee shop. The main food and beverage items served in the lounge are morning coffee and afternoon tea. These are served in the lounge, partly for guests' comfort and partly because the hotel restaurant needs to be cleaned and prepared between each meal service. Lounge service also provides for the service of alcoholic drinks to residents at times when the hotel's bar must close to comply with the licensing laws. Nonetheless, lounge service is labour-intensive and demand is erratic, which accounts for its decline. Nowadays it is common for a member of the restaurant staff to be rostered on lounge duties.

Room service

Room service must be provided in those hotels who wish to attain a four- or five-star rating, but like lounge service, room service is expensive to operate and demand is uncertain. Many hotels have replaced some room service facilities with vending machines, such as in-room cocktail bars (as at the London Hilton) or soft-drinks vending machines and shoe-cleaning facilities in corridors (as in the Post House chain of hotels). To comply with the licensing law that only residents and their bona fide guests may purchase alcoholic drinks throughout the 24 hours of a day, they must be sited in the guest's room or designed only to operate for residents, i.e. using a special key. For those hotels that continue to provide traditional room service, breakfast is the meal that most guests choose to eat in their rooms. To simplify the service, hotels have encouraged the trend towards continental breakfasts, either by making continental breakfasts inclusive in the room tariff and charging extra for a full English breakfast or by making the latter only available in the hotel's restaurant or coffee shop.
    There are two basic systems for providing service in a guest's room.

Floor pantry system

Floor waiters are based on each floor or every second or third floor and operate from a service pantry. The pantry is stocked with the goods and equipment necessary to provide beverages and snack-type meals for those rooms that the pantry has to service. Any dishes or drinks unavailable in the pantry are collected from the main kitchens or dispense bar as required. The main advantages of this system are two-fold:

1. Waiters should be able to respond quickly to a request since they are located close to the rooms.
2. A customer who uses room service a great deal can achieve some rapport with the floor waiter responsible and feel a greater sense of well-being from the personal attention.

There are, however, several disadvantages with the system:

1. Demand is erratic, peaking at breakfast time and in the early and late evening, so that extra staff must be employed at peak periods.
2. A hotel with ten floors may employ five room-service staff, one for every two floors. If several guests on the same floor require service, one waiter is rushed and provides poor service, while others are doing nothing.
3. A waiter stationed in a floor pantry at times of slack demand feels isolated and lacks job satisfaction.
4. Control of materials, foodstuffs and beverages is made more difficult by having several service points and stock-taking also takes longer.
5. Ordering by guests is made difficult. Either they telephone the floor pantry directly, in which case they may be unable to place an order if the waiter is busy, or they telephone the switchboard or reception to order, from where it is relayed to the floor waiter, which is time-consuming and places extra strain on telephonists and receptionists.

Centralized floor service

To overcome most of those problems identified above, many hotels operate a central floor service, from which all floor waiters operate. As each order is telephoned into room service, the floor waiters serve the orders in turn, irrespective of the floor the orders come from. This type of service is possible using high-speed lifts. The advantages of a centralized system are:

1. Fewer staff are required to provide a comprehensive service, especially during off-peak periods.
2. Control is made easier since the central point is usually located close to the main kitchen.
3. Equipment stock levels are lower, since it is not necessary to equip individual floor pantries with beverage-making facilities, etc.
4. Valuable and expensive floor space is saved on each floor that may be better used for revenue making.
5. The room-service telephone is staffed 24 hours a day by a member of the team.
6. Job satisfaction is enhanced by working as a member of a team and by sharing out the work load equitably between the waiters.

Case study 2.3   Europa Hotel floor service

The Europa Hotel in London is a four-star hotel with 275 rooms. The maximum occupancy is about 440 guests and in 1982 the occupancy rate was running at 85 per cent. As one of the criteria for achieving four-star status the hotel must provide 24-hour room service, and Fig. 2.7 shows the food and beverage items available. Previously all the items on the hotel's à la carte menu had been served in the guest's room, but an analysis in 1981 showed that only a small proportion of certain dishes were ever ordered, so that the floor-service menu was revised to include the most popular items from the à la carte menu, plus some snack items from the hotel's coffee shop. In fact, out of a weekly turnover of around £5000, food and drink sales were only responsible for 30 per cent of the total at around £750 for both. The bulk of sales were derived from breakfasts, with a continental breakfast priced at £3.25 and English breakfast at £5.75, since breakfast is not included in the hotel's tariff.

Figure 2.7 *Floor service menu (Europa Hotel).*

The organization of the floor-service department reflects this demand (Fig. 2.8). The service is carried out from a central floor-service pantry on the first floor that the customer can contact directly by dialling 7 on the telephone. The pantry comprises a cash desk, wash-up facility and storage space for equipment, still room, small dispense bar and breakfast kitchen. Thus for breakfast service, the unit is self-contained, while for other food items during the day, the dishes must be collected from the restaurant or coffee shop kitchen. The staffing structure emphasizes the importance of breakfast service.

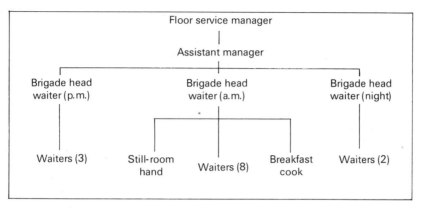

Figure 2.8 *Organization of the floor-service department.*

All staff work eight-hour shifts as follows:

Morning (a.m.) shift   7.00 to 3.00
Afternoon (p.m.) shift   3.00 to 11.00
Night shift   11.00 to 7.00

In addition to the full-time staff, there is an order taker employed from 7.00 a.m. to 11.00 a.m. In addition to their floor service function, the staff are also responsible for serving all food and beverage items in two small banqueting suites located on the first floor, near to the pantry; while the night floor-service waiters, between 1.00 a.m. and 7.00 a.m. are responsible for the service of items in the hotel's lounge.

Floor service uses a Lamson Paragon checking system, in conjunction with a Hoskyns computer-linked terminal. When guests place an order, it is written out on a triplicate check; the bottom, yellow copy is retained in the sealed machine and sent to the control office, the pink copy is sent to the dispensing department (i.e. floor service itself, restaurant or coffee shop kitchens) and the top copy is presented to the customer. Guests can choose to pay, in which case as a cash sale, it is paid into reception at the end of the shift, or they can sign the bill. In the latter case, the transaction is recorded on guests' bills via the computer terminal. The computer link means that floor service sales can be billed to guests' accounts within seconds of them receiving the items, which is essential when so many guests have breakfast in their rooms just before checking out. In order to control closely the movement of liquor stocks, day and night shifts have separate stocks and regular stock-takes monitor sales.

2.6 BANQUETING

Banquets, conferences, wedding receptions and dinner dances are an important source of revenue for most hotels. But it would be a mistake to believe that the hotel sector exclusively carries out function catering—outside caterers, banqueting houses, institutional and industrial caterers are other types of catering business involved in the 'banquet' trade. Nowadays banqueting is rather an old-fashioned term, being superseded by 'function catering'. Functions vary in size from small private parties for 10 or

12 people up to large affairs for 1000 or 1200 people; they may be family celebrations, social events or business functions; the meal may be lunch, dinner or wedding break-fast; and the dishes may range from only canapés, as at a cocktail party, up to those to be found in a six- or seven-course menu. This diversity means that each function is different and must be approached individually, taking particular note of the function organizer's particular requirements. To enable the caterer to do this, details of each function are usually entered on a function form or banqueting memorandum (see Fig. 2.9). The advantages of using a function form are:

1. A well-planned form ensures that the caterer discusses all the essential points with the function organizer.
2. It may be used as a contract between caterer and organizer.
3. It can be circulated to all relevant departments of the hotel or establishment so that all staff are informed about the function.

Task 2.2

Identify those departments in a hotel that should receive a copy of the banqueting memorandum shown in Fig. 2.9.

Banqueting personnel

The staffing of the banqueting department of a hotel will depend on many factors: the size of the banqueting rooms, time of year, popularity of the hotel, availability of staff, management philosophy and so on. Broadly speaking a distinction can be made between hotels that have a banqueting manager and full-time staff and hotels that do not. Obviously the larger and more popular the banqueting facilities, the greater the likelihood that full-time personnel will be employed. The advantages of establishing one member of the management team as banqueting manager responsible for func-tions are as follows.

1. All enquiries by customers are dealt with by one person, which should ensure no double bookings.
2. The customer appreciates the personal attention of the same manager from the first enquiry through to the day of the function itself and beyond.
3. The co-ordination and control of functions is simplified if made the responsibility of one person.
4. In groups of hotels, liaison with a central sales office is made easier if one manager is made responsible for selling and organizing functions in each hotel.
5. Normally the banqueting manager works the hours that his or her job demands without being expected to take a turn as duty manager.

The number of full-time staff working will also vary from unit to unit. However, due to the seasonal nature of function catering and the tendency for demand to peak on Wednesdays, Fridays and Saturdays, it is likely that many banqueting staff will work on a part-time basis.

Part-time workers are more cost effective as they are paid only when they are required, National Insurance contributions paid by the employer are less than for full-time staff, and rates of pay may be lower for part-timers. Although staff may be

```
┌─────────────────────────────────────────────────────────────────────────────┐
│                         FUNCTION INSTRUCTION SHEET                            │
│                                                                               │
│   NO BANQUET IS TO BE ACCEPTED WITHOUT PRIOR APPROVAL OF BANQUET MANAGER      │
```

Type of Function: *Wedding Reception*	Day & Date: *Saturday 19 February*
Contact: *Mrs. L. Mowforth*	Room: *Florae*
Phone: Bus. *1234567* Res. *888//////*	From: *3.30 p.m.* To: *6.00 p.m.* Charge: £

Organisation: No. of Persons: *120*

Address: *20 Clogthorpe Grove, Hull.*

Account to: *Mrs L. Mowforth*	Arrival Time: *3.30*
Address: *as above*	Deposit Rec'd: £ *200* Cr.

Instructions for Billing:

ALCOHOLIC BEVERAGES & TOBACCO		FOOD	Time Served: *4.00*
Reception: *Sherry only*		*120* @ £ *5.50* per person.	
Bar: *Cash bar*			
With Meal:		*Finger buffet menu "C"*	
Wine: *20 x Moet et Chandon with speeches*			
After Meal:			
Extension:			
Tobacco:			
Accommodation Req'd:		Special Requirements:	
Changing Rooms: *1 Twin 4.55 — 5.30*			

Cloakroom:	Photographer:		
Band:	Entertainment:		
Meal for Band, etc:	Time:	Coffee at @ p.p.	
Decorations & Novelties:		Tea *120* at *5.45* @ *50p* p.p.	

Flowers:	Toastmaster:	Meal for Toastmaster:
Candelabra:	Cake:	Stand & Knife: *Yes*
Table Plan: *Yes*	Place Cards: *Yes*	Menus: *Yes*
Table Covering, Linen & Napkins: *White Linen*		

Figure 2.9 *Function form or banqueting memorandum.*

employed on a casual basis, the hotel wherever possible will employ the same casual staff regularly since they may be trained up to the standards required by the caterer and they are familiar with the layout of the banqueting rooms and service areas. The number of service staff required for a particular function will depend upon the style of service (see below).

Function planning

Although we have stressed the individual nature of every function, the hotel management attempts as far as possible to pre-plan functions in several ways. First, clients are provided with a selection of menus to choose from. The advantages to the caterer of this are that:

1. Pre-designed menus can be given a great deal of thought by the caterer to ensure that the principles of good menu planning are adhered to. Function organizers with little catering experience may select dishes that they themselves like, without considering the impact that these dishes may have upon the meal as a whole.
2. Menus that are planned in advance enable the banqueting manager to quote a price to the customer immediately, since they are pre-costed. The cost of a menu determined by the customer has to be calculated from scratch.
3. Menus can be designed which accommodate the availability of both kitchen equipment and service equipment, without placing unnecessary strain upon the stocks of plates, cutlery, pans, etc.
4. The quality of food served is likely to be higher if the kitchen staff are preparing dishes that they are familiar with and have prepared often.

The dangers of pre-planned menus are:

1. They may not be flexible enough to cater for the wide range of demand from customers.
2. They may be too stereotyped and lacking in originality.
3. They may be unresponsive to changes in the conditions of supply of goods and commodities, especially fresh meat, fish and vegetables.
4. They may reduce job satisfaction due to staff having to prepare and serve the same dishes repetitively.

For these reasons, it is wise for banquet menus to be changed every two or three months and both banquet and kitchen personnel should be involved in their compilation.

The second element of planning is applied to seating and table plans for functions. The guidelines which are discussed in Chapter 12 indicate the space requirements of different styles of table, but in most cases all the possible seating arrangements of a particular function room will be well-established from constant use. An old-fashioned way of calculating the varying numbers of covers that could be served in a banqueting room is by the following formula:

$$\text{Maximum number of possible covers} = \text{length of room (metres)} \times \text{width (metres)} \times \tfrac{2}{3}$$

but this varies enormously depending on the type of seating, service style, whether there is a dance floor required or not, so that the banqueting formula can only be taken as a very rough guide. It is also not very accurate for small rooms. The two main table arrangements for functions are formal (top table with sprigs) and informal (rows of round tables) (see pages 181 and 182).

The third element of planning is ensuring the proper number of staff are available and fully briefed before the start of the function, especially if they are casual staff. The briefing should include details such as the location of guest and staff toilets, the table or station each waiter is to serve, the menu and details of each dish, the order of service, who to see if a guest requests something unexpected and so on.

Case study 2.4   Hotel Piccadilly

The extent to which menus and seating plans are pre-planned can be seen in the package from the Hotel Piccadilly, Manchester (Figs. 2.10–2.12).

Styles of service

Different service styles are adopted because of the diversity of functions. Broadly speaking these service styles are:

1. Silver service.
2. Family service.
3. Plate service.
4. Buffet service.

Each of these service styles is discussed elsewhere and are listed here in decreasing order of staffing requirements. The choice of which particular style of service to use will depend upon:

1. How much the customer is prepared to pay.
2. The availability and expertise of the service staff.
3. The size of the function room in relation to the number of guests to be served.
4. The nature of the menu items selected.
5. The time of year, since cold dishes rather than hot tend to be served from buffets and are therefore more appropriate for the summer months.

Buffet service

A buffet can be defined as a refreshment bar and the original style of buffet for a hotel or restaurant was a counter stocked with cold drinks, beers, wine, hot beverages, tobacco, pastries, cakes, sandwiches, and ice cream. Today, of course, such a buffet is more likely to be found at a railway station than in a hotel or restaurant (see snack service Chapter 5). Buffet service in the modern restaurant refers to the presentation of a wide selection of dishes on a buffet table or counter from which customers help themselves. It is a style of service particularly suitable for banquet catering or catering for guests staying on demi-pension or full-board terms, since the all-inclusive price can be calculated to allow the guests the freedom to select their own meals. The type of dishes served tend to be salad items, although there is no reason why hot dishes cannot be served. If they are, however, equipment such as plate warmers and hot-plates must be made available to keep the food hot and more service staff will be needed to help the guest with the service.

The main advantage to the caterer of adopting this style of catering is that it greatly reduces the number of staff required for the meal service, while a neatly laid out buffet presents the food in an attractive and spectacular way. It is not a service style that is appropriate for formal occasions.

Important points to consider in operating a buffet are as follows. In order to accommodate the food for a large number, the buffet table may need to be quite long, in which case it may be advisable to either have two separate service points or to split the buffet in two identical sections so that guests may start at either end of the table. Dishes and flats must be replenished as soon as they are empty and where necessary redressed to maintain an attractive presentation. Staff must be available behind the buffet to advise the guest and help with their selection. Thought must be given to presenting the dishes on the buffet in a colourful and appetizing manner. There must be an adequate supply of plates and service equipment, and finally the buffet table should not be placed near to a radiator or in direct sunlight.

Figure 2.10 *Conferences and banquets sales package (Hotel Piccadilly).*

There are, however, problems with buffet service that must be recognized and dealt with. Wastage may occur if the quantities of each dish are not estimated accurately in advance. This is made difficult by the variety of dishes presented, so that predicting accurately which dishes will prove most popular is made more difficult. The type of

Figure 2.11 *Function menus (Hotel Piccadilly).*

food suitable for buffet service is perishable, and the method of presentation at normal room temperatures will tend to hasten the rate of spoilage. Suitable buffet dishes tend to be highly priced: cold joints of meat, dressings relying on oil, and so on. In addition, to present the food as attractively as possible, the decoration of the dishes will increase both food and labour cost. The preparation of a good buffet is a skilled job, making difficult demands upon the expertise of the kitchen staff; and furthermore, by placing a buffet in a room the seating capacity is reduced, and thus revenue also is potentially lost.

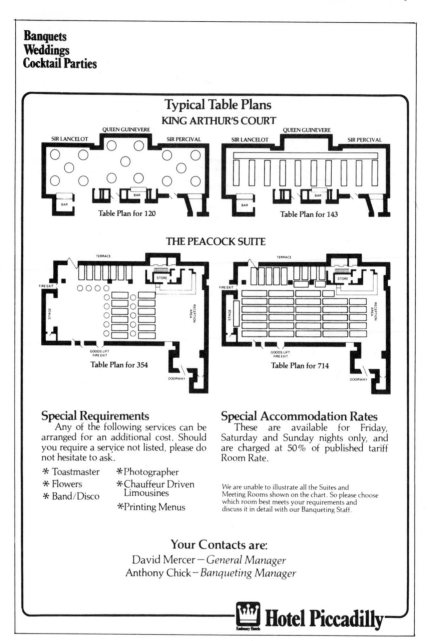

Figure 2.12 *Function table plans (Hotel Piccadilly).*

2.7 CONCLUSION

The food service manager in a hotel has a wide range of service styles and operations to deal with. Each of them has its special problem and the manager must be familiar with all the different needs and requirements. It is hoped that the case studies have illustrated this, but it is important to remember the customer's view of eating in a hotel (see Chapter 10). Each of the three areas will have a different clientele. In the restaurants, the customers will either be residents or non-residents. For many years, the residential diner was regarded as the cornerstone of hotel restaurants. Today, however, the hotel cannot rely upon residents to provide them with the turnover required to operate a successful restaurant. Thus the hotel's restaurant must compete, in its own right, with other food service operations found locally. Thus, the larger hotels have a selection of restaurants, to compete with the variety of restaurants found in any main street—an upmarket, speciality restaurant, a coffee shop or fast-food operation, a grill-room or steakhouse-style restaurant and so on. Furthermore, to enhance this competitive stance, these restaurants have a strong base and are marketed with the aim of attracting customers who are non-residential.

The floor service customer has a different need. Any guests who require refreshment do so for reasons of thirst or hunger that need to be satisfied quickly and/or discreetly and their expectations are that the service will be prompt and as good as they might get in the hotel's bar or restaurant. Finally, the guest at a function or banquet is there because it is a special occasion, be it a social event or business meeting. Therefore, the essential qualities of a good banquet are a smooth running, efficient service, care to keep to the arranged schedule and food that is as good as that a customer in the hotel's restaurant might receive.

Exercise

Analyse the day-to-day activities of a food and beverage manager in a hotel and attempt to categorize them into the functions of planning, organizing, directing, co-ordinating and controlling.

3 Restaurants

The quintessential food service operation

OBJECTIVES: to discuss the various types of restaurant operation found in the UK . . . to evaluate the problems and operational procedures of this type of operation . . . to outline the size and scale of this sector of the industry . . . to identify the operational features of family service . . . to explain the role of franchising in the food service industry.

[The average British] customers can't tell the difference between well-cooked food and badly cooked food, they don't mind what is put before them, they don't object if one waiter does the work of six and they seldom dispute the price, however exorbitant . . .

Cooper, D. (1967) *The Bad Food Guide*, London: Routledge.

3.1 INTRODUCTION

THERE is no easy way to identify this sector as clearly as the hotel sector. A restaurant has been defined as an establishment where refreshments or meals may be obtained (*Oxford English Dictionary*) and as such many different types of establishment may be included: snack bars, cafés, speciality restaurants, popular catering units and so on. This chapter therefore attempts to bring together the main points concerning restaurant operations. It excludes from its survey two types of operation which are considered in the next two chapters, namely public-house catering and fast-food operations, both of which have particular operational features applicable only to them.

In many respects the difficulty in generalizing about this sector lies in the origin of restaurants. As Derek Taylor pointed out in *Fortune, Fame and Folly*, before the Second World War 'the most common route for restaurateurs was to acquire a following when acting as a head waiter elsewhere and then to set up their own shingle'. The famous Quaglinos restaurant was established in just this way. Thus restaurants tend to be owned and operated by individuals and individualists. There is no neat formula for opening and operating a successful establishment. That is not to say that some firms have attempted to do so, which has led to the development of the popular catering market. Such chains of restaurants depend for their success on mass appeal, so that two broad groups of restaurant can be identified, namely popular catering units and 'speciality' restaurants.

3.2 OPERATIONAL FEATURES

In a 1980 survey* of 680 establishments of all types, the commercial operation of speciality restaurants was investigated. Restaurants identified as selling French or Italian cuisine were the smallest of all the restaurant types surveyed—43 per cent served less than 50 covers per day and only 7 per cent recorded over 200 covers on average per day. This was a reflection on the average amount spent per head of £7.50 exclusive of VAT and service, which is considerably higher than the average for other sectors. 'Ethnic' restaurants (which include Indian and Chinese cuisine) had an average spend of around £3 per head, but a correspondingly higher turnover with 70 per cent of them having a turnover of 50 covers or more per day. One result of this is that French and Italian restaurateurs 'were shown to be more perturbed than anybody else about the effects of price increases—the feeling was that customers could not afford the higher prices and therefore trade would be cut'. On the other hand, it seems that the owners of ethnic restaurants reacted to increased costs by absorbing them and not passing them on to the customer, possibly reflecting the family ownership of such businesses.

There was also a significant difference in policy with regard to takeaway food sales. Only 15 per cent of French and Italian restaurants had some takeaway trade, and this only accounted for approximately 10 per cent of their sales. For 'ethnic' restaurants, however, takeaway sales were important—'over a quarter of Chinese and Indian restaurants got between 20 and 50 per cent of their business from takeaway meal purchases.' It seems that many caterers recognize that a change in service style, towards more self-service and takeaway operations, is one of the most significant developments in the industry.

3.3 SPECIALITY RESTAURANTS

Fifty years ago, there were only 20 companies which operated restaurants quoted on the Stock Exchange. Speciality restaurants in particular tend to be owned and operated either by individuals, families or as partnerships. This is reflected in the erratic development of this sector. Factors that have influenced the growth in speciality restaurants include:

---

* Gallup Survey in *Caterer & Hotelkeeper*, 19 June 1980.

1. Individualism—restaurateurs are strongly motivated by the desire to work for themselves. Running one's own restaurant satisfies needs for freedom of action, personal reward for hard work and contact with customers.
2. Ethnic origins—for many reasons, people from countries such as France, Italy, Spain, India, Pakistan, China and so on, have come to live in this country. Many of them have a catering background and the relative ease with which businesses can be set up in Britain has enabled them to set up their own catering operations with fairly modest amounts of capital.
3. Eating habits—ethnic restaurants have been encouraged by the changing eating habits of the British, who began travelling abroad in large numbers for the first time in the 1960s following the introduction of package holidays. The public is much less conservative in its tastes and there has been a general trend towards savoury and spicy foodstuffs.
4. Industrial catering—during and following the Second World War, firms took it upon themselves to begin catering for their employees. Many people who had only rarely eaten out, began to do so regularly at work. With the gradual rise in living standards, more and more people were willing to spend money on this.

In the restaurant sector the size of the business has a significant impact on the way in which the restaurant operates. There are three main types of business, but it is worth noting that 20 per cent of the total workforce in hotel and catering are self-employed.

Styles of operation

In view of the wide diversity, no clear service style can clearly be identified. Gueridon, silver and plate service are used throughout the industry and tend to reflect the sophistication and scale of the operation. However, there is one service style particularly suited to the provision of Indian and Chinese cuisine, and that is family service.

Family service

This style is ideal for use in restaurants serving Far Eastern cuisine. Eastern eating habits differ from the European concept of eating a sequence of courses, including a principal dish or main course. In India, for instance, food is traditionally served on a large tray or that containing different dishes and accompaniments, and people help themselves to small amounts from one dish at a time, although there is no hard and fast rule for the order in which food should be eaten. Likewise, in China every bowl, from a wide selection, is available to all diners and they serve themselves from each dish with chopsticks. Thus, in opening restaurants in Britain, Indian and Chinese restaurateurs have adapted their service style to meet Western demands, in a similar way to their adaptation of their cuisine to Western tastes. Family service is the service of food in dishes, from which customers are expected to help themselves as they are placed on the table. Apart from maintaining links with tradition, the style of service requires fewer staff than silver or gueridon service would require; and also less training in service skills is necessary. The key element to the success of such operations is ensuring that the temperature of the food is maintained. This means that the kitchen must serve very hot food into heated dishes, customers must be supplied with hot plates (which should always be the case in all types of service where customers are eating hot meals) and that

FORMS OF BUSINESS ENTERPRISE

There are three main forms of business enterprise in the private sector of Britain's economy:

Sole trader, a business owned and controlled by one person. Many small hotels, restaurants, guest houses, free houses and outside catering businesses are likely to be operated by sole traders. Under the Registration of Business Names Act 1916 any person carrying on a business under a name other than his or her own must register with the Registrar of Business Names, display a certificate of registration at the principal place of business and print the true name of the trader and nationality if not British on all literature, catalogues, letterheads, circulars and so on. Thus for instance, a restaurant operating under the trade name *Mario's* or *Joe's Cafe* must comply with the above.

Partnership, 'the relation which subsists between persons carrying on a business in common with a view of profit', as defined by s. 1 of the Partnership Act 1890. A partnership is usually formed in order to establish better resources (assets, finance or staffing) than one person could provide. It, too, is subject to the Registration of Business Names Act, as well as the Partnership Act 1890 and the Companies Acts 1948, 1967, 1980 and 1981. The Partnership Act outlines the rights of partners if they have not been modified formally by a partnership agreement. These basic rights are the right to: participate in the business; share equally in any profits or losses; prevent admission of new partners; examine the books whenever he or she wishes; and receive interest on loans in excess of agreed subscribed capital.

The Companies Acts limit the number of partners to a maximum of 20, otherwise the business must register as a company.

Limited companies, although there are other forms of company, limited companies are by far the most significant form of large-scale business enterprise to be found in the catering industry. There are two kinds of limited company:

1. *Private companies.* These are usually small businesses that were formerly sole traders or partnerships, but that have now expanded and need the protection of limited liability. This refers to the fact that shareholders' liability for any debts incurred by the firm is limited to the nominal amount of the shares they hold. For a private company, the transfer of shares is restricted, the maximum number of shareholders is 50 and shares are not quoted publicly.

2. *Public companies.* These firms are free to advertise their shares to the public in order to raise capital and these shares are freely transfer-able. Some of the larger firms in the industry are such companies—Trusthouse Forte PLC, Grand Metropolitan PLC, etc.

Task 3.1
Consider the advantages of operating a business as a sole trader com-pared with a limited liability company.

the dishes are kept hot by lamps or hotplates placed on the table. The caterer may also find that disposable table linen is preferable, as in serving themselves, the customer may not be as efficient as a waiter and spillages often occur.

3.4 POPULAR CATERING

This sector of the industry was established nearly 100 years ago when ABC and Lyons tea shops first opened. Popular catering units are usually part of a chain operation, relying on relatively low profit margins and high turnover to stay in business. It is fair to say that customers select this type of establishment more from necessity or conveni-ence than to entertain or 'dine out', and in many respects this is what differentiates popular catering from speciality restaurants. In order to achieve the necessary turn-over, popular catering units are sited in two main areas: High Street locations to cater for shoppers, office workers and tourists (e.g. Wimpy, Golden Egg), and roadside locations to cater for motorists and the travelling public (e.g. Little Chef, Happy Eater).

Until the opening of the first McDonald's in Britain in 1975, these operations oper-ated table or plate service, or, in small snack-bar units, counter service. As the Wimpy case study shows, however, the High Street restaurants are finding it increasingly difficult to continue this style of service for several reasons:

1. The very large increases in High Street rents and rates have necessitated maximiz-ing the seating capacity of restaurants.
2. Table service does not necessarily have higher staffing costs than a comparable fast-food operation but the staffing cost per unit sale is lower due to the higher turnover of fast-food restaurants.
3. Customers' tastes have changed and effective marketing by the new operators has forced the traditional popular catering units to rethink their policies.

Roadside restaurants are less worried by the growth in fast food and will probably continue with table service because:

1. Site and investment costs are less than for High Street sites.
2. Operating costs are lower for sites drawing on local labour outside major towns and cities.
3. Customers stop to eat as a break from motoring and prefer to be served with fairly substantial meals rather than fast-food snacks.

Motorway catering

The first motorway service area was opened on the M1 at Newport Pagnell in 1960. An editorial in the *Daily Mirror* in the late 1970s stated that 'British Rail catering, on the way up, passed motorway cafes, on the way down, some time ago'* and certainly during that time motorway catering faced a great deal of criticism. In fact in 1978, the situation was so serious that the Government set up the Prior Commission to look into the whole question of motorway service areas. The report said that the service areas provide many things including petrol, breakdown/repair facilities, toilets, retail shopping, catering in a wide variety of units and even overnight accommodation. In view of this the operators of these services, however, have to face special problems that other caterers do not:

1. They are obliged to provide certain free facilities that have very high levels of usage (notably parking and toilets).
2. Service areas are often located in remote and isolated places so that staffing is very difficult, and staff cannot be employed as flexibly as demand would allow.
3. Trade fluctuates wildly through the year.
4. Under their contracts with the Department of Transport, they must provide catering 24 hours a day.
5. Despite insisting on coaches by appointment, unauthorized coach parties cost sites up to £150 000 per year due to vandalism.

At present there are 2500 km of motorway and 40 service areas throughout Britain. The major operators of these sites are Trusthouse Forte, Granada and Roadchef.

Case study 3.1   Granada motorway services

Granada operates 12 of the 39 available motorway service areas and would like to expand its network both on and off motorways. Granada was the first company to take advantage of the sale of leaseholds and purchased them in 1980 for £13.25 million. The company is organized both at head office and site level into three divisions (retail, petrol and catering) with each site being managed by a general manager. The catering division is the most profitable of the three, as well as being the most demanding in terms of operation and staffing. In 1982 the company started an image-building exercise which has included displaying their name more prominently on the motorway, introducing 'Country Kitchen' free-flow cafeterias, developing fast-food stores under the name 'Burger Express' and rationalizing the company's display materials and media throughout their sites.

The company conducts annual market research programmes and has found that a very high proportion of its customers are male adults, although the proportion of women and families increases substantially during summer months. Although trade fluctuates over the year an average site would be expected to turn over £6000 in a typical day shift, which represents 4000 customers. In contrast with this, the Carlisle site has had 190 fifty-seater coaches parked at the same time for lunch on the Saturday beginning Glasgow's holiday fortnight in July.

Granada finds that to cope with seasonal demand the staffing of their sites is

---

Quoted in *1879–1979: Food and Drink to Us* (1979) British Railways.

doubled between April and October, relying quite heavily on student labour. Toddington service area which is fairly typical of their sites, has the following catering facilities:

Northbound   Burger Express fast-food store
              400-seater Country Kitchen cafeteria
              Transport café and club for lorry drivers
Southbound   Burger Express fast-food store
              200-seater Country Kitchen cafeteria
              Transport café

Counter service

Counter service has been developed in units where customers have limited time available for their meal and are very often alone, e.g. airport terminals and motorway service areas. The system is not self-service but enables one waiter to serve a large number of customers per hour. The concept rests upon the concept of a series of bays or U-shaped counters (see Fig. 3.1), around which the customers sit, usually on stools. Each bay has a waiter to serve the customers sitting at the counter. Meals are usually plated and each bay is fully laid with all the equipment normally found on a sideboard, including cutlery, condiments and sauces, coffee-making machine and so on.

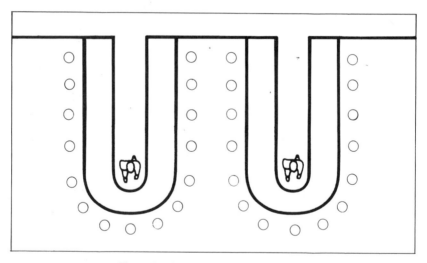

Figure 3.1 *Counter service with bar stools.*

Takeaway food sales

Counter service has also come to mean sales for consumption off the premises. The fast-food sector is obviously one that relies heavily upon sales from food that is taken away. However, it must be recognized that other types of restaurants have takeaway food sales. A survey* in 1981 of eight different types of unit showed that all of them

---

* *Caterer/Gallup Poll* 1981.

had some trade derived from such sales, even hotels. Out of a total sample of 741 units the results of the survey are shown in Table 3.1.

Table 3.1 *Takeaway food sales.*

Type of unit	Takeaway sales as a percentage of total sales
Pub—counter service	7.56
—restaurant/steak house	13.88
Restaurants—speciality	43.66
—English	16.60
—continental	15.75
—ethnic	40.24
Hotel restaurants	2.00

Thus the style of restaurant where takeaway sales are significant is fish and chip shops (not surprisingly) accounting for 89 per cent of all takeaway trade, and speciality and ethnic restaurants, where over 85 per cent of them serve takeaway food.

3.5 FRANCHISING

Franchising in Britain is a relatively recent import from the United States of America. Many types of business, including catering establishments, may be franchised, but the catering market is particularly suited to this form of operation. A franchise has been defined as a form of licensing under which an individual or company joins in partnership with an experienced organization for their mutual benefit. Such an agreement can be seen to extend advantages both to the franchisor (the organization granting the franchise) and the franchisee (the person buying the franchise). See Table 3.2.

Table 3.2 *Franchising's advantages.*

Advantages to franchisor	Advantages to franchisee
Enable franchisor to establish a chain of restaurants with relatively small amount of investment capital.	Investment costs are reduced due to the provision of expertise and advice from the franchisor.
The risk of opening and operating units themselves is removed.	Is provided with marketing knowledge and operational expertise developed by franchisor.
Establish guaranteed outlets for franchised products.	Supported by a recognized brand-name and regional or national marketing activities.
Receive regular income from franchise operations.	As an owner-operator, the franchisee is self-motivated and enthusiastic.
Operational overheads are kept to a minimum.	Guaranteed that no direct competition will be established in the locality of the franchise by the same franchisor.

The number of franchise operations in Britain is changing all the time, particularly with the development of fast food, but restaurants that are francise operations include Kentucky Fried Chicken, Wimpy and Golden Egg. See Table 3.3.

Table 3.3 *Main franchise chains*

Name of chain	Operator	Number of UK units (1978) Company owned	Franchised
Wimpy		2	610
Kentucky Fried Chicken	Kentucky Fried Chicken (Great Britain)	45	200
Little Chef	Trusthouse Forte	167	17
Golden Egg	United Biscuits	0	100
Dayvilles	City Hotels	12	70
Kardomah	Trusthouse Forte	22	17
Seafarer	Associated Fisheries	0	22
Pizza Hut	Pizzahut	12	3*
Bake 'n' Take	Bake 'n' Take Franchises	0	30

Source: *Fast Food*, November, 1978.
* 1979 figure from *Catering Times*, 27 September 1979.

Case study 3.2   Wimpy International

Wimpy was first introduced into the UK in 1954 when Lyons opened a Wimpy Bar as part of the Oxford Street Corner House. Soon afterwards Lyons purchased the world-wide trade-mark from the original founder and franchising began in 1957. There are now approximately 500 franchised outlets in this country, including 28 new 'fast-food' Wimpys. In addition to the units in this country, there are over 400 others in 38 different countries around the world. The company is owned and operated by United Biscuits, one of the largest food groups in Europe, which has chosen to diversify its snack, biscuit and convenience foods business into catering.

The company lists the services it provides to its franchisees as follows:

1. Right to use the registered Wimpy International trade-mark.
2. Assistance in finding and evaluating potential sites.
3. Assessment of the profit possibilities of the site suggested.
4. A complete lay-out of the suggested sites including decoration and equipment needs, upon receipt of an advance payment of the franchise fee (£10 000 in the case of counter service).
5. Assistance in obtaining planning and building regulations approval.
6. Advice on opening and publicity.
7. Training of manager and of staff both before and after the opening and particular assistance during the critical opening period.
8. An operations manual for the successful running of the unit.
9. Regular advertising, promotions and merchandising support.
10. Instruction on book-keeping and VAT calculation.
11. Delivery of deep-frozen Wimpy products and of freshly baked Wimpy buns.
12. Regular contact with head office by way of an operations supervisor.

In return for all the above, a franchisee is expected to invest between £150 000 and £350 000 in the operation, depending on the size and location of the site. Wimpy expect that to represent about 50 per cent of the first year's expected turnover. Wimpy derive their revenue through an 8.5 per cent royalty on turnover (net VAT).

The major problem confronting Wimpy's management is the competition from new units set up by operators such as McDonald's, Wendy and Burger King. Before the introduction of fast food, which is served over a counter, Wimpy Bars used traditional table service, but the company recognized that in order to compete, it too must offer a similar product served in the same way that the newcomers in the popular catering sector serve it. Due to the high investment costs, most of these 'new' Wimpys are owned and operated by Wimpy themselves, but seven out of 28 of the new units have found franchisees with the necessary capital of up to £500 000 to invest. Wimpy estimate that it costs almost three times as much to build a new store than that of a comparably sized table service outlet. At the same time, turnover is likely to be three times as high. Wimpy cite their Notting Hill Gate unit that prior to conversion had a weekly turnover of £1500, whereas in November 1981 as a fast-food store this had increased to £7000 per week, four and a half times as high.

3.6 CONCLUSION

Restaurants in some form or another have a very long history, and there is no doubt that they will continue to serve food and drink for many more years. Despite the growth of fast-food outlets and takeaway restaurants, people enjoy dining out, and restaurants satisfy this demand, whether they are unique or part of large chains. Furthermore, it appears to be the latent ambition of many people in the catering industry to run their own restaurant business. This sector, perhaps more than any other, offers the opportunity to individuals to fulfil this ambition. A restaurant requires less investment than a hotel, it is smaller in scale than many other types of operation and has greater status attached to it than public houses or outside catering. In many respects, it fulfils the criteria of a business suitable for any budding entrepreneur. However, at the same time, it must be recognized that a restaurant is a risky business venture. Although there are examples of staggeringly successful restaurateurs—Prue Leith, Bob Patton, Robert Carrier, to name but a few—there are equally many unsuccessful restaurateurs. The main reason for this is that apart from being proficient and expert caterers, restaurateurs must also understand the market in which they operate. It is no coincidence that many of the case studies in Chapter 11 are drawn from the restaurant sector. The restaurateur is selling a non-essential product, it is a luxury item, and must compete with other products for the customers' hard-earned disposable income.

Exercise

Survey the popular catering sector of the industry and identify the way in which the manager's role varies from that of a food and beverage manager in a hotel.

4 Public-House Catering

The art of supplying food to people out for a drink

OBJECTIVES: to understand the ownership of public houses in the UK . . . to explain the growing involvement of brewing companies with catering and hotel firms . . . to outline the operation of public-house catering . . . to describe the role of pub-style steakhouse restaurants.

Most of the problems facing brewers today stem from fluctuations in the demand for beer and the rising costs of producing and distributing it. In addition, the traditional retail outlet for beer—the pub—is facing stiff competition from supermarkets and the rapid growth of drinking clubs.

Caterer & Hotelkeeper, 26 June 1980

4.1 INTRODUCTION

THE distinction between public-house catering and operating a restaurant is essentially that in a public house, food sales are ancillary to the principal business of serving alcoholic beverages. At least, until fairly recently that has been the case, but during the 1970s there was a tremendous growth in speciality restaurants, usually so-called steakhouses, based in public houses. In some cases, such operations are now more like restaurants than public houses, but as their origins are firmly related to public-house catering, we shall review this style of operation in this chapter. 'Pub' meals vary a great deal—from the service of simple bar snacks up to five-star cuisine.

Public houses represent the largest sector of the catering industry. This sector employs more people than any other—nearly 300 000 workers—and estimates of the number of units vary between 63 000 and 70 000. More importantly, the estimated turnover of the sector in 1979 was £4 350 million (at retail selling price)* including sales of alcohol; while £544 million of this was derived from sales of food or meals alone. The Caterer/Gallup survey 1980 reinforced the view that there are two separate markets. With regard to pub snack counters, the average number of covers served per day was quite low, about 50, and the average amount spent per customer was less than £1.50, reflecting the limited menu choice and the ancillary nature of food sales in public-house catering. However, in considering steakhouse and pub-restaurant operations, turnover of customers is greater and the average amount spent per customer around £6 per head in 1979. The survey described this style of operation as 'falling squarely in the middle of the eating-out market'. In order to establish how it is that catering in public houses has developed in this way, we must examine more closely the question of public-house ownership and management.

4.2 THE GROWTH OF THE BIG BREWING COMPANIES

There was a rapid concentration of the brewing industry in the 1960s which led to the emergence of the so-called 'Big Six' brewers, namely Bass Charrington, Allied Breweries, Whitbread, Watney Mann, Scottish and Newcastle, and Courage. By the end of the 1960s these companies controlled nearly 70 per cent of beer production, 50 per cent of the breweries and 50 per cent of the outlets (public houses).

The story of the mergers and takeovers is outlined in Table 4.1.

Table 4.1 *Brewery companies' consolidation.*

Year	Mergers and acquisitions
1960	Courage and Barclay merged with Simmonds.
	Joshua Tetley merged with Walker Cain.
	Scottish Breweries merged with Newcastle Breweries.
1961	Ind Coope, Tetley Walker and Ansells merged to become Allied Breweries (eventually).
	Bass merged with Mitchells and Butlers.
	Courage, Barclay and Simmonds acquired Georges.
1962	Charringtons merged with United Breweries.
1963	Allied acquired Friary Meux.
1966	Charringtons acquired Masseys.
1967	Bass acquired Bents.
	Bass and Charrington merged.

Thus between 1960 and 1970 Whitbreads took over 23 brewing companies; Courages acquired breweries in Reading, Bristol, Tadcaster and Plymouth; and Watneys bought up breweries in Manchester, Trowbridge, Northampton, Norwich, and Edinburgh. By 1970, the Big Six operated 57 breweries (see Table 4.2).

The size and output of the Big Six's breweries far exceed that of the other brewing companies, with the possible exception of Guinness.

The reasons for the sudden increase in the size of certain brewing companies are

---

* Mintel.

complex and varied and to a certain extent depended upon the particular circumstances at that time, but there were three major factors:

1. The asset value of the property owned by brewing companies in the late 1950s was often grossly undervalued, and so to buy control of such a company was a cheap way of acquiring property.
2. Industry in general, and the brewing companies in particular, began to realize that large-scale production would result in a cheaper product, or if the price remained the same, greater profits.
3. Some companies, in order to protect themselves from takeover bids, took over other companies. This had the added advantage of reducing the number of competitors in the market.

Table 4.2 *Brewery ownership in 1970.*

Company	Number of UK breweries
Whitbread	19
Bass Charrington	12
Watney Mann	8
Allied	7
Courage	8
Scottish & Newcastle	3
Others	120 (approx.)

These brewing organizations were at the time of their creation the largest catering businesses operating on a national scale. In many respects they led the way to the development of large companies in other sectors of the industry, notably hotels. But an immediate result of growth, coupled with the need to promote keg beer through advertising, was the implementation of clearly identifiable national brand images—not only for their brewing products, but also for their in-house catering operations. Almost overnight national chains of pub-restaurants emerged, e.g. Chef and Brewer. This growth was helped by the recognition that other types of catering operation developed in the 1960s, notably the popular catering sector, were competing for business with the public houses. To retain and stimulate trade, the brewers had to become caterers and provide eating-out facilities as well as bars. The logical development of this was the creation of very large companies with interests in all aspects of food and drink sales.

Table 4.3 illustrates the extent to which the brewing companies have diversified their operations into non-brewing, but related fields of enterprise. In two cases the brewing firms are the predominant firms in the conglomerates, whereas in the case of Watney Mann, they have been taken over by a hotel company.

Task 4.1

Investigate the other three big brewing companies to establish the extent of their diversification. Why has their diversification taken place and in what ways has it differed?

Table 4.3 *Diversification in the brewing industry.*

Company	Allied Breweries PLC	Grand Metropolitan PLC	Bass PLC
Brewing interests	Allied Breweries (UK) Ltd Ansells Ltd Ind Coope Ltd Joshua Tetley Ltd Tetley Walker Ltd Skol	Watney Mann and Truman Ltd Holsten	Bass UK Charrington & Co. Ltd Mitchells & Butler
Retail interests	Victoria Wine Co. Ltd		
Wholesale interests	Grants of St. James's		Hedges & Butler Ltd
Spirits and wines	Coates Gayners Ltd Harveys of Bristol William Teacher & Sons Ltd	International Distillers & Vintners	
Soft drinks	Britvic Ltd	Club	Britannia (35 per cent owned by Whitbread)
Hotel operations	Embassy Hotels Ltd	Grand Metropolitan Hotels Ltd	Crest Hotels
Restaurant operations	J. L. Catering Ltd	Berni Inns Schooner Inns Chef and Brewer	
Others	Lyons Maid Ltd Lyons Bakery Ltd	Mecca Express Dairies	

4.3 PUBLIC-HOUSE OWNERSHIP

The vast majority of public houses are owned by the brewing companies. Those that are not are called 'free houses' and may be operated with the same entrepreneurial skills as a restaurant.

In recent years there has been a trend away from tenancy of brewer-owned public houses towards direct management of these outlets. Nonetheless a large proportion of public houses are still run by tenants, which has implications not only for the structure of the industry and the extent of integration therein, but also for the market orientation of the brewers. The advantages of tenancy can be outlined as follows:

(1) To tenants

(a) Historically it has been a successful system, enabling many people to begin a business with a comparatively small investment.
(b) Since the breweries also stipulate recommended selling prices of their products, there is little or no price competition between public houses owned by the same brewery; or for that matter by public houses of different breweries. This is accentuated by the fact that the ownership of pubs by the breweries tends to be regionally concentrated, e.g. Bass Charrington in the Midlands, and so on.

(c)   The system satisfies the desire of publicans to work for themselves, but with all the added advantages of large-scale company sales, advertising and marketing; financial expertise and the availability of cheap loans; assistance and guidance with regard to refurbishing and designing premises, etc.

(2) To breweries

(a)   The company is assured of an outlet for its products, and for its products only.
(b)   The company is assured of regular income in the form of rents for all its tied-house properties, which helps to overcome the seasonal nature of sales in the industry and any resulting cash flow problems.
(c)   As the property belongs to the brewery it can show such outlets as assets on the balance sheet, and in recent years property has risen considerably in value, so that the ownership of property is a good investment in its own right.
(d)   The system also enables the Big Six to exert a tremendous amount of control over the market, i.e. the prices at which their products are sold, what type of beers are sold and where they can be bought. All of this reinforces the barriers to entry into the market that economies of scale and restrictive licensing laws have helped to establish.

(3) To consumers

(a)   The system assures customers of a standard product at a standard price, if that is what they want. Many people (including the Campaign for Real Ale) argue that consumers want more choice and are prepared to pay for it, but this is a matter of opinion. 'Defenders of the tied-house system argue that its abolition, even if practicable, would be of no real benefit to the customer in terms of cheaper or a wider choice of beer.' (*Guardian* 27 November 1979.)

Tenancy agreements

Nearly 80 per cent of the brewery-owned public houses are operated by tenants, and most breweries have waiting lists of people who have applied for such a tenancy. Each tenant will complete a comprehensive questionnaire and undergo a personal interview before being offered a public house. Upon taking up the tenancy, the licensee will sign an agreement to pay the rent and rates of the premises and to purchase beer stocks, and probably a wide range of other products, exclusively from the brewery. The rental is often relatively low, but tenants will pay slightly more than non-tenanted licensees for the brewery's products, which in the trade is known as 'wet rent'. Any profits on sales that tenants make are their own, but there are considerable ongoing expenses in becoming a tenant. First, it is usual to place a deposit with the brewery equal to the approximate value of two weeks' stock. The brewery will pay the tenant interest on this sum, though not necessarily at a very high rate. Second, the new tenant must purchase from the previous tenant the stock in hand, any business equipment and furnishings, and so on. Finally, the tenant must have sufficient working capital to run the business on the basis that staff wages will probably be paid weekly and that the brewery may well require settlement of their account within two weeks of delivery.

Managed houses

Breweries tend to appoint managers to run their larger licensed premises. The manager is a salaried employee of the brewery, in the same way that hotel groups employ hotel managers. The salary level is established according to scales negotiated by the National Association of Licensed House Managers, and will probably be supplemented by a bonus related to the profitability of operation. Like tenants, managers will be required to deposit a sum of money as a surety, although in most cases this will be for about one or two days' takings. Managers will be expected to carry out the company's control procedures and will be subject to regular external stock checks to ensure profitability is maintained. In all other respects however, managers of public houses have to work under the same constraints as tenants.

4.4 HOW PUBLIC HOUSES OPERATE

Running a public house in this country is subject to a variety of factors.

1. The tied-house system means that in terms of product, packaging, marketing, pricing and so on, the freedom of the operator is considerably proscribed.
2. The sector is highly competitive due to the enormous number of public houses.
3. Trade is particularly vulnerable to changes in the economic climate. For instance, the National Union of Licensed Victuallers reported that in the recession-hit West Midlands 'trade is down about 12 per cent' (*Caterer & Hotelkeeper*, 11 June 1981).
4. Business success is closely related to the demand for beer, the sale of which varies with the weather (sales were good during the very hot summer of 1976), changes in consumer taste, marketing and the impact of one of Britain's most successful consumer pressure groups—the Campaign for Real Ale (CAMRA).
5. Licensing legislation means that the publican must open every day for specific periods of time (see Chapter 16).

Economics of pub operations

Such is the competitive nature of the business that pub economics have changed quite drastically since 1975. In the London area in 1975 a public house was expected to achieve a turnover of about £3000 (of which 25–30 per cent would be derived from food sales) while in the provinces sales ranged between £1500 and £2000 per week, with little or no contribution from food sales. The gross profit margin at that time was 45–47 per cent on drinks and 60–65 per cent on food, with labour costs representing only 10 per cent of turnover, so that net profits were around 20 per cent. However, with sales falling due to high taxation, colour television and the growth of discotheques and clubs, many publicans introduced live entertainment in order to attract custom. They found that turnover had to increase substantially, however, to cover the cost of providing that entertainment. At the same time most of the breweries were rationalizing their operations, which included the size of their pubs. The 'ideal' pub became one occupying between 760 and 915 square metres (2500 and 3000 square feet) of floor space, so that smaller units were closed and large sites redeveloped as new smaller pubs, plus office blocks as a further source of site revenue. Furthermore, many of the older, larger pubs had space available for the development of a food out-let, which had the advantage of attracting custom, as well as being a revenue earner in its own right. The development of in-house steak restaurants also coincided with the brewers' desire to diversify their interests into other products and markets, and led to the rise of such chains as Chef and Brewer, Berni Inns and Schooner Inns. In 1982 the weekly turnover of a pub has risen to £3000 (including inflation) and the proportion of revenue received from food sales is 38.7 per cent. 'Factors influencing a pub reaching its wages to takings percentage target', P. Noble, Brighton Polytechnic thesis.

Pub-style catering

The development of food sales in public houses has followed two broad patterns:

(1) Snack meals

Snack meals are consumed while having a drink in the bar and range from sandwiches to hot plated meals. The service style is typically food displayed in glass-fronted cabinets and plated by counter staff according to customers' requirements, although in smaller establishments where there is not enough space for display purposes, a cus-tomer may have to select his meal from a menu. Whichever is the case, the customer usually collects the plated meal, along with the necessary cutlery and accompaniments from a service point, and sits down in the bar area. From the consumer's point of view such a meal is quick and simple in a congenial and relaxed atmosphere. However, it may mean that the furniture is not ideal for eating a meal, tables are generally smaller in area and lower in height than those found in a restaurant, while bars tend to be noisy and smoky, with frequent movement of people. None the less, the consumer is prepared to put up with these limitations, since meals are usually competitively priced, the public house is probably conveniently located, and the meal is an ancillary to having a drink.

(2) Restaurant meals

Larger pubs have established restaurants on their premises, where the design and function of the room is for the consumption of food. Such restaurants are in the main steakhouse operations, certainly as far as the larger chains are concerned, and their origins and continued success are based on the following:

(a) A menu based around steak requires a limited amount of kitchen equipment, i.e. grill and deep-fat fryer, and hence capital investment.
(b) Staff, both in the kitchen and restaurant, require little technical expertise for the preparation, cooking and service of steak-based meals.
(c) The product itself is extremely popular, for instance in the Caterer/Gallup Poll 1982 it was by far the most popular dish, and it appeals to the socio-economic groups frequenting pubs.
(d) The product is usually supplied already portioned which helps very accurate cost control.
(e) The product is easy to store and has a reasonable shelf-life if refrigerated.
(f) With sufficient turnover of stock, there is little or no wastage as the steak is cooked to order.

Most pub restaurants serve plated meals with a table d'hôte menu, comprising three starters, usually soup, prawn cocktail and one other; rump, sirloin or fillet steak grilled to order; ice cream or cheese board; followed by coffee or a selection from a range of speciality coffees. The price of the meal is based on the cost of the main item, and since to attract custom pricing is competitive, strict portion control is employed. Most operators specify exactly the presentation of each of the dishes on the menu and support this with illustrations of how each dish should be presented on the plate.

Whether or not this style of operation can be classed as a 'pub' is contentious. Ben Davis in *The Traditional English Pub* (Architectural Press, 1981) argues that Berni, Schooner Inns, and 'others like them must be classed as non-pubs'. He believes that the great merits they have are not those of pubs which exist to encourage social drinking. However, I have included this type of operation here for two reasons. First, as Davis complains, 'many formerly good pubs have been lost in such transformations' [to steakhouses], so that their location, style and design is similar to a pub's. Second, some of the operators of such units are the breweries themselves, such as Watney's Chef and Brewer chain.

Significantly in 1982 a new operator has entered this market in direct competition with the so-called steakhouse operation, but employing some of the marketing and operating techniques of the fast-food sector. *Caterer & Hotelkeeper* reported (1 July 1982):

> The opening of the first Ponderosa steakhouse—a 166-seat unit—in Watford [in June 1982] could be almost as significant an event for Britain's food service industry as the opening of the first British McDonald's in Woolwich in 1974, but only if the [US] steakhouse chain can find customers to match its remarkably low prices. A 5 oz steak, jacket potato or French fries, side salad and a roll and butter all for £2.50 including VAT and service ('no tipping please', says the menu) plus free refills of tea, coffee and soft drinks will not make easy profit in a restaurant which cost £700 000 to open. It will equally be hard to compete with.
>
> Though Ponderosa, whose 700 restaurants make it the largest US steakhouse chain, is initially lining its prices up with those of McDonald's and Wimpy rather than with Berni or Beefeater restaurants, whose prices it undercuts substantially, there's no doubt that if it succeeds, it will represent a more serious pricing challenge to the steakhouse than to the hamburger chains.
>
> Ponderosa's pricing policy seems to be following the principle established by McDonald's when it first came to Britain of undercutting all competition, trimming its own margins to the bare bones and setting aside losses as a long-term investment.

It is hoped that the average amount spent by customers will be £3.50 and turnover is planned to be 4000–5000 covers per week.

> Ponderosa, like McDonald's in 1974, is clearly thinking big and will want to take quality control and pricing to the utmost edge of competitiveness.
>
> Present targets are for five restaurants in the next 18 months and 100 in the next five years. The success of such plans must, however, depend on factors like Ponderosa's franchising policy, which is likely to be directed towards companies with chain operating experience, and the availability of such operators ready to invest on a suitable scale.

Another significant development during the 1970s has been the emergence of wine bars. British drinking habits have shifted considerably since the Second World War, and in some respects operations such as Berni Inns and similar steakhouses have gone some way towards the popularizing of wine, although the major marketing effort has been made by wine shippers and manufacturers.

Non-vintage blended wines such as Hirondelle and so on have been specifically developed to meet British tastes and demands and the availability of these wines through supermarkets and off-licences has boosted sales. Riding high on the increasing popularity of wine have been the wine bars, which may or may not sell just wine. They differ from public houses quite significantly in ways that can make them much more profitable. For instance:

1. Their range of stock is confined mainly to wine, so that given enough chilled space for white and rosé wines, the scale and complexity of storage is less than for a public house which has to store draught and bottled beers, spirits and soft drinks as well as wine.
2. Wine is sold by the bottle generally, so that customers need to frequent the bar less often than in a pub, thus reducing the staffing needs of a wine bar.
3. The image and marketing of wine bars are more up-market than pubs.
4. Wine bars occupy premises that are generally smaller than most public houses, so that overheads and operating costs are reduced.

4.5 CONCLUSION

The British public house is unique, although efforts have been made to market the 'pub' abroad, particularly in locations frequented by British holidaymakers such as Spanish resorts, Paris and the Low Countries.

Food service operations within public houses vary enormously from just snack meals to internationally known gourmet restaurants, and this reflects the structure and nature of the licensed trade.

The great majority of public houses are owned by large companies, whose principal activity is the manufacture and sale of alcoholic beverages, beer in particular. However, the operation of the outlets is left to the entrepreneurial skills of tenants, who are in effect working for themselves. In only a few instances, relatively speaking, has a large company introduced managed outlets and stardardized presentation and service of food. It is not surprising that Egon Ronay and others have published guides to 'good pubs' since the style and quality of public-house catering can vary so widely.

Exercises

Discuss the impact that new-style food service operations such as wine bars and fast food have had upon public-house catering and outline the response of public-house operators to these new developments.

Outline the arguments for and against maintaining the present opening hours of licensed premises.

5 The Fast-Food Explosion

The art of supplying people in a hurry with a meal package

OBJECTIVES: to outline the development of the fast-food sector in the UK . . . to understand the operating principles of a fast-food outlet . . . to identify staffing requirements . . . to outline central and in-store control procedures.

The June/July issue [1980] of Fast Food *devotes a whole page to the opening of the latest fast-food chain to hit Britain, Joe Kwan's Mandarin Kitchen . . . But the September issue of* Fast Food *reports, in just two paragraphs: 'Joe Kwan closes first unit.' That really is fast.*

Sunday Times, 14 September 1980

5.1 INTRODUCTION

The impact of fast food has been incredible. The concept has swept the UK and some of the largest names in British business have invested in the market—United Biscuits, Grand Metropolitan and Tesco. It is calculated that Britons spent £750 million on fast food alone in 1979 and yet more than one firm has had to pull out of the market, and it is predicted that more failures are likely. International Stores claimed in 1981 that 'together, convenience and takeaway food are outstripping the growth in spending on all food and account for one quarter of all expenditure on food—£5 billion.' Nevertheless the first three months' survey of British eating habits* in 1982 showed that growth had slowed dramatically.

---

* *British Survey of Eating* (1982) London: Gallup.

Table 5.1 *Fast food—past, present and future.*

Chain	First British unit	Total units July 1982	Closures	Projected new units
Kentucky Fried Chicken	1965, Preston	356	6	25–30 in 1982–83
McDonald's	1974, Woolwich, London	76	none	100 by December 1982
Spud-U-Like	1974, Edinburgh	19	none	40 by 1983–84
Burger King	1977, Coventry Street, London	10	none	No information given
Burgermaster	1979, Stratford-upon-Avon	4	under consideration	None
Julie's Pantry	1979, M6 Corley service station	5	none	No information given
Huckleberry's	1980, Shepherds Bush, London	10	none	Under consideration
Wendy	1980, Oxford Street, London	4	none	No information given

5.2 REASONS FOR GROWTH

The origin of fast food is not new, fish and chip shops have been around for 100 years. Bejam's chain of outlets called 'Hungry Fisherman' recognize that fish and chips are a fast food. But the startling growth of the sector and diversification into new product areas has been a result of several factors.

1. A change in eating habits—there are two inter-related factors here. First, people are tending to spend less time eating lunch and second, there is a modern pre-occupation with eating less.
2. The growth of the teenage market—teenagers represent a significant percentage of the population. This age group is less conservative in its eating habits and more likely to accept convenience products.
3. Forty per cent of the working population are women, and convenience foods have experienced a growth due to demand from women who do not have the time to prepare meals.
4. High Street rents. During the last ten years, property values, rents and rates of High Street premises have increased substantially, so that catering operations had to increase sales/profitability to cover these increased costs.
5. Influence of US firms. The growth has been boosted by the influx of US firms into Britain such as McDonald's, Burger King, Kentucky Fried Chicken, etc. This development was a result of reaching saturation point in the US market.

5.3 WHAT IS FAST FOOD?

Peter Bertram has said that 'fast food is not so much a system as a way of life'.* The food sold in fast-food outlets varies widely, but the basic concept depends upon the following factors:

---

* Bertram, P. (1975) *Fast Food*, London: Barrie & Jenkins.

1. Cheap food.
2. Products that can be cooked quickly and held in the short-term without deteriorating.
3. Large throughput of customers.
4. Demand for takeaways as well as consumption on the premises.
5. Precise portion control.

For many operators, the hamburger is the ideal product but fried chicken, fish and chips, pizza, Mexican tacos, baked potatoes and crêpes are all available over fast-food counters. As fast food has evolved from the impact of McDonald's on the popular catering sector and the traditional fish and chip shops, two broad types of operation can be identified, US based and British based.

The US-based companies are mainly the hamburger chains that have entered the British market directly, such as McDonald's; arrived by way of franchising, such as MAM, a development of Burger King; or under licence, such as Berni Inn's involvement with Wendy's and Chef and Brewer's development of the Huckleberry chain, which in the USA is the Burger Queen chain. Another US company, Kentucky Fried Chicken, is also very well established, although it differs from the archetypal fast-food outlet, as it has relied almost exclusively on takeaway sales. This has influenced the siting of units in residential areas, as well as High Street sites of the fast-food chains.

British based—although not necessarily selling 'British' food, many fast-food outlets have originated in Britain. Pizzaland, Pizza Express and Pizza Hut are well-established and take advantage of the growth in this sector. Other British firms have attempted to emulate their American competitors by starting their own hamburger chains: Trusthouse Forte's Julie's Pantry, Granada's Burger Express, Woolworth's Burgermaster and British Rail's Casey Jones. Other companies have chosen alternative products to sell—Bejam's have launched the Hungry Fisherman chain and the British School of Motoring is associated with Spud-U-Like.

Case study 5.1   McDonald's

McDonald's can claim to be the original driving force behind the fast-food boom. As Alan Melborne writes, 'how many households realized they had a need for a fast, inexpensive, fun, out-of-home eating experience until McDonald's hamburgers came along?'* Their pilot outlet opened in Woolwich in 1974 and they had opened another 56 units by the end of 1981. Almost unbelievably, the company, and more importantly the customer's, brand image of their product was allowed to develop almost unchallenged for a long period of time. As we have seen, it is only since 1980 that Wimpy have responded to the fast-food threat. Unlike many other firms in the fast-food market, McDonald's own and operate their sites themselves and do not as yet franchise, although this is their normal practice in the United States. In this country, the operation is 45 per cent owned by the US parent company, 45 per cent by the British chief Robert Rhea, and 10 per cent by another individual. During the 1980s, however, McDonald's plan to begin franchising but investment will not be low. Much of the hamburger chain's success was due to a deliberate policy of only opening units within the London television area, so that an intensive promotional campaign costing £1 million per year in this region could be launched and maintained. In addition, the south-

---

* *Management Today,* February 1981.

east of England in particular has the sort of high population density that is essential to fast-food operations.

Capital investment

One of the reasons that many fast-food chains have not been franchised is the very high investment costs required, up to £500 000 for an average High Street store. These high costs are due to three main factors:

1. A fast-food outlet is very much an integrated product—operators consider every detail of the product and image that they are selling to their customers, including the style of staff uniform, packaging of the product, but in particular the decor and design of the stores (see Fig. 5.1). As we have seen the cost of the new Wimpy in Notting Hill was £400 000 (in 1981) so that interior design is a significant cost factor. Furthermore due to heavy wear and tear and the need to continue attracting custom, many stores are refurbished after only two or three years.
2. A second cost factor is the installation of highly sophisticated food production equipment. In 1982 it cost approximately £200 000 to equip an average fast-food outlet. The equipment is expensive since it is designed to process large quantities of food quickly and efficiently over protracted periods of time. For instance grills and fryers have to be 'snap action', that is to say they must be able to return to their correct operating temperature almost immediately the frozen burger is placed on the grill or the frozen french fries dropped in the fat. At the same time to maintain consistent quality control, sophisticated timing devices, thermostats and even microcomputers are used to monitor the cooking process. Wimpy, for example, use a fat fryer that lowers the basket of french fries into the fat at the touch of a button and removes them automatically after the appropriate time; similarly in Huckleberry's, the operator on the grill presses a button after placing burgers on the grill; a buzzer sounds after 20 seconds to tell the operator to sear the meat and again after a further 40 seconds to turn it; finally at 100 seconds a buzzer tells the operator to 'pull' the cooked burger.
3. An additional investment and operating cost for fast-food operators is that of leasing prime High Street sites. The average fast-food outlet is between 1200 and 1500 square metres, although larger stores such as those in Oxford Street in London are 1800 square metres in size. Fortunately, the growth in fast food has coincided with a trend for retailers such as W. H. Smith and Curries to vacate shops of this size for larger premises. Nonetheless the cost of prime sites has remained high. McDonald's have accepted this but have attempted to spread the initial cost over a period of many years by buying freeholds or long-term leases.

Task 5.1

Identify the materials used and colour schemes devised for three fast food chains. In what ways are they similar to each other and how different is their interior design to restaurants found in other sectors of the catering industry?

The fast-food concept

It could be argued that fast food should not be included in a book about food service or

Figure 5.1 *Fast-food restaurant (Casey Jones).*

catering at all. After all, food is not prepared by conventionally skilled chefs in the traditional way, nor is it served in the traditional way, nor even consumed necessarily in a restaurant, since customers can take it home or eat it in the car or walking along the street. In many respects selling fast food has more affinity with product retailing than catering and it is no accident that fast-food outlets are referred to as stores rather than restaurants. Before going on to look at how fast-food stores operate it is well worth identifying those factors that make it so very different from other branches of the industry:

1. Compared with other sites of a similar size, a fast-food store has a much greater

throughput of customers, ranging from 8 000 per week in average units in smaller cities up to 35 000 per week in London.

2. Profit is derived from high levels of turnover rather than high gross margins.
3. The product is packaged like a retail product, whether for consumption on or off the premises. The packaging must be attractive, distinctive, easy to handle and have a low unit cost.
4. The operation is based usually on one specific product and its variations, with the necessary qualities identified earlier.
5. Operators hope to market the units successfully to all sectors of the population, not relying on their appeal to one particular market segment.

Consumer perception of fast food

The fast-food industry has a maxim that the three most important principles for successful operation are location, location and location. Certainly in the late 1970s, when the concept was new to the British public, there had to be a steady stream of potential customers passing by the unit: a traffic flow of 500 pedestrians per hour was widely accepted as the minimum. Of course in some locations the number of pedestrians is so high that several stores can be located quite closely together, for instance in London's Oxford Street there are seven units within one mile of shop fronts, and each of them is probably serving at least 30 000 customers per week. More recently, however, in some provincial locations, operators have found that customers are prepared to go out of their way to get to the store and they no longer have to rely on passing trade. The reason for this is a result of the industry's four major preoccupations—quality, cleanliness, service and value—which have gone a long way to changing customers' perceptions of fast food.

Quality. When fast food was introduced into Britain it was synonymous with 'junk' food. It was looked down on by food writers and other caterers because it was cheap and US, and therefore by definition not of high quality. Operators have therefore placed a great deal of emphasis on the quality of their product, which in fact is really very good. They have pointed out that a hamburger, for instance, is a complete, balanced meal in a bun; emphasis has been placed on the fact that hamburgers are pure beef; and the fast-food chains are constantly researching consumer tastes to improve the product and its image. Wimpy, for instance, have introduced the first wholemeal bun.

This need to create and maintain a high quality product means that food in a store is prepared and cooked before it is needed in order to ensure its constant availability, but if it is not sold within a specified period of time it is *thrown away*. Operators are quite rigid in their application of this principle and each of their products has a specified holding time, for instance french fries may be held for three minutes if 'bagged' or seven minutes if they are in a 'dump station'.

Service. The essence of this particular style of food service is speed, that is why it is called *fast* food. An almost universal principle in the industry is that 'door time' should be no longer than three and a half minutes, i.e. that is the maximum length of time customers should be in the store for them to be served. Of this two and a half minutes should be the maximum queuing time and once the order is placed customers should be served in no more than 60 seconds.

Cleanliness. Operators in the industry will readily admit that the industry is almost paranoid about maintaining the cleanliness of their stores. This is primarily because their food preparation areas are open to display, although they need not be, as part of the image of the operation. They are also influenced greatly by the US practice, where hygiene is significantly more important to US consumers, recognizing, however, that they have been aided in their promotion of fast food by the bright, attractive and *clean* image that their stores present. A particular problem is that of litter, which has often been responsible for delaying or refusing planning permission to open new stores. To overcome this particular problem, staff are employed with the task of clearing the streets e.g. McDonald's 'litter-patrol'. 'Keep Britain Tidy' is printed on disposables and firms also sponsor litter bins along the street.

Value. An increasingly important factor in the industry is value for money, as consumers become discriminating over fast food and its trendiness wears off. Now that the novelty of fast food has declined, customers are far more price-conscious than previously, especially at a time of economic depression. This finds the industry in a dilemma, since the emphasis on quality products makes it particularly susceptible to price increases in food, particularly meat, dairy produce and fish. The industry therefore prefers to modify its prices as and when necessary, making small changes frequently. In the first six months of 1982 McDonald's marginally increased their prices five times. They were able to do this relatively easily since they have no printed menu cards to replace, simply an illustrated display over the service counter.

Competition in the industry

While the significant increase in the number of firms in the industry has led to the need for careful pricing strategies, it is probably fair to say that competition between firms is not price-based. A hamburger, shake, or coffee are all priced more or less the same from one chain to the next. In fact there is a tendency for operators to recognize McDonald's as the market leader and consequently to match their prices. If, however, there are several firms competing with each other for a share of the market, all of whom have adopted almost identical attitudes towards the quality, service and price of their product, how do they compete? As we have seen already more than one operator has gone out of business and it is predicted that more will follow. The principal marketing strategy that firms have adopted in order to attract customers has been to differentiate their product or product range from that of their competitors. Although at first it may be thought one hamburger is much like any other, operators stress the differences between them.

McDonald's—the 'original' hamburger, the 'home of the hamburger'.

Wimpy—the British hamburger in a wholemeal bun.

Wendys—one basic hamburger but 27 different fillings.

Burger King—the 'whopper', bigger and better than anyone else's.

Huckleberrys—not only burgers, but fried chicken and fish and chips.

Task 5.2

Carry out a small-scale market research programme to find out whether or not consumers do prefer one hamburger to another as marketed by different operators in your area.

5.4 OPERATIONAL FEATURES

As we have seen, the concept of fast food demands a totally new approach to catering—a fast-food outlet should perhaps be thought of as a small factory and retail shop rolled into one, a combination of mass-production techniques and sophisticated retailing.

Food production and service

Throughout this book a clear distinction is drawn between the production of meals and their service—no such clear distinction can be made in the fast-food industry. Staff in such units are not employed as cooks or counterhands, cleaners or clearers, but just as 'crew'. As part of their training and development a crew member will be shown how to do several tasks, both preparing food and serving it. Moreover, to enhance job satisfaction and provide variety, a crew member will be involved in several different tasks during one shift alone, depending upon proficiency and training. This may at first appear confusing when compared with the traditional, rigid structures of the kitchen brigade of Escoffier's time, but it does not mean that there are not clearly identifiable tasks or job areas to be filled, just that different personnel fill such areas as demand dictates. This is well illustrated by an analysis of how a hamburger is prepared in a typical store using solid-top grills (as opposed to broilers). This is illustrated in Fig. 5.2. Note how the staff must work closely as a team and each member of the team has a simple but specific task to do.

Staffing

There is a popular misconception that fast food is relatively cheap because its labour costs are lower than conventional restaurants. In fact the fast food industry is very labour intensive indeed and has very high levels of staffing for the size of the average unit. For instance, a store in a provincial High Street might employ over 30 full-time staff, and double this number on a part-time basis. To give some idea of the staffing levels, let us take the example of an outlet operating at peak demand in a busy location in a large city. Such a unit might be staffed as follows:

Lobby: 1 Floor manager
         5 Crew—clearing and cleaning tables, directing customers, exercising social skills, etc.
Service counter: 1 Manager
         1 Floor manager
         10 Service till operators
         5 Backers
Back of counter: 1 Manager
         1 Floor manager
         2 Soft drink pullers
         1 Shake puller
         3 Production callers
         4 Crew preparing french fries
         2 Backers

Time in seconds	Task carried out by crew member			
	1	2	3	4
0	Call out order for six more	Place top half of bun in toaster		
5			Place frozen 1.6oz burger on grill	
20			Sear burger	
50		Remove top half from toaster Begin toasting base of bun		Begin dressing top half of bun
60			Turn burger	
80				Dressed bun to grill
90		Base of bun to grill		
100			Meat pulled and burger assembled	
110	Wrap completed burger			

Figure 5.2 *Production of a hamburger.*

    5 Crew grilling meat
    4 Crew dressing burgers
    2 Backers
    3 Back room crew—tidying up, cleaning, restocking, etc.
Total: 55 Personnel

Of course, the number of staff will vary according to predicted demand; the same store may only have a total of 10 personnel present when it first opens in the morning, gradually increasing the staff levels during the morning as demand increases. Fig. 5.3 is an example of a duty rota for a fast-food store. This emphasizes the need to implement very precise rostering of staff to keep labour costs down to an acceptable figure—too few staff and the store will be unable to cope with demand; too many and profit levels will be reduced. Thus managers are very flexible in their approach to rostering and staff will work shifts of different duration on different days.

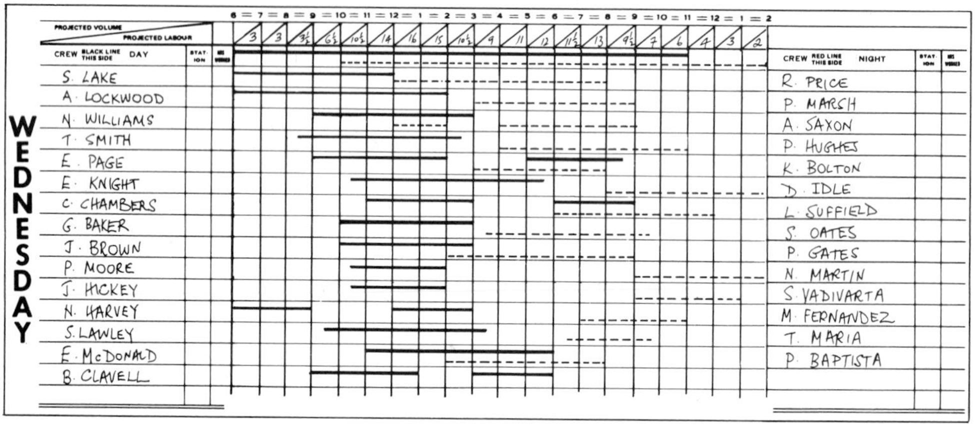

Figure 5.3 *Fast-food employees' work schedule.*

Control

Not only must the labour cost input be structured carefully, but all aspects of fast food operations are rigorously controlled. The systems developed and used in this sector make some of the control procedures adopted elsewhere look positively antiquated. Fig. 5.3 is the *daily* control sheet prepared by the manager of a store working for one particular company, it is nonetheless typical of the types of control conducted. As the sheet demonstrates the following factors are analysed.

Sales per service till analysed to establish net cash sales in total.
Hourly analysis of sales in relation to staffing level to establish sales per work-hour, and total daily sales per work-hour.
Spot checks on particular tills and particular staff to monitor cash security.
Analysis of all non-cash sales transactions.
Analysis of yields on high-cost products that are portioned within the store.
Analysis of average amount spent by each customer.
Total number of customers served.
Net sales figure after VAT and staff meals.

This analysis sheet is supported by other documentation returned daily as outlined in the bottom right-hand corner of Fig. 5.4.

Such comprehensive data enable the operator to monitor closely the three elements of cost—food, labour and overheads—and then relate them to throughput of customers. Where particular aspects of the operation are unsatisfactory, corrective action can be taken immediately. The effectiveness of this can be illustrated by a few examples.

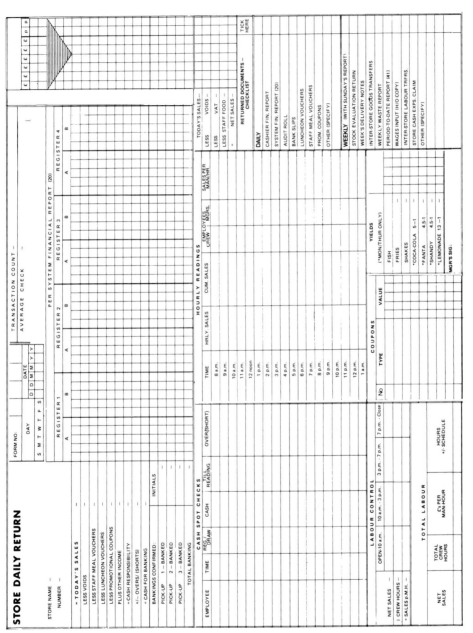

Figure 5.4 *Fast-food store daily return control sheet.*

With regard to food cost if expected yields are not achieved the ratio of syrup to liquid in the soft drinks or shake dispensers can be modified or staff retrained to reduce waste.

Overhead costs are mainly fixed, notably rent and rates, but where possible, measures can be taken to reduce the variable costs, notably energy use. The cost of electricity can be reduced by avoiding power surges so that items of equipment are not all switched on at once, thermostats should be used not only to control product quality but to minimize power consumption, and all equipment should only be switched on when required and switched off again as soon as demand falls. As well as controlling costs closely, the daily summary sheet also enables revenue to be closely controlled. As well as conducting spot checks on tills to balance cash against recorded sales, it is usual for two stock takes to be done every day—in the evening to compare receipts with stock use, and in the morning to ensure no pilferage or spoilage overnight and as a cross-check on the previous day's closing stock figure.

There is no doubt that such tight control procedures are time-consuming and costly, but the industry operates within very tight margins and such constant monitoring is essential to ensure the financial well-being of the operation. In particular, the industry is particularly vulnerable to changes in demand, for a wide variety of reasons. A graph showing unit sales of a store would have many peaks and troughs which could be attributable to the weather, television, school holidays, transport strikes, bomb scares and so on. It must always be remembered that the system of fast food relies on the prediction of sales in advance—food is not cooked to order, but before the customer sets foot in the store so that it is ready for immediate, *fast* sale. There are two stages to this prediction process: first, the manager must attempt to predict on the basis of previous sales figures the level of sales over the next 10 days so that the unit can be efficiently staffed, and second, on a minute-to-minute basis at the time of service the crew must prepare enough of each item to be always available for sale without waste.

Management control

All units in the catering industry operated by firms are subject to some degree of control from head office.

Task 5.3

Refer back to any other chapters you have read in Part A. Attempt to identify examples of such control.

The fast-food industry has instituted the concept of 'inventory control' whereby all aspects of an operation are analysed regularly on a weekly or fortnightly basis. This is common practice in franchise operations since the franchisor is anxious to ensure that independent franchisees achieved acceptable levels of operation, but even in those fast-food chains that are not franchised such inspections are still carried out, as part of the emphasis on quality, cleanliness and service. The inspection may be carried out by a district manager, responsible for several stores, by personnel from head office or on occasions by US experts who visit to check on the British operations of their original systems. The detail of such inspections is minute and it may take two inspectors a whole day to carry out. In most cases the unit is given a score for its performance so that comparisons can be made with previous analyses. To give some idea of the complexity and detail of such inspections, part of a typical inventory sheet is shown below.

Customer service	Target	Actual
A. *Speed of service*—Rush periods only (times from — to —)		
1. List 10 door to thank-you service times: 3½ minutes max.	100	
— — — — — — — — — — Avge—		
2. List 10 assembly times: 60 seconds max.		
— — — — — — — — Avge—	100	
B. *Service steps* (tick against each one for each crew member)		
1. Greeting (enthusiasm and smiles)	50	
2. Properly taking order (and back line reacting properly)	10	
3. Suggestive selling and customer assistance/selling up	10/10	
4. Receiving payment/tendering cash properly	5/5	
5. Correct collection of fries, sandwiches, etc.	10	
6. Assembling order properly	10	
7. Presenting the order	10	
8. Thanking and/bid for return	10/5	
9. Condiments correctly dispensed by cashier	15	
10. Children's prizes given	15	
11. Proper handling of 'grill' products	5	
12. Evidence of training and understanding of present promotions	10	
13. Napkins and straws full and in tidy condition	5	
14. Crew hustle—backing each other	20	
	405	
C. *Employee appearance*		
1. Employees and management clean and properly groomed	15	
2. Uniforms clean/good repair	10/10	
3. No unnecessary jewellery, etc.	10	
4. Male uniforms correct: hats/slacks/smock/nametags/shoes, etc.	2/2/2/2/2	
5. Female uniforms correct: hats/slacks/smock/nametags/shoes, etc.	2/2/2/2/2	
6. Management in proper uniform: ties/nametags, etc.	10/5	
	80	
D. *Customer relations*		
1. Restaurant using birthday parties, tours, or other devices	10	
2. Management or host spending time in dining room	10	
3. Restaurant actively soliciting for business through local advertising and community relations	5	
4. Management aware of forthcoming promotions, etc.	5	
5. Tables being kept clean at all times	10	
6. Thank-you bins being emptied before they overflow (including outside)	10	
7. Lobby floor always clean	5	
	55	
Total	540	

5.5 CONCLUSION

Despite the fact that the fast-food concept has been in Britain for several years now, I believe that the catering industry and the public have yet to come to terms with it. It has had and will continue to have a tremendous impact on the hotel and catering industry—motorway service areas are rapidly having fast-food stores built. Wimpy have completely modified their catering concept, every High Street in every large town and city has at least one if not two such operations.

Many people, notably traditional caterers, catering teachers and some of the catering press, believe fast food to be a flash in the pan and that like many other popular catering concepts, such as milk bars in the 1930s and coffee bars in the 1950s, it will decline in popularity and fade away. At the same time the industry is looked upon somewhat disparagingly as cheap and brash. Such die-hard opinions are, however, gradually being eroded by the undeniable success of fast food as operators insist that their sales are still rising and that they have by no means reached a peak of popularity.

What people must recognize is that fast food is different from catering, but that far from being a threat to traditional caterers it has much to offer them in improved standards and performance. Throughout this chapter three factors have been emphasized about fast food—service, quality and cleanliness. All of these things have been known by caterers for years, and successful restaurateurs have provided them to their customers. It has been difficult for larger firms to impose acceptable standards on units run by employees rather than entrepreneurs. Fast food has shown, however, that such control is possible and in fact has set probably the highest level of hygiene standards to be found anywhere in the industry. For all its popular appeal, its brashness, its 'junk-food' image, fast food has brought bright and imaginative marketing, incredibly high standards of hygiene and a youthful outlook into catering. Caterers may not like it but they cannot ignore it. Finally perhaps the most significant factor about fast food is that a magazine called *Fast Food* was launched in 1980 to provide news and information to this sector alone—a sure sign that fast food is an industry in its own right.

Exercise

Discuss to what extent the success of fast food has been based upon its novelty. How has the industry sought to consolidate consumer acceptance?

6 Industrial Catering

The art of supplying food and drink to people at their place of work

OBJECTIVES: to outline the size and scope of industrial catering in Britain . . . to identify the food service systems operated in this sector, in particular cafeteria operations . . . to evaluate the role of automatic vending in this sector and in catering in general.

Pressure for the continuation of canteen facilities comes today mostly from the trade unions but the moral obligation of making at least hot drinks service available to its working force is accepted by management as an important factor of industrial life.

Vending (1977) Kingston: Automatic Vending Association.

6.1 INTRODUCTION

FOR many years, industrial catering was regarded as one of the least attractive sectors of the industry from the point of view of status and career opportunities. The 1970s, however, saw many changes in industrial catering practice that greatly improved attitudes towards this sector. This is symbolized by the fact that the term 'factory canteen' is no longer current, having been superseded by 'staff dining room' or 'staff cafeteria'. Before the Second World War, only a few enlightened or larger companies provided refreshment facilities; most workers were expected to provide their own, in a thermos or lunch box, or go home for lunch (or go without). Even today, it is estimated that 60 per cent of industrial workers still do provide their own refreshments. Nonetheless, this sector now serves 40 per cent of the total number of meals served in the catering industry, and 30 per cent of the people who eat out do so at their place of work.

The impetus to expand catering facilities in industry arose during the Second World War, when the Emergency Powers (Defence) Factories Canteen Order 1940 and 1943 made canteen facilities compulsory in all factories employing more than 250 workers. After the war, these facilities continued to cater for employees, and trade unions have usually succeeded in guaranteeing the continuation of the service and improving the facilities provided.

The personnel director of Sutcliffe Caterers, a large industrial contract caterer, was reported as saying,* 'There have been many occasions when lay or full-time union officials have been instrumental in the firm keeping or losing a particular contract.' In addition to the influence of trade unions, there has been a trend towards larger firms and bigger plants and factories, so that feeding workers has become increasingly more difficult, with hundreds and sometimes thousands of people all requiring refreshment at mid-morning, midday and mid-afternoon. The Industrial Society's survey of catering prices, costs and subsidies reveals that only the larger companies can achieve a profit on food and beverage sales and that over 60 per cent of firms surveyed subsidize their catering facilities.† This has led to firms having to decide whether they will operate the catering facilities themselves or employ contract caterers such as Sutcliffe, Gardner Merchant or Grandmet Catering.

6.2 INDUSTRIAL CATERING MANAGEMENT

Company operated facilities

In this case the firm operates its own catering facilities, employing staff directly and managing the operation in its entirety. Expert advice may be sought from consultants, though, especially when establishing new facilities or modifying existing operations. This means that a firm involved in engineering or manufacturing becomes responsible for an area outside its normal field, and usually delegates its personnel department with the task of managing the catering operations. This may present problems for the firm but it has the distinct advantage that catering facilities are entirely controlled by them, so that the extent of the service provided can be determined according to the firm's own particular philosophy and policy. ICI, for instance, operate their own catering facilities and state as a part of their company's policy that 'it is the policy of the company to ensure that, wherever practicable . . . its employees have access to a good quality meal at a fair price in pleasant surroundings.'‡

Contract catering

Dennis Coates has defined a contract caterer as 'an individual or company, who, in recognition of a financial reward, will undertake to administer, control and direct a specified catering operation within the guidelines stipulated by the company.'§ There is a growing trend for companies to use the services of such contract caterers to pro-

---

* *Personnel Management*, November 1980.
† *Catering Prices, Costs and Subsidies Survey* (1979) London: Industrial Society.
‡ 'Industrial catering—the ICI concept' in *Catering Equipment and Systems Design* (1977) G. Glew (ed.) London: Applied Science.
§ Coates, D. S. (1971) *Industrial Catering Management*, London: Business Books.

vide catering for their workforce, although the company usually has to provide the facilities. The advantages for the firm are:

1. It is logical for an industrial organization to deal with other specialized companies for their raw materials or components, usually because specialist firms can provide a better product at a lower cost than the firm itself could provide. Thus, just as BL buys its electrical components from Lucas and its windscreens from Pilkington Glass, it can buy its catering from a contract caterer.
2. As we shall see, most industrial catering is subsidized by the firm. At a time of inflation, a catering contract enables the firm to establish a fixed cost for its catering, leaving the contractor to work within the established budget, thus removing the worry of operating in the red from the firm and placing it with the contractor.
3. If the caterer does not provide a satisfactory service, the catering contract can be terminated and offered to a rival company, so that the contractor has every inducement to provide a superior service.
4. The contract between caterer and client usually specifies the following information:

    (a) a specification of the standards expected with regard to meals and beverages served;
    (b) operating times of catering facilities;
    (c) budget available for feeding workers, as cost per head or percentage of annual payroll;
    (d) responsibility for cleaning, maintenance and replacement of equipment and plant;
    (e) stipulations with regard to any closed-shop agreement in force in the client company.

    The contractor will also usually stipulate penalty clauses if the contractor fails to maintain the standards as laid down and will accord the contractor the sole right to the catering operations within the client firm.

Case study 6.1   Grandmet Catering Services and Wiggins Teape

Wiggins Teape is a large, multinational firm with its head offices in Basingstoke, which it has occupied since 1976. All the catering in the head office is contracted out to Grandmet Catering Services, which includes:

Main restaurant	feeding up to 500 people each day
Senior staff dining room	seating for 50, average of 35 covers per day
Directors' dining room	a maximum of 18 covers, average of 13 covers per day
Three guest (function) rooms	up to 24 covers per day
Automatic vending	throughout the building.

The policy at Wiggins Teape is that catering facilities are very much part of their employees' conditions of service, so that they are prepared to subsidize the provision of meals quite substantially. Thus all employees using the main restaurant pay just 30 pence for a three-course lunch, senior staff pay 40 pence, and all vending drinks are free. With the food cost of a standard meal averaging 80 pence, the prices charged are very low, so that Wiggins Teape must cover the balance of the food cost, all the labour cost of catering staff, catering overheads and the fee charged by Grandmet Catering. In 1982 the budget for these costs was approximately £300 000.

In the contract between the firm and the caterer, the choice and quality of the meals to be provided is specified. In the main restaurant a choice of four hot dishes and a variety of salads are available each day; in addition, soup and fruit juices are always available, along with a selection from two hot sweet items, as well as cold sweets and a selection of cheeses and fruit. Senior staff have their own menu, although only one main course item and the sweet actually differ from the menu in the main restaurant. In the directors' dining room, a short table d'hôte menu is provided, although once again some of the dishes reflect the choice in the other two units. The three types of menu are shown in Fig. 6.1.

In the main restaurant the service style is cafeteria with counters arranged in eche-

MAIN RESTAURANT

ROAST PORK
STEAK & KIDNEY PUDDING
SAUSAGE LYONNAISE
MUSHROOM TOASTY

CARROTS
BRAISED CELERY
ROAST & CREAMED POTATOES

SALADS
WALDORF
QUICHE LORRAINE
CHEESE

BAKED SULTANA ROLL
CREAM HORNS
LEMON SEMOLINA

25 March 1982

WigginsTeape

SENIOR STAFF DINING ROOM

COCKALEEKY SOUP
FRUIT JUICE

STEAK & KIDNEY PUDDING
COLD BUFFET SELECTION
CARROTS
CELERY HEARTS
ROAST & CREAMED POTATOES

BAKED SULTANA ROLL
CHEESEBOARD

COFFEE

MAIN RESTAURANT

ROAST LEG OF PORK
SAUSAGE LYONNAISE
MUSHROOM TOASTY

25 March 1982

WIGGINS TEAPE

HAM & CAULIFLOWER AU GRATIN
COCKALEEKY SOUP

ROAST LOIN OF PORK

COLD BUFFET
ROAST TURKEY

CARROTS
CELERY HEARTS
CREAMED & BOULENGERE POTATOES

BAKED SULTANA ROLL
CHEESE & BISCUITS
COFFEE

MAIN RESTAURANT

ROAST PORK
STEAK & KIDNEY PUDDING
SAUSAGE LYONNAISE
MUSHROOM TOASTY

25 March 1982

Figure 6.1 *Menus from Wiggins Teape.*

lon (see page 87), senior staff have plated waiter service, and two waitresses serve the directors using semi-silver service.

Although Grandmet have held the contract for some years now, Wiggins Teape put the contract out to tender every two years, since it helps them to check that they are getting good value for money and to keep Grandmet up to standard. The decision to renew the contract is made by Wiggins Teape's Gateway House manager who is responsible for all the in-house services, and conducts negotiations with Grandmet's regional director after taking into account the performance of the caterers, their budget forecast and the wishes of the workforce. The workers have a restaurant committee through which their feelings can be expressed.

The contract between the two parties allows Grandmet a large degree of freedom, and apart from specifications concerning menus, the major constraint is exercised through the budget that both sides agree each year. Thus Grandmet purchase all foodstuffs, select their own suppliers and are entirely responsible for the staffing of the catering operation. Grandmet's workers' wage increases reflect Wiggins Teape's wage review, rather than Grandmet's, while discounts on bulk purchases go to the client and not Grandmet. The annual catering budget is broken down for control purposes month by month, on the basis of the number of working days in the month and the time of the year, and this is further broken down into sales forecasts for the different outlets. Each month, performance is measured against the forecasts and Wiggins Teape meet the total cost including the contract fee provided that any fluctuations can be reasonably accounted for.

6.3 OPERATIONAL GOALS

Industrial catering is subject to two interacting but opposing forces, namely the need to provide an adequate service within stringent financial limitations. While these considerations apply to all sectors, they are particularly important in this sector where firms are concerned with maximizing profits and in consequence with minimizing costs, and the return on capital employed in catering facilities is much less tangible than that for plant or machinery. None the less, most firms subsidize their dining room and refreshment operations, in some cases only expecting to cover food cost, or food and operating costs despite the fact that these subsidies have increased substantially. In the 1960s it is estimated that the subsidy for employee feeding increased on average by 350 per cent. ICI's decision to introduce a cook–freeze system for their catering operations was motivated by the fact that 'when we looked at our costs in the mid-1960s . . . in the next five-year period, the subsidy required from the company could double and the prices we would have to charge our diners would also double. This was a situation that would please no one, and that was at a time when the rate of inflation was considered reasonable.'[*] But, both for the company and contract operators, there are good reasons why prices should be kept as low as possible. Although employees often have little or no alternative facilities for refreshment, either because the factory is situated on a new factory estate out of town or because local catering facilities are unable to cope with the sheer weight of numbers requiring food and drink at lunchtime, this does not mean that employees automatically use the on-site catering facilities. The firm, however, would prefer them to do so and therefore makes its dining-

---

[*] Glew, G. (ed.) (1977) op. cit.

rooms as attractive as possible and keeps prices down. The firm wants its employees to use these on-site facilities because:

1. It reduces the time needed for tea, coffee and lunch breaks. In factories this can make significant differences to productivity, since it shortens the time that plant or machinery is shut down during breaks; while in offices, shorter refreshment breaks can shorten the working day and thereby make considerable energy savings, especially in winter.
2. At times of high unemployment, the provision of good catering facilities may not apparently be necessary to attract or keep staff, but job satisfaction is enhanced by such facilities and hence productivity is also maintained or improved.
3. Once the firm has committed itself to the capital cost of setting up catering facilities, it wishes to maximize the turnover and use of them in order to get the best return on capital expenditure that it can. High turnover should also help to minimize the subsidy required by the operation too.
4. As previously mentioned, trade unions protect their members' rights to refreshment and service areas. They have contributed to keeping prices down to the extent that it is estimated that their pressure has caused dining-room prices to rise at a slower rate than the costs of providing the service.

6.4 THE SCOPE OF INDUSTRIAL CATERING

The industrial caterer expects to serve all employees of the firm, from factory workers up to board level. Depending upon the management philosophy of the firm, the catering facilities will be available to all personnel or there will be segregated dining rooms for different grades of staff. The egalitarian approach is adopted because it is believed to foster better industrial relations and is likely to be cheaper to operate than several different dining rooms. Most certainly this approach has been adopted by Japanese firms in this country and is often cited as one of the reasons for the good industrial relations record of these firms. Companies that operate several dining facilities argue that their senior management use lunch to discuss business and confidential matters or to entertain visitors and customers, so that it is not practicable to have only one facility. The style of service in senior dining rooms may be silver, family or buffet service and in many respects is similar to the banqueting operations of a hotel. Some days may consist of company executives dining together, while on other days there may be a small cocktail party or buffet lunch. In this respect, industrial catering is not substantially different to the features discussed in Chapter 2 concerning function catering.

Of particular interest are the service systems adopted to feed a large number of people at minimum cost and it is with these systems that we concern ourselves primarily in this chapter.

6.5 INDUSTRIAL FOOD SERVICE SYSTEMS

Offices and factories have two different service requirements:

The service of a main meal.
The service of morning and afternoon beverages and/or snacks.

By far the most significant type of operation for the service of meals is cafeteria or counter-service restaurants, but for the service of morning and afternoon beverages, vending and trolley service are significant.

Table 6.1 *Method of distributing snacks and beverages in the morning and afternoon.*

Food/Drink	Vending	Counter	Trolley	Kiosk
Beverages	66%	55%	29%	9%
Snacks	26%	78%	27%	12%

Source: *Industrial Society Survey* 1979.
(Figures may add up to more than 100 per cent where firms use more than one method of service.)

Cafeteria operations

The cafeteria is the basic self-serve operation, designed to feed large numbers of people quickly with the minimum number of personnel. Basically, food and drink are displayed on counters at which customers either help themselves or are served by service staff. As we shall see, there are different arrangements for counters, but there are certain features of the operation that apply to all cafeterias, irrespective of their design. The manager must be aware of these essential features:

1. The menu should be displayed prominently, before the customer arrives at the counter, allowing him or her to make an early choice of meal. This is particularly important in cafeterias where customers must wait or queue before being served.
2. Food and beverage items listed on the menu must be available at the service point throughout the service period. Staff must ensure that display cabinets, bains-marie, heated and refrigerated units are replenished according to requirements.
3. Self-service by the customer should be encouraged to reduce bottlenecks, so that items should be pre-plated and pre-portioned wherever possible.
4. Non-consumable items that the customers require, such as cutlery, napkins and condiments should be situated apart from the service counters and after the cash desk to avoid congestion.
5. Quality and portion control is essential since the food is on display and customers are serving themselves. If one dish appears to be better value or is presented more attractively than its alternatives, flow will be slowed by customers changing their minds, the popular item will become unavailable to later customers causing dissatisfaction and the less popular items will not be sold causing wastage. Therefore all items must be displayed to their advantage and staff must be provided with the proper equipment and clear instructions to ensure portion control.
6. The menu should provide a good choice for the customer, but not be too extensive which creates problems for the customer of knowing what to choose, and problems for the staff in arranging counters to serve an extensive menu and remembering the prices.
7. The same staff should regularly act as cashiers to improve their proficiency. Their task is made easier if pricing policies are consistent and variations between prices are kept to a minimum. Some units operate on the basis that all meals are the same price, for instance at the Bank of Ireland each diner is entitled to a starter, main course and sweet for a voucher worth 70 pence.* The number of cashiers

---

* *Hotel & Catering Review*, 17 January 1981.

and cash desks will depend upon the flow of customers. (See also Chapter 12 where the task of a cash till operator is analysed in greater detail.)

8.   Seating must also be closely related to the numbers that can be served. There is nothing more frustrating for the customer, who may have had to queue to purchase a meal, to then find that there is nowhere to sit. It is essential therefore that places are cleared as soon as they are vacated. Clearing may be achieved by getting the catering staff or the customers themselves to do it.

    Catering staff are employed to clear away. The advantages of this are that the caterer is sure, provided that her or his staff are doing their job properly, that tables are cleared quickly, breakages are less likely, dirty items are stacked to help washing up and customers are provided with a better service.

    Customers clear away themselves. The advantages of customers clearing away are that it is less costly to get customers to clear than employ staff, and tables are cleared immediately each customer leaves. The major disadvantage is that customers may not participate, so that the caterer must do everything possible to encourage it. This can be done by providing trays from which the customer may eat without needing to unload plates from the tray on to the table before eating, siting trolleys for dirty items near the exit points and so on. To avoid congestion with trolleys sited at exit points, mechanized tray removal systems also exist. A gravity feed system may convey dirty items directly to the wash up on a belt conveyor, or the Trayveyor system can remove trays from the dining area to the wash up located some way away, perhaps on a different floor.

9.   Lastly, although the catering supervisor is not responsible for the design of equipment and counters for cafeterias, there are certain features of good design that the supervisor should be aware of to ensure that they are maintained in working order. Such features include sneeze guards where foods are openly displayed, tray rails with 'outboard protector bars' to prevent trays from sliding off at corners or at the end of the run, drainage points at beverage service points, containers of alternative sizes compatible with the counter that permit presentation of foods according to their likely sales, and by-pass areas to allow customers to pass at points where there may be a delay. Tray slides and floors should be level and the tray slide should extend beyond the cash desk to prevent delays. It should be unnecessary to state that all display and service units must be kept scrupulously clean.

There are three main variations of the cafeteria system:

The 'in-line' cafeteria :

This consists of a single counter along which customers pass to select food and beverage. It is sometimes described as the 'straight-line' cafeteria, but not all such counters are in fact straight, although there are advantages in ensuring the counter is straight, primarily because customers pushing trays along the counter may be distracted enough to either push the tray off the rail where it changes direction away from them or into the counter, thereby spilling items, where it turns towards them.

    This style of cafeteria can serve between 4 and 8 customers per minute depending upon those factors mentioned above such as the speed of the service staff, proficiency of the cashier and the menu display, and also the customer's familiarity with the unit and the order of presentation of items along the counter. Some experts believe that the counter should be arranged logically in the order of the menu so customers select a starter, main course, a sweet and beverage in the 'correct' sequence, while others advocate that all those items served at room temperature or chilled should be at the beginning of the counter, so that hot items are served last and therefore have less time to cool before they are eaten. Whichever method of presentation is adopted, it is important to be consistent so that customers will become familiar with the layout, and will know at which point along the counter they will find particular items.

The length of a cafeteria counter will depend upon the number of menu items, but will be between 6 and 15 metres (20 and 50 feet). The longer the counter, the slower the service is likely to be. This has led to some modifications of the basic idea:

1. One counter is divided into two, with both halves serving the same selection of items. Customers may start at either end and move towards the cash points located at the midpoint of the counter, or start at the midpoint and move towards either end (see Fig. 6.2).

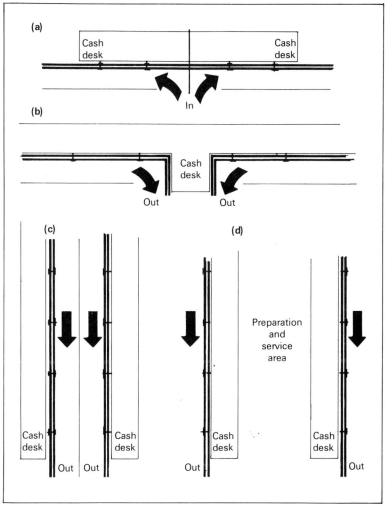

Figure 6.2 *In-line cafeterias—different designs.*

2. Parallel counters, with the customer flow between the counters on either side.
3. Two counters are placed either side of a central service point running in parallel with each other.

Task 6.1

Most schools, colleges and department stores, as well as industrial catering operations, have cafeterias. Try to compare two or three such operations and evaluate the extent to which they meet with the essential features listed above.

Case study 6.2   British Home Stores

The operational policy of department store cafeteria is determined at the head office of British Home Stores, so that all of the public restaurants in the group conform to the same standards. This includes the display of food items along the cafeteria counters. For each menu that may be used, the order in which the food items are to be arranged is specified. For example, the grill menu in September 1981 comprised the following dishes:

Main meals

　　　　Grilled gammon steak with pineapple
or　　Three sausages
or　　Grilled hamburger in a bun
with　Chips, peas or baked beans

Children's meals

　　　　Junior burger
or　　Junior fillet of plaice
or　　Two sausages

Sweets

　　　　Strawberry flan
　　　　Lemon meringue pie
　　　　Blackcurrant cheesecake
　　　　Egg custard tart
　　　　Cherry pie
　　　　Apple pie
　　　　Two tone jelly
　　　　Chocolate dessert
　　　　Crème caramel

The hot-food display was specified to be arranged in bains-marie along the counter as shown on the left-hand side of Fig. 6.3.

For the cold items it was specified that 'displays to be vertical through all shelves . . . rolls, butter and cheese . . . in baskets off the counter.'

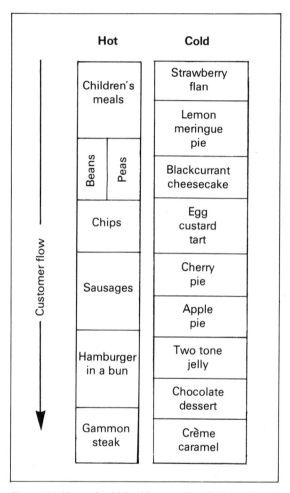

Figure 6.3 *Hot and cold food layouts (British Home Stores).*

Similar layout charts are provided for the group's fish menu, breakfast menu, main menu (morning) and main menu (afternoon).

The free-flow system

This is also known as the 'scramble system' or 'hollow-square'. Whereas in-line cafeterias comprise usually one counter in whatever configuration thought suitable, the free-flow system has several counters each serving different meal items, such as hot foods, sandwiches, salads, desserts and beverages. The major advantage of free flow is that it avoids the necessity to queue and, although short queues may form at periods of high demand, the number of customers that can be served may be as high as 15 per minute. Customers prefer this layout because the service is quicker, there is less queuing, the customer who only wants a snack does not have to use the same counter as someone who requires a three-course meal and a wider selection of menu items may be offered. In particular, it is possible to operate a call-order counter for grills that in a conventional cafeteria is impracticable. From the caterer's point of view, the free-flow layout has the advantage of flexibility. During periods of slack demand, some counters may be closed, counters may be removed in the event of breakdown and greater use may be made of self-service by customers since the flow of the entire system is not held up by one slow customer.

There are two main types of layout of the free-flow cafeteria:

1. The hollow square (see Fig. 6.4) has counters placed around three sides of the service area in a U-shape, with customers entering and leaving via the open side. This is used particularly in operations where there is a steady flow of customers throughout the service period, such as in department stores.

Figure 6.4 *Free-flow cafeteria (Granada motorway services).*

2. The echelon (see Fig. 6.5) counters are arranged at an angle next to each other. This is used particularly where there are a large number of people to be served, as in the industrial sector.

With both layouts it is important that the counters are well signposted so that customers can easily identify the particular counter they wish to use and counters should be arranged so that as little cross-flow takes place as possible.

Figure 6.5 *Echelon counter service (Royal Surrey Hospital).*

Carrousel

The Carrousel was first introduced into Britain some years ago and has been a limited success. It comprises a large rotating arrangement of shelves, approximately two metres in diameter, on which food and drink are presented. Thus customers remain stationary as the Carrousel revolves once every minute to enable them to select items from it. Only one half of the Carrousel is in the service area, so that as items are removed, the shelves can be replenished in the serving area behind the unit (see Fig. 6.6). Trays, cutlery, napkins and beverages are usually separately available from dispensers so as to avoid congestion at the unit. Cashiers are situated between the Carrousel and the dining room.

Advantages of the Carrousel. (1) As a method of self-service, it has a customer throughput of between 8 to 10 per minute, which is higher than the traditional in-line counters. (2) It requires less space than many other self-service layouts, particularly in the service area of the operation.

Disadvantages of the Carrousel. (1) Operators must be well trained to re-stock the shelves quickly and efficiently to maintain a steady flow rate of customers. (2) Customers may cause delays waiting for a complete revolution of the unit before making their selection. In this respect, the Carrousel is most suited to operations where there is repeat custom on a frequent basis.

Case study 6.3   Middlesex Polytechnic

Early in 1982, Middlesex Polytechnic opened their first cafeteria in their Bounds Green

Figure 6.6 *Carrousel system (Middlesex Polytechnic).*

site. It is based around a Regithermic Carrousel which during lunch makes three main meal choices available, as well as a variety of sweets. Customers may also select salads or sandwiches and snacks from two adjacent counters, or use the call-order fast-food bar which is open all day. Beverages are available in the cafeteria and throughout the site via vending machines.

The Polytechnic's catering is operated on a centralized cook–chill production system, so that meals for the unit are prepared in the central kitchen on another site, seven miles away. At Bounds Green, the food is reconstituted in infra-red ovens. These are the only items of kitchen equipment on site apart from deep fryers, one steamer and a convection oven which are used to prepare any additional items for a day's menu. This has resulted in a servery taking up very little of the available space, so that seating is maximized. There are 1200 staff and students in this part of the Polytechnic and although they do not all use the catering facilities the cafeteria is operated by just ten staff. Only one or two staff are needed to load the Carrousel during the service, as all the meals are prepared and reheated before the service and held in the storage area immediately behind the unit. The pre-plated items are then transferred by the staff from the heated meal holders to the Carrousel as required.

Automatic vending

The Automatic Vending Association recognizes that the development of vending machines in Britain was closely related to the industrial catering sector. 'By the 1950s . . . it was clear that the future [of vending] lay in servicing the worker and his [sic] refreshment needs.' In 1980, there were 325 000 vending machines in Britain. Of these many were in offices and factories and had a turnover of £650 million.* The AVA list 82 different types of goods or services that may be vended by machine, but from the caterer's viewpoint, the most important products are:

Beverages—hot or cold.
Confectionery and snacks.
Sandwiches.
Meals—hot or cold.

Machines vending such products may be found in cafeterias, refectories, hotel corridors, student common rooms, clubs and pubs, and many other types of location. In order to show just how pervasive machine vending has become, count the number and types of vending machines encountered during the course of an average day.

Types of machine

The type of machine will depend upon the product being vended. Those vending pre-packaged goods, such as confectionery, soft drinks and sandwiches need only electricity supplied, whilst cup-vending machines need water supplied also. Machines are also temperature controlled and may be ambient, refrigerated or heated. The operating mechanism varies from machine to machine but they include cup, drop-flap, rotating drum, compartment, endless belt, lift and column and drawer mechanisms.

Machine operation

Since the caterer is not expected to be technically capable of maintaining or repairing these machines, the complexities of their mechanisms will not be dealt with here. In those cases where machines are sited by a vending company on contract to the caterer, all maintenance, cleaning, restocking and control is likely to be carried out by the vending operator's staff. The caterer need only report a machine defect or failure if this should occur. In other cases, machines are not on contract from a vending operator, but are purchased, leased or hired, in which case technical support is usually provided by the suppliers according to a maintenance agreement. Caterers operating their own vending machines must therefore have well-trained staff responsible for the regular cleaning, replenishing, maintenance and control of the machines. In 1975, 80 per cent of machines were self-operated, but there is a growing trend towards contract operation, reflecting US practice, where 95 per cent of all machines are on contract.

The vending question

The advantages of installing vending machines include the following.
Flexibility. A vending machine, properly maintained provides its product 24 hours a

---

* *Mintel*, 1981.

day. It allows workers in offices and factories to take refreshment whenever they wish, according to their individual needs. So long as industry and commerce are prepared to accept their workers having flexible break times, there is no doubt that their perform-ance is improved by providing tea, coffee or other beverages throughout their working day.

Accessibility. Machines may be sited in close proximity to the work place, be it fac-tory or office, thus reducing the amount of time required by the user to get to and from the service point. This is particularly important in offices and factories covering several hundred square metres.

Control. The machine dispenses an exact measure or amount of the vending com-modity for the correct value of coins or tokens, therefore wastage, pilferage and loss are eliminated and exact control is made possible, which was not always possible with trol-ley service.

Labour saving. It is estimated that one machine can be serviced by a member of staff in 20 minutes each day. With the use of disposables (see Chapter 9) which reduces the need for washing up, this probably involves fewer work-hours than a conventional food and drink service would necessitate.

The disadvantages of vending machines have been:

Speed. A well-trained cafeteria operator can probably dispense teas more quickly than one machine, but even so a machine using instant ingredients takes only 10 seconds to serve one customer. Where speed is particularly important, several machines located around the service area would be needed.

Quality. Initially there was a great deal of resistance to tea-vending and coffee-vending due to the poor quality of the product, reinforced by its dispensing in a plastic or paper cup. This resistance has been eroded by definite improvements by the manu-facturers of vending products and a change in consumer attitude towards the product and disposables. To illustrate this the reader may wish to conduct an experiment. Serve 10 people with two cups of tea in identical cups. Obtain one from a vending machine and make the other using a teapot in the traditional manner. Ask the 10 tasters to identify the cup of tea made by the vending machine.

Impersonality. The vending machine has effectively replaced the tea-trolley (see below). It is a factor that vending manufacturers are aware of and have researched in order to design machines that reduce the lack of personal contact. They believe that 'brightly coloured and well-lit machines can do much to overcome any resistance encountered from the "impersonal tag".'*

Vandalism. Perhaps because of the above, damage, malicious and otherwise, may be caused by frustrated consumers. No machine is entirely vandal proof, but modern machines are very robust, despite their increasing sophistication. On contract oper-ated sites, the contractors have a vested interest in ensuring the security of takings, since they get a share of them; while a damaged or broken-down machine affects the operators' or caterers' turnovers.

Vending operations

From what has been outlined so far, the catering manager in an operation where vend-ing machines are installed must have three clear priorities:

---

* *Vending*, p. 32.

1. To ensure that the machines are sited effectively to maximize their use and pro-
    vide the best possible service.
2. To ensure that a member of staff, if a self-operator, is well trained and capable of
    replenishing, cleaning and regularly maintaining the machines and if it is a con-
    tract operation, that the contractor fulfils these same obligations properly.
3. To agree a clear policy with regard to customer dissatisfaction due to machine
    malfunction or breakdown. For instance, if a customer complains that the
    machine accepted money but failed to vend or refund the same, there must be a
    consistent policy with regard to refunding money or not. In any event, it is in
    everyone's interest to ensure that the machine is kept in proper working order, so
    it is advisable to place a notice on each machine that says who should be contacted
    in the event of any dissatisfaction.

Case study 6.4   Hospital vending

The East Surrey Health District began a scheme in 1971 that replaced night catering
staff in eight hospitals with a refrigerated merchandiser, linked to a 2 kW microwave
oven, and a hot and cold beverage machine. The District catering manager estimated
by 1977* that this resulted in savings of £30 000 per annum, primarily as the result of
reduced operating costs at a time of higher wage demands, but also due to increased
sales which doubled during the night hours. Additional advantages that benefited the
hospital were that vending allowed food and drink to be served in more comfortable
rest rooms, rather than dining rooms, which allowed the latter to be closed for cleaning without discontinuing the refreshment service for staff.

  On the other hand, two hospitals have found that the social cost of replacing the
night cook with vending machines has been too great and sales fell drastically.
Middlesex General Hospital installed machines for sandwiches, salads and beverages,
but still employs a call-order cook, while Lancaster Infirmary discontinued vending
operations and re-employed a night cook.†

Trolley service

Despite the advent of automatic vending, some operators still operate a tea or beverage trolley which tours the factory or offices providing mid-morning and mid-
afternoon refreshment. The principal advantage of such a service is that the refreshment goes to the employees rather than the employees having to leave their work
place to have refreshment. Also, trade union influence has tended to support the person bringing round the tea rather than make her or him redundant through replacement with machines.

  Like any other form of service, there are essential features that the catering supervisor must be aware of.

  One trolley can serve approximately 200 people, if they are not dispersed over too
wide an area or on too many floors. It should provide a choice of beverage and snack
items, but choice should be kept to an acceptable minimum to simplify administration,
control and stock turnover. From experience, a trolley on a regular route will establish

---

* *HCIMA Journal*, July 1977.
† *Staff and Welfare Caterer*, January/February 1981.

a well-defined pattern of sales—so many teas, coffees, glasses of milk, and so on—which enables the operator to stock the trolley sufficiently to satisfy predicted sales without excessive waste.

The trolley should be regularly cleaned and maintained so that beverages and food items are served hygienically and presented in an appetizing way.

The route of the trolley should be carefully considered and reviewed regularly to take into account the starting, break and finishing times of staff, the distance to be travelled and any obstructions to a smooth schedule, such as lifts. No route will be ideal since it will take about 1½ hours to serve 200 people, for some of whom the trolley will arrive too early, and for others it will be too late. Therefore the caterer should be in close consultation with management and unions to maximize satisfaction with the service.

The trolley operator should only serve from designated stops to ensure an efficient service, since experience has shown that it takes longer to serve people when they stop the trolley to purchase than if the trolley stops for a while to serve several people. This also helps to establish a routine so that employees who move around the building know where to find the trolley at any given time.

The control of trolley service is just as demanding as any other food service system. Items may be easily pilfered and cash is particularly vulnerable. Much depends on the security-consciousness and honesty of the operator and in some cases, caterers have adopted a procedure whereby the stock is 'sold' to the attendant before the service, which she or he then pays for out of receipts, less any returned stock. The attendant is therefore much more likely to guard the stock and cash than otherwise. This system is particularly used outside industrial catering when trolleys are used for refreshment services at sporting events, such as hot dog stands at football matches and so on.

6.6 CONCLUSION

This sector has seen very significant changes in the last 30 years in both the attitude of clients and customers towards catering and the systems adopted to meet this client demand. Contract catering has developed to become a significant sector of the industry and has been instrumental in developing the trend towards large-scale catering firms operating on a national basis. It is also a sector of the industry about which much clear cut information is unavailable. Those firms that run their own catering operations are not identified as such in the Government's collection of statistics concerning industrial output. Nonetheless, it is clear that industrial catering is now recognized as being an important part of the hotel and catering industry and the economy in general. Its image has changed from being very much the poor relation to that of a standard setter with regard to sound catering applications and development of systems designed to feed large numbers of people.

Exercise

Discuss some of the issues, such as industrial relations, economic, social, etc. that may be raised by the decision to replace a factory's trolley service with automatic vending machines.

7 Institutional Catering

The art of feeding people unable to feed themselves

OBJECTIVES: to outline the importance of the institutional and welfare sectors of the industry . . . to explain the particular needs of the client group in this sector . . . to describe the catering systems adopted in the service of food in hospitals . . . to describe the organization of catering within the National Health Service and local education authorities.

Educational catering is a vital element in Britain's hospitality industry

John Fuller*

7.1 INTRODUCTION

'INSTITUTIONAL catering' is a rather old-fashioned term these days and has to a great extent been replaced by 'welfare catering'. While the latter may be more acceptable, it is less precise than the older and somewhat derogatory phrase. But unfortunately 'institutional' succinctly describes this sector—catering for schools, colleges, universities, old people's homes, hospitals and prisons. For a long time, the standards associated with such places have been thought of as inadequate—the Dickensian image of Oliver Twist asking for more seems to have lingered on until long after the Second World War. But in recent years this sector has been revitalized by the building of brand new universities and polytechnics with modern purpose-built catering facilities, the introduction in the hospital service of European and US systems of food service such as Ganymede and the development of large comprehensive schools which has led to much development and innovation in the provision of school meals. By the 1980s, this sector was recognized as being a significant and influential part of the catering industry.

---

* In an introduction to Evans, J. (1974) *Catering in Schools and Colleges,* London: Barrie & Jenkins.

7.2 NEEDS OF THE CLIENT GROUPS

There is no doubt that there are considerable differences in *how* food is prepared and
served in schools, colleges and hospitals and that the client groups* are very different.
Nevertheless, there are certain factors that apply to this sector in general before considering each of these types of institution in more detail.

Public sector involvement

Unlike any other sector of the hospitality industry, the great majority of catering provision is undertaken by the State in the form of the National Health Service or Local
Education Authorities. In this respect, the 'authorities' tend to act on behalf of the
client group as arbiters of what is needed as well as providers of the service. This
means that the clients—school children, students, old people, hospital patients—have
little or no say in the standard of provision. This is reinforced by the fact that provision
in this sector was, until recently, completely free, or at very low cost.

Social role

The cheap provision of meals at school and in hospitals is part of Britain's economic
and social policy. For instance, the original aim of the 1944 Education Act was to
make school dinners free of charge completely, and was seen as a supplement to the
cash benefit of the family allowances as part of the benefits of the Welfare State. It is
also no coincidence that only two years later, the National Health Service Act 1946 in
effect nationalized the hospitals.

Nutrition

Far more than any other sector, the nutritional needs of the consumer are given particular thought by institutional caterers. Ann Harris said (in *A Textbook of Hospital
Catering*, 1967) 'good nutrition is essential for every one of us, [but] more especially, it
is necessary for a sick person.' Likewise Judith Evans can state 'the school meal is
designed to provide one third of a child's nutritional requirements for the day,'
although since April 1980 the nutritive value of school meals is no longer established
by law.

Choice

In addition to providing nutritional value, clients expect some degree of variety, and
possibly choice, with regard to provision of food. In many respects, they are captive in
the institution either because they are confined to bed or a prison cell, or because

---

* The client group is presumed to be the consumer. As we shall see, the 'client' may well be the Government or local authority rather than the consumer.

NUTRITIONAL REQUIREMENTS OF DIFFERENT PEOPLE

Most foods are a mixture of the different nutrients needed for a well-balanced diet. These nutrients are:

1. *Proteins.* An average diet requires about 65 grams of protein a day; these are broken down during digestion into amino acids, eight of which are essential to adult life. Generally speaking, meat, cheese, eggs and fish are higher value protein foods and vegetables are low value foods.
2. *Fats.* These basically provide the body with energy, and yield more energy for a given weight than any other nutrient. 30 to 35 per cent of calorie needs for individuals should be derived from this source.
3. *Carbohydrates.* These also provide energy, in the form of starch and sugars. To some extent such foods have the function of providing bulk in the diet, which assists in increasing bowel movement.
4. *Minerals.* These have three functions: bone formation, as dissolved salts in the body fluids to maintain acidity or alkalinity, and as constituents of soft tissues to enable them to carry out their particular function.
5. *Vitamins.* These are present in small quantities in food and are needed to prevent specific deficiency diseases.

    However, depending upon their age and health, different people have specific dietary requirements.

Table 7.1 *Recommended intake of some typical nutrients.*

	Protein (g)	Thiamin (mg)	Vitamin A (μg)	Iron (mg)
Babies	20–30	0.3–0.5	400	6–7
Infants	35–45	0.6–0.8	300	8–10
Teenage boys	70–75	1.1–1.2	730	14–15
Teenage girls	58	0.9	730	14–15
Adult men —sedentary	65–70	1.0–1.1	750	10
—moderately active	70–75	1.2	750	10
—very active	90	1.4	750	10
Adult women —sedentary and moderately active	55	0.9	750	12
—very active	63	1.0	750	12
Pregnant women	60	1.0	750	15
Nursing mothers	68	1.1	1200	15
Old age pensioners	50–60	0.7–0.9	750	10

there are no alternatives available, or they cannot afford an alternative. The caterer must therefore provide dishes that appeal to clients and stimulate the appetite, but at the same time, meet their dietary and nutritional requirements.

7.3 CONSTRAINTS UPON THE CATERER

The four points discussed above impose specific restraints upon caterers' freedom of action as do three other identifiable and significant factors.

Cost

Like all public sector services, institutional catering operates under severe budgetary limitations, and similar limitations exist in privately run institutional catering operations. We have already seen that industrial caterers must be budget conscious, but compared with institutional catering, caterers in industry have much more money to spend. Public spending restraints mean that caterers must examine all areas of cost, although their degree of freedom to cut costs is often curtailed by the imposition of bureaucratic measures designed to monitor spending. For instance, most caterers must deal wih designated suppliers, work within rigid budgets, and pay nationally negotiated wage scales. In addition, the trend at this time is for catering to be most affected by cutbacks in spending.

Case study 7.1   Reorganization of the Berkshire school meal service

In 1978–1979, Berkshire local education authority decided to implement cutbacks on its education spending in order to comply with Government guidelines. Significantly, although the Government required local authorities to make overall cuts of 1.5 per cent, spending on the educational sector was allowed to increase while *all* the reductions were to be made from spending on school meals and milk. Nationally, the Department of the Environment expected spending in this sector to fall from £337.7 million in 1977–1978 to £244.4 million in 1978–1979. For Berkshire, this meant a total reappraisal of their spending, but they too 'preferred to make savings on those areas that were not strictly educational, but could be loosely described as welfare provision.' This provision constituted a large proportion of their budget, for although LEAs may charge pupils who are not eligible for free meals, such charges are controlled by the Government. For instance, in September 1977, charges were increased from 15p to 25p.* Thus in 1977–1978, Berkshire spent £6.6 million on school meals provision, and after deducting the income from schools' meals charges, the net cost was still £3.7 million.

Table 7.2 *School meal provision in Berkshire 1977–1978.*

Type of school	Numbers present			Meals served					
	Pupils	Teachers	Others	Pupils		Teachers		Others	
				paid	free	paid	free	paid	free
Primary	68 033	2804	3761	50 685	4969	40	1762	41	3300
Secondary	47 919	2881	1368	22 035	2380	143	1702	17	1136
Special	1 783	166	255	1 356	300	0	145	0	244
Total	117 735	5851	5384	74 076	7649	183	3609	58	4680

---

* LEAs under the Education Act 1980 are now free to charge what they like.

In order to effect these cuts, the authority set up an education panel, who were 'to review such parts of the Education Budget as appear desirable and in particular to conduct an immediate review into all school meals expenditure.' Although one councillor was reported to have suggested 'making school meals as unpalatable as possible' in order to reduce demand, the panel's actual recommendations were as follows:

1. The present policy of 'rationalization' of kitchens, with closing down of surplus capacity, be continued, necessary reductions in staff being achieved by natural wastage or transfer to other nearby kitchens.
2. The use of convenience foods be increased, coupled with a long-term investigation of the effect of such increased use on staffing levels required.
3. The continuous cafeteria system of service be introduced at all schools other than nursery and infant as a matter of policy. The effect of any staff reductions achieved by this means to be built into the investigation referred to in (2) above.
4. Where possible, the meal break should be reduced with a consequent reduction in the hours paid to meal controllers; bearing in mind the numbers of controllers who may be required following the deliberations of the head teachers' working parties.

It was also hoped to reduce the number of free meals for staff, but nationally negotiated agreements with the teaching unions give teachers the right to free meals if they are carrying out supervisory duties during lunch breaks, so that Berkshire were unable to make much saving in these areas after discussion with the unions involved.

In conclusion, this case study illustrates the extent to which the school meal service is controlled and manipulated by a variety of pressure groups, including central government, local government, teachers' unions, public sector workers' unions and parents. Commenting on the Berkshire study, Finch and Ozga* write, 'many local authorities attempted to make savings on school meals provision in the late 1970s and substantial reductions in estimates for provision of school meals were commonplace. It is doubtful if these savings were effectively achieved, however, given the many constraints on the local authorities' freedom of manoeuvre.'

Legislation

In as much as most of the provision in this sector is provided by the State the institutional caterer has been subject to a great deal of statutes and regulations that stipulate, sometimes in great detail, just what can and cannot be done with regard to provision of meals. Thus under the Provision of Milk and Meals Regulations 1969, Circular 3/66, local authorities must provide 'on every school day . . . for every pupil as a midday dinner, a meal suitable in all respects as the main meal of the day.'

Consumer

Unlike any other sectors, the caterer must be able to cope with the fact that consumers may be unable to feed themselves easily, and, certainly in hospitals, be unable to present themselves at restaurants or cafeterias. Thus in addition to the problems associated with bulk food production, there is the problem of transporting the prepared food from the production area to where the consumers are.

---

* Finch, A. & J. Ozga (1979) *Local Government of Education*, Milton Keynes: Open University Press.

Hospitals have developed many different and sophisticated systems in order to overcome this constraint. This chapter deals primarily with these systems, since schools and colleges have to a greater or lesser degree tended to adopt food-service systems such as in-line cafeteria, free-flow cafeteria, automatic vending, etc. that we have discussed previously (see Chapter 6).

Task 7.1

Discuss to what extent the needs of the client as a consumer contradict the desires of the client as a tax-paying voter.

Before going on to discuss the particular food service systems adopted in this sector, it may be beneficial to examine the organization of the two principal areas of this sector—schools and hospitals.

7.4 INSTITUTIONS IN THE WELFARE SECTOR

Schools and colleges

Although emphasis has been placed on State education, 7.9 per cent of schools and colleges are private ones (see Table 7.3).

Table 7.3 *Number of pupils in school.*

	1970	1977
	(thousands)	
Public sector	9 301.2	10 484.8
Private sector	687.8	835.6
Total	9 989.0	11 320.4

During the late 1960s and the 1970s, the number of children attending schools and students going to colleges steadily increased, so that education required a large amount of new investment and school building. This period of expansion has now come to an end and so there is a consequent retraction in the sector. We shall look at both sectors, the smaller one first.

Private schools/colleges

Broadly speaking, schools can be thought of rather like industrial catering units. As in the previous chapter, they may either operate their own catering facilities or employ the services of a contract caterer.

Case study 7.2   Charterhouse School

Charterhouse is a large public school, near Godalming in Surrey, that for a number of reasons operates its own catering facilities. During term time, the catering department serves over 620 breakfasts, 900 lunches and 700 suppers per day. The school continues to operate its own facilities for the following reasons:

1. Tradition. Originally, each house in the school was self-contained and catered for itself. In the last few years a central catering complex has been built and catering for seven of the eleven houses is now on one site, although they continue to dine separately in their own dining-rooms.
2. Flexibility. The school believes that it can be much more flexible in its approach to catering than a contractor would be prepared to be. For instance, each Saturday there are over 300 sports teas and also late suppers. Teams may arrive late and so on, all of which the existing catering staff are used to dealing with.
3. Cost. The school believes that it is more economic to run its own catering, especially as employing contract caterers would mean the additional cost of their fees.
4. Special needs. In addition to the everyday catering, the schools catering manager is also familiar with the special requirements of annual events such as the Founder's Feast, Old Carthusian reunion, Scholars' Feast and so on. These annual functions may involve anything from 200 to 4000 guests.
5. Staffing. By operating the catering, the school can take full advantage of letting out the facilities during vacation periods for English language courses, conferences and an annual School of Music.

State schools and colleges

The provision of meals in state-run schools and colleges, like the education service itself, has developed throughout the twentieth century. Since the service is diffused, with separate legislation covering England and Wales, Scotland, and Northern Ireland, the organization of meal provision varies from area to area. None the less, the principles are similar throughout the UK. Originally, the school meal service was constrained through 'almost total control by the Board of Education'* but the Education Act 1980 is likely to provide LEAs with much greater scope for action than possibly ever before. However, this is itself curtailed by centrally imposed restrictions upon public spending.

Despite the fact that when proper school meals were provided in the 1940s, it was hoped to provide all children with meals free of charge, only about 50 per cent of the total school population at any moment have ever been fed at no cost to themselves. Following the 1980 Act, free meals need only be provided to children whose parents receive family income supplement or supplementary benefit. However many local authorities, despite the cutbacks, regard it as their social and moral duty to provide meals for as many children as possible at the lowest possible cost. Some authorities, for instance Somerset, have even enlisted the services of an advertising agency in order to persuade children to use the school dining facilities. Whereas in the past Her Majesty's Inspectors were responsible for monitoring catering in educational institutions, the Department of Education and Science now has catering advisors to oversee generally the provision of food and drink.

Essentially, however, the LEAs are free to administer the service as they see fit, so long as they comply with the statutes and regulations laid down, and since education is the largest budget heading for most authorities, it is regarded as the most important of

---

* *Education,* 12 September 1980.

all their activities. Following the Local Government Act 1972, most authorities have adopted the organizational structure shown in Fig. 7.1. Thus elected councillors, on the education committee, make all the major decisions concerning education, including catering at schools. They do so, however, on the advice of the permanent staff of the education service, who are employed by the LEA to administer the service. Burgess believes that a major trend in school catering will be that 'catering in schools is likely to be more commercial in character and there will be greater opportunity for the professional caterers to use their catering skills'.[*]

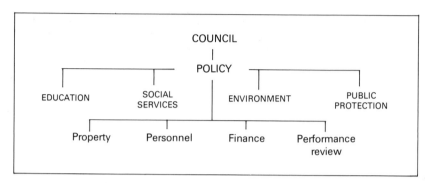

Figure 7.1 *Committee structure of a local authority.*

Case study 7.3   The school meal service in Somerset

Somerset is fairly typical of a county education authority. In autumn 1981 there were 62 865 children in schools throughout the county, of these 31 265 were pupils in approximately 250 primary schools and 30 787 were pupils in 50 middle or secondary schools. Of this total, 9.5 per cent of children, approximately 6000, take up their right to a free meal, as defined earlier. This compares with the national average of 8.5 per cent. Of the remainder, nearly a further 45 per cent purchase a school meal, which is higher than the national average of 36.8 per cent, partly because of the economic circumstances of the area and partly because of the county's policy towards promoting school meals. Thus, when all the adults such as teachers and staff who are entitled to a meal are added to the children, Somerset is feeding nearly 38 000 people every day, when schools are open. In addition, the authority is obliged to make available an area where children who bring their own food may eat, which constitutes a further 19 000 people per day. To provide this service, all Somerset's secondary schools have their own kitchen and operate cash cafeterias, so that pupils select their meals from a counter and pay at the cash desk. Ninety primary schools are supplied with food from central kitchens, but the remainder have their own kitchens too. In these infant and junior schools, the service is much simpler and children collect their lunch from counters one course at a time.

In order to finance the education service, the county council allocates to their LEA out of a total of £140 million, a budget of £86 million, of which nearly £3 million is spent on the school meal service. For the financial year 1982–1983 the service's budget was as follows:

---

[*] *Education,* 12 September 1980.

	£
Costs—labour	3 224 570
—food	1 584 450
—other expenditure	873 040
Total expenditure	5 682 060
less Income	2 822 330
Net cost	2 859 730

Included in the overhead cost, apart from a proportion of schools' fuel costs, capital investment and so on, are the salaries of the county's catering officer and staff. The service is administered by the county catering officer, to whom four area catering officers report, and three assistant catering officers. All other staff in the service are in effect part-time, because they are not employed during the school holidays (although they are paid a retainer) and they all work less than 37 hours per week, which the local authority wages council regards as full-time employment. Thus the authority employs nearly 1200 cooks and kitchen assistants, although on the basis of full-time equivalent work-hours, i.e. a 37 hour week, this works out at 857.6 school kitchen staff hours per day, 44.5 central kitchen staff hours per day and 25.5 mainte-nance fleet hours per day. There are also nearly 1000 school meal supervisors employed, but as they are only present for about two hours per day during the meal this represents 191.8 full-time equivalent work-hours.

In order to minimize labour costs, although the staffing level of supervisors is based on the school roll, the staffing of kitchens in each school is based on the take-up of meals. To achieve this, Somerset has prepared a staffing scale for their primary schools and secondary schools. Thus for instance, a primary school that serves 200 meals daily has 113 hours per week of staffing allocated, which is broken down into the posts of cook supervisor (30 hours), assistant cook (30 hours) and general kitchen assistants (53 hours). In secondary schools, where cash cafeterias operate and where large numbers are served, a school serving, say, 400 meals daily would have a cook supervisor working a 35 hour week, cook (30 hours), assistant cook (30 hours), cashier (15 hours) and general kitchen assistants working a total of 93 hours per week. In order to establish each school's point on the staffing scale, each primary school's take-up of meals is measured over a two-week period in February; while in secondary schools, staffing is based on measurements taken half-termly, since the number of meals eaten constantly falls during the academic year, whereas in primary schools the figure is much more stable. Where falling demand removes the need for a post, e.g. a cook or assistant cook, the employee in that post will effectively be downgraded at the time of the staffing review.

In order to monitor their spending on food, Somerset have devised a system for each of their two types of school. In primary schools, they have developed a menu pat-tern and quantity guide for the 'traditional' two-course meal, which they sell at 50p to infants and 55p to juniors. This menu pattern specifies that in any period of 20 days, certain dishes must be served: for instance, a roast must be served twice, fish three times, sausages four times, and so on. It also specifies the amount of meat, fish, veget-able or sweet items required to serve 100 meals: for instance, 17 dozen fish fingers, 14 lb sausage meat, and so on. However, the supervisor in each unit can decide in which order to use these dishes during the 20 days and also what actual dishes to make. It is specified, for instance, that a potato dish must accompany the main course 13 times, but the type of potato dish is left to the discretion of the supervisor.

In secondary schools, because a cafeteria operates, the children are offered a choice of between six to ten dishes. The traditional meal of a main course and sweet is priced at 55p, but other items such as snacks and beverages are priced separately, so that the average spend is approximately 43p. In planning the menu, the supervisor in each school can select the dishes from over 70 dishes nominated by the catering officer, each with its own recipe card and costing sheet. Each month the catering officer revises this list to establish the current selling price for each dish and circulates this to each school in the form of a summary of tariff, food costs and gross profit percentages. The county's policy is to achieve a gross profit of 45 per cent on sales. In order to monitor this each month, the number of meals taken up is divided into the purchases cost for each school, giving the average cost per meal per school. This is then compared with the cost analysis determined by the catering officer. Area catering officers ensure that school supervisors achieve the desired gross profit and select suitable menus in the context of the nutritional requirements of the children.

The county catering officer admits that relatively speaking Somerset's control systems are very basic and in 1982 more sophisticated computer control systems were being developed. However, this reflects the policy decision of the authority to overcome the problems of enforced cutbacks in spending and provision not by rigid cost cutting and complex control, but by increasing income through an active promotion of school meals. They began a campaign in 1980 based around a cartoon character called Mr Grub (see Chapter 11, Fig. 11.4) and in 18 months the number of children eating school meals rose by 15 per cent from 24 000 to 28 000, even though prices had to be raised. This resulted in the cost of financing the promotional campaign being met out of increased revenue and the surplus income that has been generated greatly reduced the net cost of providing the service. It also meant that the authority was able to do more than just provide nutritious meals to those that wanted them and so improved the use of the facilities and capital already invested in school meals.

Universities

Britain's universities, although receiving most of their funds from the State through the University Grants Committee, are autonomous bodies, i.e. they are self-governing. In this respect the provision of catering facilities will depend upon the particular policy of each university. They differ from LEA establishments in as much as their clients are predominantly aged over 18 and they have the freedom to employ contract caterers.

Case study 7.4   University of Surrey

This university in Guildford is fairly typical of the 'red-brick' universities that were established in the late 1960s and early 1970s. There are 3500 students and 2100 staff on the campus, of whom 2500 are resident on site. To cater for this large number the university has four main facilities:

1. *Central catering.* This department is administered and funded directly by the university, which has established an amenities committee to determine catering policy with regards to those units operated by central catering. These units are two self-service restaurants, one licensed bar where snacks are served and a coffee bar. The opening hours, style of service, menu items, pricing, and so on are laid

down by the amenities committee. While the university would like this operation to be self-financing, it is subsidized annually by £50 000 of university funds.

2. *Student union*. Like central catering, the student union catering facilities are open seven days a week. The union operates three bars, all offering hot and cold snack meals and a servery providing cafeteria meals and takeaway service. These facilities are operated as a surplus, partly because they are supported by other trading activities that the other facilities do not provide, such as games machines, automatic vending, cigarette machines, union shop, supermarket and so on. Apart from rent and rates, the Union must meet all its own operating costs which in 1980–1981 were £100 000. Turnover in the same period was £120 000 so that there was a surplus of £20 000.

3. *Wates House*. This building comprises all the catering facilities for academic and technical staff, and consists of a bar serving cold buffet meals, a self-service restaurant and two waitress service units. These facilities are only open in the day until 2 p.m. from Monday to Friday. Just as the catering manager of central catering and the student union report to a committee, the catering manager of Wates House reports to a committee made up of staff.

4. *Sports hall*. There are two bars, one in the sports hall and another in the sports pavilion, which are operated by the sports committee.

Hospitals

Like education, hospitals are state run and they too, have undergone periodic reorganizations since the inception of the National Health Service in 1946. The Department of Health and Social Security is responsible for its administration and operation. The National Health Services Act 1977 (as amended) lays a duty on the Secretary of State for Social Services to promote a comprehensive health service and requires her or him to establish regional and district health authorities to help discharge these duties. There were 14 Regional Health Authorities and 192 District Health Authorities in 1982. Each RHA is responsible (within national gudelines) for the policies and strategic planning for health services in its regions and allocating resources to, and monitoring the performance of, its District Health Authorities. DHAs are established on the basis of covering an area with a population up to 860 000. Within Districts, services are arranged into units of management responsible for a particular service, including the provision of catering. According to the DHSS, the 'DHA is accountable to the RHA for the performance of its responsibilities within national and regional policies and guidelines, but will enjoy a considerable degree of autonomy to conduct its affairs with minimum interference from higher levels.'

7.5 INSTITUTIONAL TRAY SERVICE

Institutional catering has since the Second World War seen a great deal of technological development and an increase in the systems approach to catering. This is particularly true of food service in hospitals. While schools and colleges have tended to adopt those systems used in the industrial sector, the hospital sector has developed highly specialized systems, designed to overcome problems associated with centralized kitchens servicing wards that are widespread through hospitals. In particular, tray service systems have been developed and they have proved so satisfactory that the DHSS make provision for such a system in the cost allowances for new district general hospitals. The first installation of this kind was in 1964 at Bethnal Green Hospital, where the Ganymede system was used. In a report* sponsored by the King Edward's Hospital Fund for London, it was concluded that such a system 'can be successfully applied to the patients of a general hospital; that the standard of feeding in most respects will be higher than the bulk food trolley system [used formerly]; and that the amount of time saved by nurses, ward orderlies and domestics is quite considerable.'

Tray service operations

A menu for each patient is sent to the wards for patients to select the dishes preferred and usually the portion size also, and patients usually choose their meals a day in advance. These menus, which are in three sections (breakfast, dinner, supper) are returned to the catering department for summarizing, i.e. totalling the number of each dish ordered. These totals provide the basis for food production the following day.

Food is plated in the kitchen by catering staff and assembled on trays, using a moving conveyor belt (Fig. 7.2). Trays come off the service line, in a well-organized unit at eight per minute. This speed is rarely exceeded because of the stress on the checker, all trays being checked before being sent to the ward. The speed may sometimes be

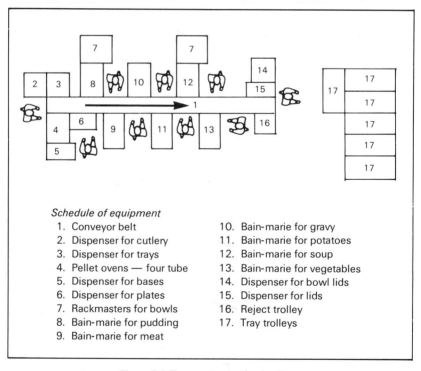

Schedule of equipment
1. Conveyor belt
2. Dispenser for cutlery
3. Dispenser for trays
4. Pellet ovens — four tube
5. Dispenser for bases
6. Dispenser for plates
7. Rackmasters for bowls
8. Bain-marie for pudding
9. Bain-marie for meat
10. Bain-marie for gravy
11. Bain-marie for potatoes
12. Bain-marie for soup
13. Bain-marie for vegetables
14. Dispenser for bowl lids
15. Dispenser for lids
16. Reject trolley
17. Tray trolleys

Figure 7.2 *Tray-service production line.*

---

* *The Ganymede Tray Service in Hospitals* 1966.

reduced to six per minute but on average a 500-bed hospital will take about 1¼ hours to serve the midday meal.

Food is kept hot in a variety of ways, either by a heated pellet, a heated base plate or a heated plate inset into an insulated tray. There are also systems which make use of disposables inset into an insulated tray. The other dishes—the soup and sweet—are served in insulated plastic, porcelain or stainless steel bowls, as they lose their heat more quickly. Beverages are normally made on wards but the use of central beverage units could be considered for hospitals with wards near to the kitchens.

Food is sent to the wards on individual trays complete with all three courses, cutlery, etc. It is conveyed in special tray trolleys of a Trayveyor lift and the ward staff hand the tray to the patients. In due course the trays are collected and returned in the trolleys or by Trayveyor lift to the kitchen, where they are unloaded. The crockery, cutlery, etc. are sorted and passed through a central crockery washing machine. They are then placed in mobile dispenser cupboards which are sited in the service line ready for serving the next meal.

Because of the length of time of service, meal times are staggered, the first ward probably having dinner at 11.45 a.m. and the last at 1 p.m. Naturally the ward which has the first breakfast would have the first midday meal and the first supper, so that the time between meals is the same for all. The trays, of course, are handed to the patient immediately the trolley arrives to ensure the patient has a palatable meal, although the system would keep the main dish hot for some considerable time. The catering department will require about 22 full-time staff or their part-time equivalents to operate tray service for around 500 midday meals. This includes staffing the dishwashing facilities. For a tray service for 500 people, an area of around 90 square metres is required; for two tray services serving approximately 1000 people, about 140 square metres will be required. Each trolley needs around 1.3 square metres.

Advantages of the system

The DHSS identify the following advantages:

1. *Selection.* Patients are able to select those dishes which they normally like but selection is made the previous day. Furthermore the patient is able to ask for large or small portions by indicating so on the menu.
2. *Effect on food.* Staggered meals give the opportunity to cook food nearer the time of consumption. For example, such items as fish, chips or eggs, could be fried and served to the patient within seven to ten minutes of cooking. Therefore this system gives the opportunity to provide a better standard with the food looking more palatable. There should be continuous cooking during the service with items such as cabbage, potatoes, etc., being cooked in batches.
3. *Effect on staff meals.* As patients' meals are staggered, it will automatically follow that staff will be able to come to meals over a period rather than in two or three sittings. This, in turn, makes it possible to have a steady flow of cooking and service with beneficial effect on the quality of the food served to the staff.
4. *Crockery washing.* The washing of patients' crockery for the main meals is automatically centralized with the obvious advantages of (a) a better standard of hygiene, (b) a higher standard of efficiency and (c) the removal of noise from the ward. These objectives are achieved by being able to install large fully automatic dishwashing machines which operate more efficiently than those which are normally installed at ward level.

5. *Trolleys.* The trolleys used for tray services do not normally have to be heated. Unlike bulk trolley services, space is not required in front of the trolley bay for loading at meal times, consequently the unheated trolleys can be double banked.

Disadvantage of the system

The major disadvantage is the reliance of the entire feeding of a hospital upon the efficiency of one central kitchen and in particular the conveyor belt. In the event of power failures, most hospitals have their own generator, and the belt may be moved mechanically by hand in the event of a breakdown. None the less, there is a high reliance upon technology.

Case study 7.5   Royal Commission Report Number 5

The extent to which patient feeding has been successful can be judged from the findings of this report.* Two main areas were researched: times meals were served (Table 7.4) and dissatisfaction with hospital food (Table 7.5).

Table 7.4 *Times meals were served.*

Patients' opinions of times that meals were served	Men and women
	Percentage
Meals were served at suitable times	74
Times were unsuitable: too long from last meal to breakfast	3
breakfast served too early	9
other meals served at awkward times	11
other answers	7

Base: all in-patients aged 14 and over = 100 per cent.

Overall, three out of four patients were satisfied. Major complaints concerned the length of time between the last meal at night and breakfast in the morning. The most dissatisfied group were women on maternity wards, who experienced problems when feeding their babies coincided with meal times, which led to dissatisfaction with the early time for breakfast.

All patients had similar views about the standard of food served, and only one in five expressed dissatisfaction, despite the popularly held view that hospital food is very poor. The major causes of dissatisfaction were that food was cold when it reached them and that it was tasteless or unattractive.

Types of system

The tray service system has produced such satisfactory results that the DHSS makes provision for its installation in the cost allowances for new district general hospitals.

---

* *Patients' Attitudes to the Hospital Services—1978 Royal Commission on the NHS.* Report Number 5, Cmnd 7615, London: HMSO.

Table 7.5 *Dissatisfaction with hospital food.*

Satisfaction with the food	Men and women	
	Number	Percentage
Satisfied with the food	652	82
Dissatisfied with the food	145	18
Base: all in-patients aged 14 and over = 100 per cent	797	100
Reasons for dissatisfaction: Base: all dissatisfied with food	145	100
food was served cold	52	36
no taste, unappetizing	54	37
badly cooked	40	28
portions too small	33	23
not enough variety	35	24
specialist needs not considered	5	3
other reasons	44	30

Percentages add to more than 100 as some people gave more than one reason.

There are several manufacturers that market such systems but they all work around the concept of a moving conveyor belt (see Fig. 7.2). Depending upon the size of the hospital, conveyor belt installations are adapted to meet different needs. The major difference between the systems available is their method of keeping food hot.

Ganymede system

The Ganymede system is manufactured by Falcon and offers a choice of two methods for keeping the foot hot, Dri-heat and Heatstor.

1. *The Dri-heat arrangement.* A metal pellet (about 225 grams in weight) is heated in a special unit to 232°C and is mechanically put into an insulated dish. The china plate is placed on top of the base, so that heat radiates from the pellet to keep the food hot. When food portions are then plated they will be kept at a serving temperature for about 45 minutes. Alternatively, the pellet can be cooled (to approximately 2°C) and will keep salads cold for up to 1½ hours.
2. *The Heatstor arrangement.* The Dri-heat arrangement for keeping the food hot is now, however, being replaced by the less cumbersome Heatstor arrangement. In this system the heat-retaining material is an integral part of the steel dish which is heated to about 130°C in a special dispenser.

The china plates used in the Ganymede system are specially made to absorb the required heat without cracking, and particular care must be taken with the stainless steel base plates as their replacement cost is high. The system is flexible enough to cater for meals in small cottage hospitals up to the very largest district hospital.

Finessa system

Finessa tray meal service, manufactured by Grundy, uses a double-walled plate warmer with a built-in pellet which is heated to about 120°C in specially designed dispensers. The outer wall of the plate warmer cools to a comfortable temperature but the built-in pellet is surrounded by insulation and will continue to transmit heat to the food for about 45 minutes. The accompanying lid, like the base dish is stainless steel, and the plate that sits on top of the platewarmer and from which the customer eats is china. The Finessa tray service is capable of catering for the smallest hospital of fifty beds, to the large district hospitals of several thousand.

Heatrex system

This is a more recent development by the same company who market the Stellex system below, and is very similar in principle to both the Ganymede and Finessa systems. Food is kept hot by the Heatrex plate base which is a one piece unit with no separate pellet. The china plate is placed on top of this base as the tray moves along the conveyor belt, the food portioned onto the plate according to the menu card, and a stainless steel lid placed over the dish at the end of the belt. Insulated stainless steel bowls are used for soups, hot and cold sweets, etc. The trays are loaded into unheated tray meal trolleys which are taken up to the wards where the trays are distributed to the patients.

Stellex system

In the Stellex system the food is kept hot by electrically heated elements which remain in situ in the trolley. Plated meals are fitted in a special cut-out tray although there is still room on it for beverages. The tray is placed into the trolley so that each plate is located over, and therefore rests on the elements: each section of dinner or sweet plates can be switched on for hot dishes or left off for cold. Part of the top of the trolley is fitted with a bain-marie unit which is used to serve soups, custards, etc. at the ward level. The electrical elements in the trolley keep the food hot even when only switched on for 15 to 20 minutes before loading, and the trays with holes are said to be an advantage because the plates do not slide about the tray. However, this system is not used extensively in hospital catering as it has been superseded by the other tray meal systems which do not require trolleys to be heated to transport the food to the wards.

Helitherm system

The Helitherm system is manufactured by Electrolux under this name. It is based on a tray set designed to keep heated food hot and cold food cold for 30 minutes. The basic tray set is manufactured in polystyrene and has indentations to receive dishes of various sizes. The porcelain plates have a specially thickened base which provides the heat source for the food during distribution, as there is no heating arrangement in the tray trolley. The large plate is divided into segments for meat, fish, vegetables or potatoes, and a ventilated lid is placed on top for added insulation.

   The trays are prepared by the use of a conveyor belt, between eight to ten per minute. Cold and hot dishes are served from different sides of the assembly line. The bains-marie are placed against the conveyor, rather than at right angles to it, so that staff portion food onto the plates in a forward movement rather than a sideways movement as in the Ganymede and Finessa systems. This system therefore enables staff to serve from more than one section should it be necessary.

Other systems

Other systems that are available but not widely used in Britain are

1. Alpha system.
2. 1216 system.
3. Sweetheart system.
4. Optacon II.
5. Integral Heat system.

Role of the catering manager

The manager of a 'hospital catering' facility will, of course, have similar responsibilities to those of any food service manager, but due to the rather different circumstances of feeding patients, there are certain activities she or he must specifically undertake. For example:

Ensure that the preparation of food meets the required nutritional standard.
Monitor the operation of the tray service system to check that personnel are operating the belt efficiently.
Visit the wards to research consumer opinion concerning the standard of meal service.
Review operational procedures to ensure the most effective timetable for trolley assembly and ward meal-times.

Case study 7.6   Walsgrave Hospital, Coventry

Walsgrave Hospital is a typical, large general hospital built in the early 1970s. The general and maternity hospitals (there are also geriatric and psychiatric units on the same site) have a total of 30 wards with approximately 25 patients on each, although on average 550 patients are catered for each day and over 1900 patients' meals are served.

Meals are prepared in one central kitchen and served to patients using the Ganymede tray service system. Menus are designed over a three-week cycle and are sent to each patient for the following day. Approximately 130 patients per day are on a special diet and their meals are prepared in the diet kitchen attached to the main kitchen.

Dinner is served between noon and 12.30 p.m., so that service on the belt commences at 11.30 a.m. There are usually 10 or 11 staff on the belt and they take on average less than three minutes to assemble the trays for each ward. All the trays for each ward are assembled in one trolley and are taken up in lifts located near to the assembly area. The service should be finished by 12.15 p.m. The sequence of despatching trolleys is determined in consultation with the senior nursing officers, although it largely depends on the location of the wards in relation to the central kitchen.

In addition to feeding patients, the catering department is responsible for feeding staff. This comprises a large cafeteria with counter and buffet service where main meals are served, coffee bars where tea, coffee and a small selection of counter lines are sold, and vending machines for sandwiches and beverages in three suites of operating theatres. The catering manager expects to make 15 per cent gross profit on sales to staff, but the pricing of staff meals is prescribed exactly by the West Midlands Regional Health Authority as follows:

Meal	Content	*Price recommended from 1 April 1981 inclusive of VAT at 15 per cent*
Full breakfast	Cereal or toast and marmalade Hot course Cup of tea	35p
Light breakfast (to be available where possible)	Cereal, toast and marmalade Cup of tea	22p
Lunch	Main course	62p
Tea	Cake, bread and butter and preserves Cup of tea	17p
Supper meal	As lunch above	62p
Snack supper	Single course snack meal Cup of tea	29p

The memorandum detailing these prices goes on to say:

> The Health Notice circular 77/173 dated November 1977, confirmed the suggestion that with rising costs it was increasingly difficult to provide a reasonable standard 2-course meal for the ASC lunch or main meal cost of 37p (1st April 1977) which has now been increased to 62p from 1st April 1981.
>
> Some Areas will want to continue to provide the improved standard for the 62p for a single main course while others may wish to provide the 2 courses with a resultant reduction in choice. For those who wish to do this the breakdown should be 50p for the main course and 12p for the sweet, including VAT.
>
> There is a need for snack items costing less than the above main courses and it is recommended that the choice of these items should be provided on the 60/40 basis (ingredients/labour) to provide a range of dishes for customers not wishing to incur expenditure of more than 62 pence.

7.6 CONCLUSION

The welfare sector of the hotel and catering industry differs significantly from other sectors in two main respects. First, it is part of the public sector with all the benefits and drawbacks this accrues. Second, the welfare caterer is concerned with feeding very large numbers of people with standard, nutritious meals, in the context of fulfilling a moral duty of care as well as satisfying the consumers' needs. Both of these factors have led to the development of food service systems designed to meet the large-scale demands using relatively unskilled and therefore cheap labour. As a result of this, it is probably fair to say that a catering manager in this sector is primarily preoccupied with food production and spends relatively little time on the food service side of the operation or in contact with the consumers. Having said that, many hospital caterers regularly visit at least one ward every week in order to gauge patients' reactions and comments upon the meals provided.

Exercise

Identify the constraints upon a catering manager in the welfare sector of the industry and illustrate this with specific examples.

8 Transport Catering

The art of supplying refreshment to people on the move

OBJECTIVES: to describe the provision of food on trains, aeroplanes and at sea . . . to identify the particular problems of transport catering.

For me, sitting in the comfort of a dining car is always full of interest and remains one of life's important pleasures

Frank Muir in *1879–1979: Food and Drink to Us* (1979) London: British Railways.

8.1 INTRODUCTION

THE travelling public has always had a significant impact upon the structure of the hotel and catering industry, as we have seen, and transport catering has developed simultaneously with the advancement of transport systems. The first public dining car service on Britain's railways was from Leeds to London in 1879, while 100 years later, British Rail served 2.25 million passengers in restaurant cars and 15 million in buffet cars in one year. For the airlines, feeding passengers has become significant as a means of differentiating one airline from another, since for many years, the national airlines in particular have had fixed fares. It is interesting to observe, however, that the concept of feeding passengers is approached in entirely different ways.

8.2 RAILWAY CATERING

Since the railway system in Britain was nationalized in 1947, British Rail has standardized and rationalized its catering operations. There are essentially three parts:

111

1. *British Transport Hotels.* Many of the newest and biggest hotels in the late nineteenth century were built by the railway companies. Under British Rail, these were organized as one hotel chain and operated separately. In 1984 they were sold.
2. *Travellers-Fare Station Catering.* This operates nearly 200 licensed buffets, 250 licensed bars, 50 unlicensed buffets, 40 railbars and numerous other operations including off-licences, foodshops, bistros and grills situated at railway stations throughout Britain. In addition, 50 kiosks and vending machines at 300 stations had a turnover of £7.4 million in 1979.
3. *Travellers-Fare Rail Catering.* This part of BR catering accounted for £1.65 million in 1978—approximately one-third of Travellers-Fare turnover in that year. The range of catering includes the provision of all the main meals (breakfast, lunch and dinner) as well as afternoon and high teas, snacks, beverages and drinks.

Operational features of rail catering

There are five important factors affecting the provision of food and drink on trains in Britain.

Logistics

The complexity of the operation is staggering, as Table 8.1 shows. In order to supply the rolling stock, there are 38 victualling points throughout the country. In most cases, the restaurant cars and buffet cars are stocked with unprepared foodstuffs and the items are prepared on the train, by chefs working in the railway galleys. For instance, meat is roasted in the galleys and the pastry made up fresh for the preparation of pies and sweets. In this respect, catering is very traditional and the service of food is very similar to that in any non-mobile restaurant or buffet. British Rail estimates that the annual rate of failure to supply the required catering services on trains is 3 per cent of the total catering vehicles run. Failures are due primarily to the priority of running the trains on schedule, which takes precedence over the revictualling needs of the catering vehicles.

Table 8.1 *British Rail on-train catering.*

Number of meals served in 1979	
Full breakfasts	914 000
Lunches	647 000
Dinners	440 000
Afternoon and high teas	277 000
Snacks	3 000 000
Beverages	12 500 000

Responsibility for the operation of on-train catering is shared between the British Rail regions and Travellers-Fare. The regional authorities provide the correct vehicle and Travellers-Fare provide the staff to operate the facility so that failure to provide a service could be due to operational or catering reasons.

Staffing

The essential problem is that once members of staff are on a train, they have to make a round trip in order to return to their original destination. Staffing levels are high throughout the working day in order to cope with peak demand, so that catering vehicles are run at uneconomic times simply because staff are available.

Control

The mobility of the catering units makes it extremely difficult to monitor, supervise and control all aspects of the operation; stock, cost and staff behaviour. The Press in recent years has reported several cases of dishonesty by catering staff on trains, and British Rail has developed systems that help to overcome these problems.

Unions

Catering staff on British Rail are all members of the National Union of Railwaymen as the organization has a closed-shop agreement with British Railways. Since 1965, they have been exempt from the provisions of the Wages Councils Orders, since the representation of the NUR is believed to represent them adequately. Thus, in comparison with other sectors of the industry, catering staff are relatively well paid, as their pay and conditions of service have parity with railway workers.

Investment

As a nationalized industry, British Rail's development of its catering operations depends upon the Government's policy towards the railways. Thus the Mark I catering vehicles introduced after the Second World War were meant to be renewed after a working life of 10 years. In fact, lack of investment in the railways delayed the replacement of stock until the 1970s, during which time, Mark III vehicles have gradually been introduced. These are not significantly different from their predecessors, although there is a greater emphasis on fast food cooked on griddles for self-service buffets.

As a result of these problems, like every other major railway operator, British Rail train catering is operated at a loss (see Table 8.2).

Table 8.2 *Some West European rail catering operations.*

	Britain		France		Germany		Italy	
	1973	1978	1973	1978	1973	1978	1973	1978
Total sales £ million	£9.09	£16.62	£12.27	£18.24	£10.15	£20.78	£4.40	£5.92
Cost (percentage of sales)								
Food and drink	40.1	45.2	32.1	33.9	38.4	32.6	27.7	30.2
'On board' staff	39.9	45.4	50.7	49.5	52.6	60.1	50.7	71.6
Other 'on board' expenses	14.0	16.0	9.8	13.3	14.1	11.9	10.6	15.9
Administration and other expenses	17.3	22.7	21.3	24.0	35.8	40.8	29.4	46.6
Net cost (% sales)	(11.3)	(29.3)	(13.9)	(20.7)	(40.9)	(45.4)	(18.4)	(64.3)

(Figures in brackets = deficit)
* Source: *Caterer & Hotelkeeper*, 13 September 1979.

However, the British Railways Board has accepted such losses as a cost item to be offset against Inter-City revenue in order to achieve a corporate gain. They argue that by providing refreshment, something like £15 million of revenue is generated by custom that would not otherwise use rail transport (*Caterer & Hotelkeeper,* 24 June 1982).

Types of catering

There are basically two types of service provided on trains. The first is the buffet car.

There are two types of buffet car—the locomotive-hauled Mark I cars and the 125 High Speed Train Mark III buffet cars. The Mark I cars are unable to use up-to-date and sophisticated items of equipment, such as microwave ovens and therefore their Welcome Buffet is more limited than the Buffet Bar 125. Nonetheless, standard food and beverage items (tea, coffee, sandwiches, ploughman's lunch and so on) are priced identically in both types of operation. Such buffets are usually operated with one or two stewards, depending upon the time of day and the particular line. For instance, a train travelling on the line from Victoria to Bognor Regis will have one steward in the Welcome Buffet, while on the Waterloo to Portsmouth line there will be two. On the 125s there may be a third member of staff in addition to the stewards, namely a cook. On those routes where it is uneconomic to use a full buffet car, one steward may operate a 'trolley' bar, which is a redesigned section of a conventional carriage, although these are gradually being phased out.

The second type of catering on trains is the restaurant car. Although many European train operators have introduced airline-style meals, British Rail has decided to continue their traditional approach to food production and continue serving meals with full silver service. The reason for this is that 'they feel that the space available on a train for a fully equipped modern kitchen able to produce good, freshly cooked food is a major advantage denied to their air and road competitors.'* British Rail identify three types of traveller who use its catering facilities and has therefore introduced three types of menu. Depending upon the time of day and the route covered, one of these will be implemented in the restaurant car.

1. *Inter-City Grill.* Mainly for families and second-class ticket holders, this consists of a simple two-course meal: main dish with vegetables, roll and butter and a sweet or cheese.
2. *Main-line Menu.* Aimed at the middle market, it is a three-course table d'hôte meal.
3. *Gold Star Menu.* For the business traveller on selected routes, a four-course 'up-market meal' with a wider choice of dishes and wines is available.

The staffing of restaurant cars is as follows:

Chief steward
Cook
Stewards (up to four per car)

The maximum number of covers that can be accommodated in a restaurant car is 64 (see Fig. 8.1), but the staffing of the car will (as for buffet cars) depend upon the line

---

* *Modern Railways,* October 1978.

Figure 8.1 *An Inter-City 125 first-class restaurant car (British Railways).*

and the time of day. One route that provides a very comprehensive service is the Clansman, which links London to Inverness; because of the distance it can provide a breakfast, lunch, afternoon tea and dinner service.

8.3 AIRLINE CATERING

The provision of food and drink on aeroplanes is very different from other forms of catering for a variety of reasons:

1. The customer purchases the flight and in effect receives the meal as part of an all-inclusive package.
2. Little or no food production takes place on the aircraft.
3. Meals are served in surroundings that are designed for the purposes of air travel rather than for eating in.
4. The catering staff (stewards) have many other functions apart from that of food service.
5. The circumstances of flight may deter people from eating either because of travel sickness or the effects of jet lag.
6. Food served must reflect the wide range of ethnic, religious and cultural attitudes among passengers on international flights.

Flight catering operations

Raymond R. Charman (Principal Environmental Health Officer for Crawley Council, which includes Gatwick airport) describes just how in-flight caterers operate.*

> At the outset, the management will have a programme of the days and times when meals will be required, together with the type of aircraft to be served and the class of meal to be provided, which may range from sandwiches to a first-class eight-course meal with all the trimmings. With this plan available, the supplies of perishable foods and dry stores, all the cutlery, crockery, china, glassware, napkins, condiments, trays and cabinets will be assembled in the kitchen. It will then be the job of the chef and staff to prepare the number and classes of meals required for each day (and night) at the specified times. This will involve several different types of meals for separate flights and types of aircraft, all departing at various times and all probably requiring the use of their own special design of equipment such as storage cabinets and flasks. To achieve this diversity in operation, it is necessary to prepare some meals well beforehand and to preserve them as fresh as possible in a chilling room until they are required. Some hot meals will be prepared, cooked and despatched for immediate use and others will be deep frozen for subsequent reheating on flights. As the departure time for flights draws near, the correct number and types of meals are assembled together in the appropriate cabinets, together with all the necessary accoutrements which are placed on the trolley and retained in a cold room, until it is transported to the aircraft in a Hi-loader vehicle.
>
> When the vehicle returns to the flight kitchen from the aircraft, it will return with the cabinets, trays and all the remains of the meals which were served to the passengers on the previous incoming flight. The refuse is removed for disposal and partially consumed food is, whenever possible, incinerated, whilst the indisposable equipment is retrieved and subjected to a cleaning and sterilising process before it is set aside for use on subsequent flights.

Most aircraft have two galleys, one forward and the other aft, and some have a middle galley too. Depending on the length of the flight, the passenger will be served with a snack meal or main meal by the cabin crew, who work together in pairs serving the meals on trays from a trolley. The aircraft type determines in which order the passengers are served, but generally service begins in the middle and works back towards the galleys. The cabin crew, consisting of a purser or chief steward and stewards, are given very intensive training and instruction in service techniques and the airlines place great emphasis on the excellence of their in-flight service. Despite the problems created by providing a choice of meals, the business is so competitive that many airlines have re-introduced a choice, particularly on their first-class flights. This requires careful market research in order to forecast the demand for the different dishes and careful control in-flight by the stewards to ensure that passengers can have what they wish, since only about 10 per cent surplus in total is loaded. Where passengers have special dietary needs, such as vegetarians, infants or invalids, these too will be catered for, although the airline would hope to be notified in advance of such requirements.

Flight catering can be provided in a variety of ways, but really there are two alternatives: airlines operating their own in-flight kitchens and being entirely responsible for their own in-flight needs, or flight catering specialists providing catering services for the airlines on a contract business. From the purely catering viewpoint, most operators would agree that food prepared in one or two major locations on a large scale is the most economic way to provide in-flight meals. However, with the high cost of aviation fuel, the savings are more than lost by the costs of transporting meals around the

---

* Charman, R. R. (1977) *Control of Food Hygiene in Flight Catering.*

world. Thus in general terms, aircraft are re-supplied at their destinations rather than stocked for the entire round trip. Just how this re-provisioning takes place depends upon the local circumstances. For instance, British Airways uses a contract caterer on its flights out of the United States; it uses the state-controlled catering organization under Kenyan law when flying from Nairobi; and in some middle eastern locations, restocks with its own London produced frozen meals that are stored there.

Storage onboard

The storage and stowage of both consumable and non-consumable items is a problem for flight caterers for a variety of reasons:

1. Stowage and galley areas are specifically located in stressed areas of the aircraft and the payload weight of each locker or space is designated precisely and cannot be exceeded. Thus an aircraft will always carry a full set of equipment with dummy units, if the passenger payload is below capacity to maintain the aircraft's payload.
2. Storage must take account of the aircraft's angle of ascent and acceleration. For example, the power and attitude of Concorde at take-off created real problems with the presentation of items on trays.
3. All aircraft types are different and the galley equipment may be installed by different manufacturers; everything loaded on board must be compatible with that on the aircraft.
4. To minimize the weight of equipment, all items are manufactured in lightweight materials, especially, plastics, to specific design criteria that facilitate stowage. For instance, the airlines would prefer to serve all their alcoholic beverages in ring-pull cans, since unlike bottles in glass or plastic, such cans are stackable, lightweight and unbreakable.

Loading aircraft

The loading of catering supplies, which includes not only meals for the passengers and crew but all the items likely to be needed by the travelling customers, depends primarily on the aircraft of which there are two types:

1. Narrow-bodied aircraft—such as the VC10 or BAC 111. These usually have a single aisle with passenger seats either side and galleys at the front and the rear of the aircraft, adjacent to the doors. The aircraft are usually loaded by hand and non-perishable stock replenished by bringing the stock level up to requirements.
2. Wide-bodied aircraft—such as the Tristar or Boeing 747. These aeroplanes have twin aisles and three lots of seats, with as many as five separate galley areas located near access doors. Such aircraft may have a 'turn round' of 45 minutes, which means that the aircraft must be fully restocked in about 20 minutes. In order to achieve this roll-on roll-off storage units are used, so that all stock is replaced entirely, irrespective of usage, and the used units are then replenished on the ground for another flight. Fig. 8.2 illustrates a typical stowage area (galley 2 on a British Airways 747) and indicates the extent to which space is at a premium and the use of space is precisely designated for every single item. There are five similar galleys on a 747 as shown in Fig. 8.3.

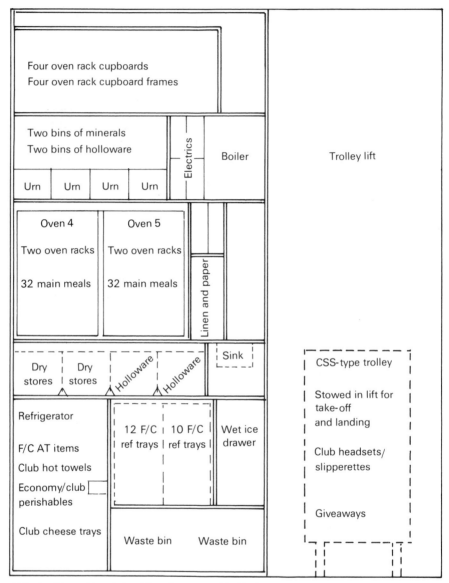

Figure 8.2 *Stowage galley 2 on a 747 (British Airways).*

Staffing

The number of cabin crew depends upon:

Type of aircraft.
Configuration of the aircraft, a 747, say, can seat various combinations of first-class, business/club and tourist passengers.

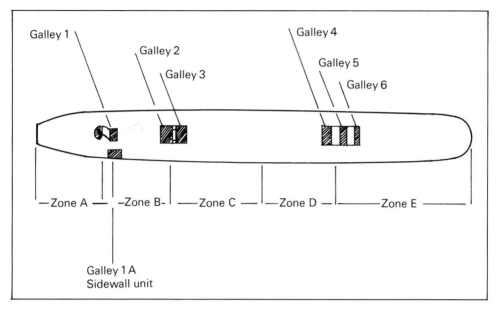

Figure 8.3 *Cabin stowages on a 747 (British Airways).*

Duration of the flight and time of take-off.
Passenger density.
On-board equipment.

A large aircraft, such as the 747, might be staffed as follows (Fig. 8.4):

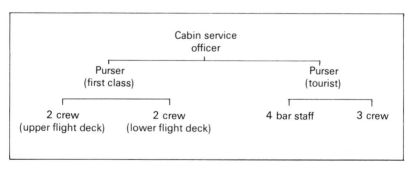

Figure 8.4 *Cabin crew of a 747.*

Smaller aircraft have a correspondingly lower level of staff, and may have a purser in charge rather than a CSO. All stewards (female and male) are expected to be capable of working in any capacity after three years' experience, so that specific duties are allocated to the crew on the basis of seniority, flight needs and staff-training needs.

In-flight food service

Every airline in planning its routes determines the level of catering for each flight.
British Airways for instance has a catering schedule for every one of its flights. Such
schedules lay down what type of refreshment will be provided within the broad
framework of policy for the standards of service for different groups of passengers. As
we shall see first-class passengers receive a higher level of service and greater choice
than other travellers. The decision to provide a meal during a flight is as much a
marketing decision as the need to satisfy passengers' needs.

Whatever the service, whether it is a main meal, light refreshment or just drinks the
service routine is determined by the aircraft type. Generally speaking, on narrow-
bodied aircraft meal trays are 'hand run', that is to say the crew take trays to the passenger by hand from the galleys. On larger aircraft the trays are taken to the passengers on trollies, holding up to 32 trays. If a hot meal is to be served it is loaded into the
convector oven on the ground. Once the aircraft has taken off, the hot food dish is
reheated for 20 to 35 minutes, depending on the dish. The hot items are then placed in
an insulated canopy on top of the trolley. The meal is then added to the passenger's
tray just as it is served.

Oven sizes and capacity equate to trolley size so that meals and tray trolleys (oven
and trolley) match precisely. By adopting this method, some of the work is removed
from the galley to the cabin and carried out in front of the passengers. In this way an
efficient cabin crew can serve all 400 passengers of a 747 with pre-dinner drinks, a
main meal, and coffee to follow in 90 minutes. The main meal routine for a large
aircraft will depend upon the configuration and loading of the aircraft, but assuming
that the aircraft is almost full and is divided into club and tourist passengers, the service would proceed as follows:

1. Starting at the forward part of the aircraft, club passengers in zones B and C (see
    Fig. 8.3) would be served with aperitifs, followed by tourist passengers in zones D
    and E, whose wine would be offered at the same time.
2. Club passengers would be offered a second round of drinks, and wine to accom-
    pany their meal.
3. The first 32 passengers on each aisle of the aircraft would be given a meal tray in
    zone B.
4. The entrées would be placed on the meal trays already served and then the next
    64 passengers would be served with meal trays through to zone C.
5. Entrées would be placed on meal trays of the remaining club passengers in zone C
    and meal trays *with* entrées in place would be served to tourist passengers in zone
    D.
6. While meal trays with entrées are being served to passengers in zone E, cheese
    would be served to passengers in zones B and C.
7. Beverage service commences in the forward seats and moves towards the rear.

The service of meals to first-class passengers is much more sophisticated. In effect
everything is served from a trolley and on British Airways, for instance, a joint is
often one selection on the menu and is carved at the seat. A typical first-class menu is
shown in Fig. 8.5 and illustrates the types of dishes that are served in-flight. In almost
all respects, the standard of service is extremely traditional and classical in its
approach and few concessions are made to the fact that service is taking place 10 000
metres up, although no flambé work is carried out, of course.

Tokyo - Anchorage

Dinner

Japanese delicacies

Seafood cocktail Hokkaido
Vegetable pâté

Pan fried fillet steak with
artichoke and tomatoes
Fillet of sole bonne femme
Barbecued pork with red ginger

Buttered string beans
Glazed carrots
Berny potatoes

Palm heart salad
Vinaigrette or créole dressing

Black Forest gâteau
Praline ice cream

Assorted cheese

Fruit basket

Coffee . Caffeine free coffee

Green tea

Friandises

We apologize if, due to previous passenger selection,
your choice is not available

Refreshments
will be served

Figure 8.5 *Typical first-class menu (British Airways).*

8.4 MARINE CATERING

No statistics are available to determine the numbers of people served meals at sea, but three clear areas can be identified:

1. Short-stay clientele travelling on cross-Channel ferries and so on.
2. Holiday-makers on board a cruise ship for at least five days and more.
3. Employees working at sea, which includes the not inconsiderable number of personnel employed aboard oil rigs in the North Sea.

Quite obviously the demands made by these three different categories of 'customer' are very different too and this is reflected in the nature and style of catering on board.

Ferries

The purpose of a ferry is essentially that of transport from one place to the next. In this respect, catering on ferries most resembles that discussed earlier in this chapter, notably rail catering. Both are monopolies in the sense that customers have no alternative catering available unless they bring their own food. There is also the need to handle large, unpredictable numbers of people, both first-time users and regulars, such as lorry drivers and frequent business travellers. Ferry companies operate catering facilities on their ships for two main reasons—first as another source of revenue in addition to the price of the ticket, and second to satisfy consumer demand. Unlike the railways, however, the consumer does have a choice of operators and therefore as with air travel, the catering facilities, as well as other factors, may influence the choice of ferry operator selected. The facilities offered by a typical cross-Channel ferry are threefold—a semi-silver service restaurant offering a three-course table d'hôte menu; a cafeteria operation serving main meals, snacks and beverages; and at least one if not two bars. For instance, Townsend Thoresen operates ferries carrying 1300 passengers on the Dover–Calais route, which have a 50-seater silver-service restaurant and two cafeterias seating about 150. P & O, on the other hand, on the same route operates only one cafeteria with just over 250 seats. P & O estimates that 65–70 per cent of all passengers use the catering during summer months and that this percentage is higher at off-peak periods (*Fast Food*, September 1980).

Cruise liners

The heyday of the cruise liner was the 1930s when the style and comfort of the great cruise ships such as the *France* and *Queen Mary* could be compared with the most luxurious of the grand hotels. Since the Second World War, and particularly the late 1960s and early 1970s, there has been a significant decline in this type of travel and holiday due to a variety of factors. First, air travel has become significantly faster and safer with a consequent and particular impact on travel across the Atlantic. Second, the cost of a holiday on a cruise ship has also increased substantially due to the high investment and operational costs of operating such a ship, particularly the sharp increase in fuel costs. Third, the hotel and tourist industries of European and Mediterranean countries have developed to cater for the needs of holiday-makers, so that by comparison cruises are less popular. Last, cruise operations are highly labour intensive, as high as one crew member to every two passengers, with the ratio of catering staff to passengers being approximately 1:8.

The aspects of catering for cruise liners that are of particular importance are the need to satisfy passengers over extended periods and the need to restock and revictual the ship during a very short turnround in port with enough stock for up to several weeks' cruising. There consequently has to be a compromise between holding in stock a very wide range of food and beverage items and a selection of foodstuffs sufficient to stimulate the appetites of a captive market. Consideration must be given to the role that food and mealtimes have as part of the holiday package. Good food of a high standard is synonymous with this type of holiday, and since all meals are part of the original all-inclusive price, passengers tend to make the most of their meal opportunities. In order to satisfy consumers' expectations, most cruise ships operate full à la carte restaurants and a coffee shop, while speciality and ethnic menus are prepared and presented daily.

Oil rigs

Until the 1970s offshore catering was almost nonexistent round Britain. By 1982 there were approximately 200000 personnel working on 100 installations in the North Sea. Some of these operations were self-catering, but for the 15 or so companies with contracts to supply and feed the rigs it is estimated that their turnover was £75 million per annum.* In many respects catering on the oil platforms is typically institutionalized and since the platforms themselves are so stable, even in quite heavy seas, it could be imagined that the facilites were on shore. However, there are specific problems that make offshore catering both complex and costly.

24 hour operation

Due to the rig personnel working shifts around the clock in order to extract oil continuously, most catering operations are open permanently, serving a choice of main meals at four meal periods in each twenty-four hours. This has implications for the caterer with regards to menu planning, staffing, cleaning and maintenance.

Food and menus

The oil companies regard the provision of good food as one of the most important factors in maintaining the morale of their personnel. Basically rig workers have little else to do apart from work, sleep and eat which they must do in relatively cramped conditions. This means that a wide variety of dishes must be offered at each mealtime while the caterer must recognize that the personnel will require well-balanced meals since the opportunities for exercise, sport and recreation are limited.

Supply

It is common practice for a catering contract to stipulate that a minimum of 21 days'

---

* *Caterer & Hotelkeeper* 8 April 1982.

supplies are kept on board any installation. Difficult weather conditions, remote location and problems of access can disrupt planned revictualling schedules and there has to be close co-operation between suppliers, caterers and boat or helicopter operators.

Equipment

The main purpose of an oil rig is the extraction of oil and installations, particularly older rigs, are not well designed from a catering point of view. The increased use of accommodation rigs, not used for exploration or production, has improved the situation, but nonetheless kitchens and galleys are often cramped, as well as being in continuous use. This places strenuous demands upon the equipment and consequently some manufacturers are installing custom-designed modular units specifically for the North Sea.

8.5 CONCLUSION

It cannot be denied that there are similarities between the nature of catering for air, rail and sea travellers and more conventional catering. In fact, rail catering is carried out on a train with little regard for the fact that the restaurant or buffet is travelling at speeds up to 125 miles per hour (200 km/h) and the menu, the style of service, and table lay-up is typical of the traditional restaurant.

Although concessions are made to the restrictions of space and equipment available, as we have seen, the actual preparation of the food is in many respects identical to that in any hotel kitchen. Whether or not this will continue into the 1980s is a matter for some speculation, however. It has even been suggested that British Rail might be prepared to franchise the catering operations on its trains to independent operators. Apart from the obvious difficulties with regards to design and equipping of rolling stock, the major stumbling block to this concept is that it would seem highly unlikely that franchisees could make rail catering any more profitable than BR can.

The airlines too are facing great difficulties in the early 1980s. In 1982 two airlines, Laker and Brannif, went out of business and all the major airlines, including PanAm and British Airways were reducing their workforce. This, however, is unlikely to affect the in-flight catering facilities, partly because the cost of providing meals is relatively a very small part of the airline's operational costs, and partly because the operators use the catering facility they provide as a marketing tool in order to promote and sell their airline in the face of stiff competition. In the case of in-flight catering, the food service system is uniquely adapted to cope with the provision of meals in particularly difficult and demanding surroundings.

Exercise

Discuss to what extent alternative food production systems have influenced and may still influence the provision of meals in the transport sector of the food service industry.

9 Outside Catering

The art of supplying food and drink in places where catering was never intended

OBJECTIVES: to outline the size and scope of outside catering operations in Britain . . . to identify the particular problems of outside catering and outline procedures adopted to overcome these problems.

Honestly, the problems and frustrations one has to face are sometimes so great that I sometimes wonder why anybody wants to take on outside catering at all!

Catering manager at Farnborough 1980.

9.1 INTRODUCTION

THIS specialized sector of the food service industry is probably one of the most difficult to operate successfully and one of the most speculative. Unfortunately it is extremely difficult to estimate the size and turnover of this sector, since by the very nature of things outside catering is not a permanent operation, as the events listed below indicate:

Garden parties—ranging from just a few people, up to a few thousand at royal garden parties.
Fêtes and other fund-raising events.
Exhibitions—either on permanent sites such as the National Exhibition Centre or Olympia, or on a much smaller scale at other temporary events.
Agricultural and county shows.
Air shows—such as Farnborough and Biggin Hill.

Sporting events of all kinds—the British Grand Prix, the Grand National, and so on.
Private functions—such as wedding receptions, clan gatherings, anniversary parties and other social occasions.

9.2 TYPES OF OUTSIDE CATERING

The events listed above can be broadly divided into two main types of function:

Contracted functions

In this case, the caterer agrees to cater for a specified and guaranteed number of customers. In this respect it is very similar to banqueting, except that instead of providing food and refreshment in a banqueting suite, the setting is likely to be a semi-permanent chalet, as in the case of many agricultural and county shows, or a marquee on the lawn for 'one-off' events such as wedding receptions or garden parties.

Speculative functions

The outside caterer in this instance is not assured of any custom, but contracts to provide refreshment on a site for members of the general public attending the event, as in the case of many sporting events. If the attendance at such meetings is high, then the rewards are great, for the caterer can achieve a very high turnover in a very short space of time. But the risks are high too, for attendance is often subject to the vagaries of the weather, to the extent that many outside caterers will insure themselves against losses due to adverse weather conditions affecting business.

9.3 OUTSIDE CATERING OPERATORS

Just as there are two types of catering in this sector, so there are also two types of caterer engaged in this business.

Professional outside catering firms

These range from sole traders with their mobile ice-cream vans or hot-dog stalls up to very large firms like Ring and Brymer, who are part of the Trusthouse Forte group, and Grand Metropolitan Catering. The larger firms are very much specialists, with a great deal of experience. Such firms do not only cater for the functions noted above, but also undertake catering for firms and organizations on the clients' premises, providing food and refreshment at meetings, seminars and conferences. This type of catering helps to even out the somewhat seasonal nature of their business, as true *outside* catering is obviously only undertaken in the summer months in most cases. Such specialist outside caterers operate very much like any other type of caterer. They have a management team in charge of sales, operations, personnel and administration, which forms a nucleus of permanent staff, fully trained and familiar with the operating standards and organization of the firm. In addition they employ as many part-time staff as they require for a particular function, since it is uneconomic to employ waiting staff permanently due to the fluctuating nature of the business. None the less, the part-time staff, more often than not, have regularly worked for the firm at the same annual events year after year. It is usual for full-time employees to fill the key personnel roles such as control clerks, chalet managers, chefs and storekeepers, while the part-time staff work under their supervision.

Non-specialist outside caterers

Outside catering is often undertaken by hoteliers, restaurateurs and others who are not regularly in the business of catering outdoors. In some cases they are very successful, but there are pitfalls awaiting the unwary. Such caterers are usually prompted to take on outside functions for two reasons. First they are aware that the rewards for success are high; and second because regular clients of their hotel or restaurant specially request them to 'do' the local fête or a daughter's wedding reception. The pitfalls are twofold. In attempting to cater elsewhere, the regular business is deprived of key personnel and equipment which results in a lowering of the hotel or restaurant's standards to the dissatisfaction of customers. Likewise, due to a lack of trained staff, inexperience in outdoor catering, shortages of equipment and so on, the quality, presentation and service of the food is not up to the standards expected by the client, who expects the restaurateur to be as successful on the back lawn as in his or her own restaurant.

9.4 PROBLEMS OF OUTSIDE CATERING

There are problems associated with outside catering that are specific to this particular sector of the industry.

Services

On permanent or semi-permanent sites some or all of the essential services are plumbed in, i.e. sanitation, running hot and cold water, electricity and gas. But more often than not, cooking has to be done on Calor gas stoves, water transported from a distance and lighting provided by gas or paraffin lamps (although the light is not such a serious problem as most outdoor functions are held in the longer summer evenings).

Hygiene

In view of the above and the sometimes primitive accommodation, it is extremely difficult for the outside caterer to meet the hygiene regulations. In addition, many semi-permanent sites are subject to regulations, conditions and specific requirements laid down by the local health authority's Sanitary Department. The outside caterer must ensure that the storage of foodstuffs, cleaning and washing of kitchen and service equipment, practices and activities of staff are all of the highest standard; not just because at all special events (like the Farnborough air show or Ascot week) health inspectors visit all the catering units on site, but because the good name and reputation of the firm depends upon the quality of the food and service that it provides.

Security

This is a major headache for the outside caterer. Foodstuffs, cellar stocks and equipment all have to be stored often in only canvas marquees or tents which are extremely difficult to make secure. At the same time, it is necessary to hold relatively high stocks of everything as the caterer is usually miles from base and would not have the time or opportunity to leave the site to replenish stocks or provide for some unforeseen eventuality. Thus theft and pilferage are not unknown. The public attends the larger events in its thousands, so that inevitably there are dishonest elements who will take advantage of the crowds and circumstances to remove anything that is not secure. At the same time, in order to staff the event, caterers have no option but to employ part-time and casual staff about whom they know very little. Such staff may not physically steal items from the site, but they may consume food and drink while at work or break equipment due to malpractice, both of which will affect caterers' profits.

Staffing

Apart from the security problem, two aspects of staffing are problematical. First, it may be extremely difficult to obtain the required numbers of staff and second, staff may require some training. At an event like the Farnborough air show, several thousand staff are required for a period of nine days. Usually, firms have well-established links with casual staff and they can find enough staff from such contacts, but for the larger events they employ housewives and students, particularly those studying hotel and catering subjects. This may necessitate bringing the staff in on the day before the event or some hours before it starts to brief them fully on the style of the operation and train them up to the required level of service.

Acts of God

This term, borrowed from the insurance companies, is somewhat dramatic but adequately describes the unforeseen and unpleasant things that can befall the outside caterer. The most obvious factor is the weather. In this country, one tends to think of torrential rain, but very hot weather can have as much impact, placing an enormous strain on coolers and portable refrigerators and making it very difficult to serve the type of food demanded by the consumer, namely crisp salads, ice cream and cool drinks. There is also the problem of insects, particularly in the summer months. Flies and wasps not only increase the risk of contamination by cross-infection, but are extremely unsightly around beautifully presented foodstuffs or circling the heads of hot, thirsty customers and may also upset staff trying to prepare or serve food.

9.5 COST FACTORS

Generally speaking the prices of food and refreshments at outside catering functions are higher than those usually charged in regular outlets such as public houses and restaurants.

The reason for this higher pricing policy is the need to cover the additional costs of catering outdoors. Such costs include the following:

Marquees. Although some catering firms may own their own tentage, usually it has to be hired from firms specializing in this area. The cost of this may be borne directly by the client or it may have to be passed on to the customer through prices.

Transportation. All foodstuffs, beverages and equipment have to be transported to the site either in the firm's own vans or in hired transportation so there are the running costs of petrol, drivers' wages and hire charges and the possible capital costs of depreciation, insurance and so on to take into account.

Fuel. Where the caterer has to provide his own fuel for the operation, particularly for cooking, the cost of this may prove to be more expensive than usual.

Equipment. The caterer must take great care to ensure the safe transportation of equipment, particularly crockery and glassware, that may have a value of several hundred pounds even for a relatively small function. This may require the use of special packing cases and boxes designed for such purposes which add to the cost. But in addition, whatever the equipment is packed in, staff are involved in the considerable task of packing and unpacking on site and in stocktaking to assess losses and breakages.

Insurance. Many outside caterers have the additional cost of insurance against unforeseen events, in addition to the normal insurance costs related to equipment and employees' protection. It is likely that the premiums are higher for outside caterers than for those who operate under normal circumstances.

Depreciation. Large sums of money are tied up by the large stocks of equipment needed for peak-season business.

Losses. Finally, caterers will probably find that despite all the care they have taken, they will still have relatively high losses of equipment due to breakages, misuse and pilferage; certainly far more than on a secure site. Such losses, of course, have to be passed on to the customers.

Task 9.1

Compare the prices of soft drinks, alcoholic beverages, sandwiches, snacks and meals sold at special events with prices charged under normal circumstances.

9.6 PROCEDURES

Due to the very wide range of catering events that may be undertaken and the wide variety of firms engaged in the business, no detailed analysis of operating procedures can be given. However, case study 9.1 'Ring and Brymer at Farnborough '82' goes some way towards serving this need, while certain critical points are outlined below.

Planning the function

In many respects an outside catering function is no different from a 'banquet' function (see Chapter 2). Full details of the client's requirements should be taken and in addition the caterer should visit the site to establish the following information:

1. Means of getting to and from the site and how close transport can get to the unit before, during and after the event.
2. Services available on site and requirements with regard to power supplies, portable generators and gas bottles.
3. Size of floor area and storage space in both preparation and service areas in order to plan the siting of cooking equipment, tables and chairs, buffet tables and service points.
4. Availability of premises before the event for the setting up of equipment and mise-en-place, and after the event to close down and remove equipment.
5. Levels of stocks that will be required and can be stored securely on site, and the provision of security personnel should they need to be left overnight.
6. Other security arrangements concerning the admission of catering staff and personnel to the site during the event.

During the function

The preparation and provision of food at outside catering events may be carried out in three basic ways:

1. All food can be centrally prepared and sent out to be reheated and dressed on flats or plates on site.
2. All food can be prepared and served on site.
3. A combination of the two.

There is no doubt that there are sound reasons for using a central kitchen or commissary.

1. Standards of food are maintained since the cooking of food is either carried out or monitored by the firm's permanent staff.
2. Wastage may be reduced due to bulk production.
3. Centrally prepared dishes may be more impressive than it may be possible to prepare on site.
4. Stricter control of foodstuffs is made possible.
5. Storage of raw materials is eliminated on site.
6. Less equipment is required on site.

7. Staffing levels on site can be reduced and fewer skilled personnel are required there.

The disadvantages of a central kitchen are:

1. The degree of organization required to ensure that all the outside units receive the food that they require.
2. Difficulties associated with transporting prepared foods safely.
3. Problems of re-heating or re-constituting dishes on site, with all the possible dangers of contamination.
4. Staff on site may not have the experience or know-how to cope with any of the problems that may arise.
5. There is little or no chance of food being returned if too much is allocated, despite strict supervision.

Thus, there can be no doubt that it requires a great deal of skill and expertise to organize an outdoor catering event successfully and achieve a profit.

Case study 9.1   Ring and Brymer at Farnborough '82

The Farnborough air show is held every two years. It is a multi-million pound venture attended by all the major aerospace manufacturers and aviation firms who exhibit their hardware in the exhibition halls. They also entertain their clients and personnel in chalets arranged in rows overlooking the runway to give the best possible view of the air show itself. These chalets are semi-permanent in that supply roads, concrete bases and essential services, such as sanitation and water are in situ. But the chalets themselves are only erected for the show and are essentially marquees and tenting fixed to scaffold poles, although the client firms renting them go to considerable trouble to make their interiors as plush and comfortable as possible (Fig. 9.1).

Ring and Brymer were the largest catering firms at the show in 1982, catering for over 40 different companies, ranging from one chalet unit up to one of the largest of the show comprising seven chalet units joined together. For purposes of administration and control, the chalets were divided into nine zones of approximately equal size, a zone manager acting as trouble-shooter for the five or six chalets under his control. Likewise, vans and drivers were allocated to carry all stores and provisions for each zone from a central compound. Both zone managers and drivers were equipped with short-wave radios to keep in constant touch with each other and the compound as telephone lines were limited and always busy. The compound was built primarily for security purposes and contained all administrative offices, the stores, cellar, linen 'room' and staff canteen. It was staffed 24 hours a day for the entire eight days of the show by full-time employees of the company and provided back-up services in all areas such as staffing, training, hygiene, public relations and so on.

Each chalet had its own manager in charge of the unit. Each manager was fully briefed two weeks before the show and given a 32-page dossier containing all the information he or she may have required, including names and telephone numbers of key personnel at the compound, notes on administrative procedures, stock control and staffing, security procedures, general hints on staff training, Calor gas safety instructions, copy of the occasional licence granted for the sale of intoxicating liquor in the chalet, function sheet and menus, and so on. In most cases menus had been determined in advance in consultation with the client, so food was issued each day according to the specification. Most items had been blast frozen at THF Supplies

Figure 9.1 *Ferranti chalet at the Farnborough air show 1982.*

Manufacturing Division at Dunstable or prepared in the compound, but it was left to the chefs in each chalet to put the finishing touches to the dishes and to present them attractively. Liquor stocks had likewise been predetermined for the chalets' bar, with enough stock to last three or four days to minimize the movement and requisitioning of new stock. Most clients dispensed their refreshments free of charge (although they were careful to control access to the chalet so that only bona fide guests were entertained) so that bar stocks were provided on a sale or return basis. Equipment was delivered to each chalet on the day before the show opened and checked against a stock sheet. It was returned on the last day, again after a stock check, so that breakages and losses could be calculated. Staffing for a typical chalet serving 100 customers a day, for morning coffee, lunch and afternoon tea, might comprise one chalet manager, two chefs, two bar stewards, six waiting staff and two kitchen porters.

During the course of the show, Ring and Brymer were responsible for the service of tens of thousands of meals. They employed many hundreds of staff, most of whom were working for them on a part-time basis and travelled up to sixty miles each day to get there. They also employed staff from as far away as Birmingham and provided hostel accommodation for them to live in during the show. Every member of staff had to be provided with a uniform and passes to get into the show, and they had to be directed to a particular chalet and eventually paid at the end of it all. Chalet managers were responsible for the standards and performance of staff and were given guidelines concerning this, including: 'All customers to be greeted with a THF smile and Good Morning/Afternoon'. As you can imagine, after a week of very hard work under trying conditions and in difficult circumstances, that smile was wearing thin. But Ring and Brymer had a very successful 1982 and will be back at Farnborough in 1984, just as they have been for over 30 years.

9.7 CONCLUSION

Outside catering is a specialized sector of the food service industry covering a wide range of functions and events. Although the Farnborough case study highlights an event much larger than most outside catering events, it illustrates the essential point— it is a risky business that requires a great deal of forethought and planning, down to the last detail with regard to all aspects of the operation. And once the function is under way, it is essential to *control* very closely the movement of stocks and perform- ance of staff, for without strict control the potential profit from an outside catering function may not be realized. In many respects this type of catering provides a real challenge to the professional caterer and a great deal of job satisfaction is to be gained from the diversity of operations and difficulties surmounted.

Exercise

Discuss the reasons why the costs of providing meals and service at an outside catering event are greater than the normal costs associated with function catering.

PART TWO
OPERATIONAL ASPECTS OF FOOD SERVICE

10 The Meal Experience

What affects the customer's enjoyment of eating out

OBJECTIVES: to explain the influence upon a consumer's meal preferences . . . to identify the reasons why people choose to eat out . . . to indicate the factors that affect the customer's enjoyment of a meal and the eating out experience.

Anyone who follows this profession of selling food and drink without being a real host to the guests is on the wrong track.

Bachman, W. (1952) *Professional Knowledge*, Vol. III, London: MacLaren

10.1 INTRODUCTION

IN his book, *The Bad Food Guide*, Derek Cooper wrote—'I have the utmost sympathy for caterers who are trying hard to do a self-respecting job in the face of almost universal indifference . . . There is, alas, no reason for optimism on the eating front. For the minority prepared to pay for the privilege, there will always be a small number of good restaurants. The majority of us will continue to put up uncomplainingly, perhaps even with a sort of masochistic pleasure, with this kind of bad food and bad service.' Thus Cooper puts the blame, if blame there need be, for poor standards of catering in Britain fairly and squarely on the consumer. He argues that if the consumer refused to accept food and service that was inadequate, then the caterer would have to improve those standards or go out of business. But he was writing in the 1960s. Do the British public still have such low expectations? Why in fact do people go out for a meal in the first place?

10.2 EATING OUT AS AN EXPERIENCE

Probably everybody in this country has 'eaten out' at some time in their life. Taken in its broadest sense, eating out could be said to be all those meals not prepared and eaten in the home, so that dining with friends in their home would be included. Quite obviously we are not concerned with that type of catering, although if people become more proficient and confident with preparing meals for others in their own home, this may affect business in the food service industry. We are concerned with the 25 per cent or so of consumers' expenditure on food which is spent in the catering industry. As we have seen, there are many, many different sectors of that industry, each catering for very different consumer needs. Essentially, however, there are some sectors of the industry that cater for people who have no choice but to eat there—hospitals, institutions, prisons and so on—which have a captive market; and those restaurants, cafés and cafeterias where the consumer chooses to eat. In some cases, this choice is very restricted, on a train for instance, or in a staff dining room, but in most cases, the choice is vast, and it is this choice that we shall be examining.

If people decide to eat out, then it follows that they have decided on this course of action in preference to some other. In this respect, the caterer is competing with alternative experiences that might attract consumers' hard-earned disposable income, and these may be far removed from any gastronomic delights. The consumer may choose to go to the theatre, cinema, opera or ballet; to play squash, bridge or football; to visit the races, the zoo or the seaside; and so on and so forth. So let us look a little more closely at why a person chooses to eat out instead of some other pleasurable activity.

10.3 REASONS FOR EATING OUT

Graham Campbell-Smith* lists a total of 43 different reasons why people may choose to eat out. It is really no surprise then that there is such a rich diversity of eating-out establishments available to the public. However, we can identify six basic reasons why people eat away from home:

1. *Convenience.* This factor includes all those people who are away from home for some reason—shoppers, commercial travellers, commuters—who are physically unable to return home at normal meal times. It would also include people who do not have the time to eat at home and eat out in conjunction with some other leisure activity.
2. *Variety.* Just as people do not go to see the same film every week, people are stimulated by trying new foods or drinks in different restaurants. Also, people who live in circumstances where meal experiences are limited, such as in hostels at universities or colleges or in poorly equipped bed-sits, may choose to eat out for this reason.
3. *Labour.* The desire to have someone else prepare, cook, serve and wash up a meal most certainly influences some people's decision to eat out. Or for medical

---

* Campbell-Smith, G. (1967) *Marketing the Meal Experience*, Guildford: University of Surrey.

and other reasons domestic help may be required and may not be available. The popularity of fish and chip shops is a long-standing example of this, as is the recent growth in takeaways and fast-food operations.

4. *Status*. Both for personal and business reasons people may choose to impress their guests by taking them out to a fashionable and/or expensive restaurant. In many parts of the world, the business lunch is an accepted way of sealing successful business transactions, while in the United States, the executive even has a working breakfast. On the personal level, eating out may be partly attributable to conforming with the social pattern of the neighbourhood.

5. *Culture/Tradition*. Peter Bertram (in *Fast Food*) described eating as 'a part of our cultural heritage, and is a manifestation of kinship'. In Britain, celebrations of special events such as anniversaries and birthdays are often associated with eating out, although not to the same extent as the Belgians and French under such circumstances.

6. *Impulse*. This is rather like saying that sometimes people have no particular reason for eating out, they do so on the spur of the moment, so that it is a catch-all for any circumstances that have not been included previously. But there is no doubt that in certain businesses, notably retailing, impulse-buying is very significant and that it contributes to sales in the catering industry too.

But whether there are 6 or 600 reasons for eating out, the important point that is being made is that *people do not eat out just for the food*. It is all too easy for the catering student and professional caterer to believe that because the food is the most visible product of a restaurant, and that is what the customer most obviously pays for, the food is the be-all and end-all of successful catering. As we have seen, however, customers may be eating not to satisfy hunger at all (although in most cases they will be) but to satisfy other needs like social contact, status and curiosity.

10.4 TYPES OF CUSTOMER

So far we have been looking at the 'customer' as if there was such a typical person. But obviously there are many different types of customer—male and female, young and old, single people and families, rich and poor. It is essential that caterers are aware which of these customers their operation will attract. It may attract all of them, although this is unlikely. In Chapter 11, we look at marketing in some detail, but before that, we need to recognize why different restaurants attract different customers.

Task 10.1

From the list below, quickly match up the type of customer with the different types of restaurant.

The Savoy Grill	Car-owner
Happy Eater restaurant	Husband and wife
McDonald's	Rich
Berni Inn	Holiday-maker
Seaview restaurant	Shopper

This only goes to show that you have pre-conceived ideas about the suitability of certain catering establishments for certain types of customers, and in this respect, you are no different to the vast majority of people. For the purpose of economic analysis and research, the population in Britain has been broken down into 'socioeconomic groups' to help us identify the different types of customer. Basically it is the sub-division of the population into groups with broadly similar incomes, occupations, education levels and resources (Table 10.1).

Table 10.1 *Socioeconomic groups in Britain.*

Group	Examples of the group
A	Higher managerial, administrative or professional
B	Intermediate managerial, administrative or professional
C1	Supervisory, clerical, junior managerial or professional
C2	Skilled manual workers
D	Semi-skilled and unskilled manual workers
E	State pensioners, widows, casual and lowest-grade earners, unemployed

The implications for the caterer of such groupings are many since research has shown that 'expectations, values, usage and attitudes are likely to vary between groups. Members of different groups are likely to give different priorities to certain needs, and the upper socioeconomic groupings are likely to be able to satisfy certain needs more easily than others.'* Thus to answer the question, 'What factors contribute to the customer's enjoyment of a meal?' is by no means easy. For each type of customer, with each type of need to be satisfied, there is a restaurant that will be satisfactory. All we can do is look at those factors that contribute to the meal experience in some way or another and draw some general conclusions about how they affect the customer.

10.5 FACTORS INFLUENCING THE MEAL EXPERIENCE

Food

After reading the above, you might almost be forgiven for believing that food is not the most important part of the meal experience, but of course, food is what it is all about. But because everybody in the Western world eats every day, everybody is an expert about the subject. People know what they like and expect to be served it, even if you as a caterer disagree with them.

From the caterer's point of view, it is extremely unlikely that we can change the consumers' preconceived ideas about food. The customer has partly chosen the restaurant on the basis of what type of food is served and will select from the menu those dishes that are most appealing. This is particularly true of people aged 30 and over, and those from socioeconomic groups CDE, whereas younger people and people from groups AB are far more flexible and adventurous in their eating habits. Nonetheless, the caterer must have a very clear idea about how food reacts with people in order to maximize the pleasurable aspects of the meal. The palate is a delicate instrument

---

* Cannon, T. (1980) *Basic Marketing*, Eastbourne: Holt, Rinehart & Winston.

FOOD ACCEPTABILITY

Why do we eat what we do? This is an extremely complex question, so we can only give a brief summary of factors influencing our diet.

Cultural

Cultural beliefs, often of a religious nature or in the form of taboos, affect what may or may not be consumed. Notable examples are the kosher diets of orthodox Jews; Islam, which forbids the consumption of pork or alcohol; and Hinduism which regards the cow as sacred.

Social

Societies differ in their eating and drinking habits. For instance, in France it is quite usual for young children to drink wine with a meal, while in Britain, no person under 18 is allowed to consume wine in a public house.

Geographical

Where you live will obviously affect your diet. Britain's stereotypical diet of bread and butter, fish and chips, roast and two vegetables plus foaming pint of beer is essentially a result of our economy, climate, soil, and our fishing and agricultural practices, whereas the Nigerian diet of chicken, kola nut, cassava, rice and plantain is likewise determined largely by geographical factors.

Physiological

Our diet is affected by our age and health. Babies, invalids, diabetics, the aged and so on all have differing dietary needs. Although there is some doubt as to whether or not most people are aware of food's nutritional value, there is also the modern preoccupation with body weight that has caused up to 30 per cent of the population to diet at some time or another.

Also, foods affect people in different ways and what may be acceptable to one person may be indigestible to another. The body can react in a variety of ways to food that it does not like: indigestion, wind and an allergic rash being but three.

Psychological

The consumption of certain items is determined by psychological influences. Thus beer drinking is supposed to be a 'masculine' pursuit, Coca-Cola's popularity during the Second World War among GIs abroad was due in part to the memories of home it evoked, and oysters are eaten, along with other foods, because some people believe them to be aphrodisiacs.

Economic

Not only will people's income influence how much is spent on food, but what proportion of that income people decide is to be spent on food determines whether they eat pork or suckling pig, chicken or pheasant and so on.

Advertising

In the West at least, we cannot exclude the influence that advertising has upon our eating habits. The popularity of many foods is based predominantly upon the success of marketing those products: Coca-Cola, yogurt, margarine and crisps being just four examples.

The food itself

The colour, odour, flavour and texture of food influences acceptability. There are many examples but the colour of tripe, odour of curry powder, flavour of garlic and texture of liver are four examples that affect many people.

Task 10.2

Investigate the cuisine of one of the following: the Caribbean, India, Indonesia, Iran, Israel, Japan, Mexico, Portugal, Scandinavia, West Africa or the USSR. Compare the proteins, vegetables and fruits used, methods of cookery and specialities with those in Britain.

which should be cared for and educated; all the various sensory impressions or sensations such as odour, taste, texture and variety complete the gastronomic experience throughout life. The successful caterer is the one who ensures that

appearance
aroma
taste
texture
and temperature

are all just as the customer expects them to be.

Appearance

The expression 'looks good enough to eat' has not become a cliché by chance. Food has to look good on the plate—a factor that all the major catering firms are aware of. They spend a great deal of time and effort in ensuring that their units sell a product that looks good.

Aroma

The second thing that will affect customers' reaction to the food, even before they eat it, is its smell. Dining out in an Indian restaurant or buying fish and chips would not be the same without their own particular aroma. Some operators even exploit this factor by ensuring that the ventilation leads out onto the street in order to attract customers, and although this may be very effective for fresh bread shops and doughnut houses, not all cooking smells are desirable. While eating food, much of the sensation is derived from the olfactory centre of the nasal cavity, without which most of what we eat and drink would lack its subtlety. In drinking a vintage wine or a good brandy, much of the enjoyment is derived from its 'nose' and the same can be said of other gastronomic experiences. To illustrate this point take a cup each of pineapple juice, fresh lemon juice and vanilla-flavoured water. Get friends or colleagues to taste each of these in turn, while holding their noses or by wearing nose clips (as worn by swimmers). Ask them to identify the three liquids.

Taste

The taste buds of the tongue are only able to detect four basic flavours—sweet, sour, salt and bitter. It is the many variations of these four that combine to create the unique flavour of a particular food. For the consumer, the combination of flavours is quite important and can be used to good effect in various dishes: sweet and sour pork, lamb with mint sauce and so on. It is also relevant to the sequence of dishes since generally sweet items are left until the end of a meal lest they upset the palate.

Texture

There are many textures to food—rough or smooth, hard or soft, fluid or solid, dry or moist, and tough or tender. The consistency and shape properties of food are experienced by pressure and movement receptors in the mouth. It is these that signal our dislike of food that is rubbery, slimy or tough and a customer's choice of a rare, medium or well-done steak is partly derived from the influence of texture upon the palate.

Temperature

Customers enjoy the variety that temperature can add to a meal—a piping hot stew followed by ice cream for instance. Wealthy Victorians ate a sorbet in the middle of their long banquets in order to refresh their jaded palates as the citrus-based ice was refreshing. But temperature not only provides variety, it affects flavour too. The sweetness of a dish is accentuated when served hot, while the saltiness of a soup is reduced at a high temperature.

Service

Customers are not familiar with nor care for the problems of providing service. They are only concerned that the service is of the standard that they expect. If they are in a hurry then they will go to fast food outlets which will provide a speedy meal; if they are out to impress, they will go to a sophisticated restaurant providing gueridon service. As we have seen in Part One of this book, there are many differing styles of service, each tailored to meet the particular needs of a certain type of clientele. For social groups AB, service is very much part of the experience, since as Campbell-Smith puts it—'Powers of discrimination and degree of richness of life are most fully developed'.* Whether this is the case or not, this social group do spend more than any other group (40 per cent of their expenditure on eating out) in restaurants, hotels and steak bars where 'service' is provided, whereas groups DE spend 30 per cent of their expenditure in cafeterias, pubs and cafés. This of course reflects the cost and value for money as much as an attitude towards service, but there is no doubt that consumers who are not used to full silver service or gueridon work feel uncomfortable in those situations where it is provided. Campbell-Smith goes so far as to argue, 'At the lowest level of socioeconomic grouping, there is probably no need to have more than four or five types of eating establishment, from a general café to a fish and chip shop, hamburger bar, bacon-and-egg speciality restaurant and possibly a simple snack and sandwich bar.'

Cleanliness and hygiene

In the United States, the preoccupation with hygiene is much more developed than in Britain, but it seems probable that along with the influx of US style operations, some of their ideas about cleanliness will be introduced. As we shall see, disposables, which are probably the most hygienic means of serving food, are becoming more acceptable, and we shall probably see other ideas, such as cellophane-wrapped cutlery, crockery and so forth, assuring us of their pristine state, on tables in restaurants in Britain quite soon. The power of advertising and the media to influence people is also making consumers more and more aware of personal hygiene and hygiene in the home which is bound to affect attitudes to eating out. Already there is a growing movement towards the banning of cigarette smoking in public places as they have done in Belgium, and many places, cinemas, canteens, and public transport have segregated areas for smokers and non-smokers.

Whether justified or not, Britain does not have a very good reputation for cleanliness. Tourists from abroad find our streets, parks, buses and public buildings dirty and litter-strewn in comparison with their own countries, and this attitude is extended towards our hotels and restaurants. The archetypal British eating establishment had encrusted sauce bottles on a not very clean table, with waitresses having a quiet cigarette in the corner. Hopefully, this image is fading, if not gone forever. The

---

* Campbell-Smith, G. (1967) op. cit.

THE GUIDES

Journalists in general, through their columns in local and national newspapers, undoubtedly influence sales in the food service business. In particular, the so-called 'good food guides' can affect the success of new hotels and restaurants. The fact that there are several such guides suggests that the public are influenced by and act upon their recommendations, although caterers themselves are quick to point out that all such guides can only exist with the aid of sponsorship of some sort.

The Good Food Guide—founded in 1951 by Raymond Postgate, it was edited by Christopher Driver and published by the Consumers' Association and Hodder and Stoughton. In 1980, the *Guide's* circulation was 50 000 and included entries on 1000 different establishments. The information presented depends on contributions from 'ordinary' restaurant customers and part-time inspectors who are usually members of the Good Food Club. It is for this reason that the guide has 'never been particularly popular in the industry'.*

Egon Ronay's Lucas Guide—published by Penguin and sponsored by Lucas. It has the largest circulation of all—over 150 000 and the 1980 edition had nearly 5000 entries. Ronay uses full-time professional inspectors with catering backgrounds to research his choice of where to eat in Britain. He stresses that 'the organization maintains complete independence in its editorial selection and judgements'. This view is reflected in the industry where he is regarded as 'the country's main authority on restaurants. He is more concise, more informative and fairer than other food guide writers'.†

Hotels and Restaurants in Britain—published by the Automobile Association, it originated in 1908 and now has a circulation of 50 000 and grades approximately 5000 establishments. These are inspected by full-time staff, although information supplied by AA members is also used. Hotels generally apply for recognition and are subsequently inspected incognito, prior to full inspection. Restaurants, however, are inspected on an *ad hoc* basis.

RAC Guide—similar to the AA guide, its circulation is larger, about 80 000 and it grades 5600 establishments. But this guide deals only with hotels and does not grade restaurants.

Michelin Guide—in 1980, the *Guide* had 4800 entries, both hotels and restaurants. The organization is reluctant to reveal circulation figures and *modus operandi*, but it can be assumed that their full-time inspectors operate in a similar way to the other guides.

---

* Hempel, S. in *Caterer & Hotelkeeper*, 8 February 1979.
† Sassie, V. (proprietor of the Gay Hussar restaurant) in *Caterer & Hotelkeeper*, 8 February 1979.

caterer is aware that cleanliness and hygiene are selling points and that the regulations laid down are only a minimum standard to be met. Essentially there are three areas of concern for the caterer: staff, equipment and environment.

Staff

Customers will not expect staff to wear a uniform, although most catering operations do encourage staff to wear a uniform as part of their overall image: fast-food outlets are a good example of this. But staff will be expected to be smart and clean. People tend to ascribe cleanliness to four particular aspects of appearance—clothes, which they expect to be well-pressed and stain free; hair, which should be clean and looked after well; nails, which should be clean and manicured; and body odour, which should be non-existent, i.e. neither sweaty nor overly perfumed.

Equipment

Customers will notice if equipment is not clean since it is literally put under their very noses. All table appointments, cutlery, crockery and so forth must be clean and polished and not defective in any way, for instance, cups chipped, plates cracked or forks bent.

The environment or room itself

Because most restaurants and food service outlets have direct access onto the street and have a great deal of human traffic in and out of them, they collect a lot of dirt and dust. The caterer must ensure that floor and wall surfaces are cleaned regularly and fittings such as pictures and prints and lights are dusted properly. 'So often one sees lamps that have run to the limit of their life just left in service until they fizzle out and have to be replaced while the customer watches the dead flies shaken out of the fitting'.*

At this point one might reasonably presume that the next factor that influences the customer's enjoyment of a meal will be that indefinable factor—atmosphere. Ask anyone why they go to a particular restaurant and they will probably say one of three things (a) they like the food; (b) it is good value for money; or (c) they like the 'atmosphere'. But, if you ask someone to explain what 'atmosphere' is, they will probably be tongue-tied. They may say that they like the surroundings, the music played there, the other customers or some other aspect of the operation, but usually they will not be very clear about it. This is because so many of the factors that contribute towards creating an atmosphere are received by the customer on a sub-conscious level. So rather than talk about atmosphere in vague terms, we will look at these factors in some detail.

---

* Newall, M. (1965) *Mood and Atmosphere in Restaurants*, London: Barrie & Rockliff.

Task 10.3

Conduct a survey of 100 people. Ask them what is their favourite restaurant and why do they like going there. Get them to list in order their reasons for frequenting the restaurant and see how often the word 'atmosphere' (or something similar) is in the first three reasons given.

Decor

'In the year since redesigning its Notting Hill, London, outlet, Wimpy International has trebled turnover there. And at the THF Cavendish Hotel, a redesign has improved bar turnover by 50%.'* So good interior design is obviously important to an establishment's success. But to analyse what is good and what is not so good is very difficult. Malcolm Newell at the very beginning of his book (*Mood and Atmosphere in Restaurants*) writes, 'Atmosphere is ethereal, evasive and indeterminate. The response of an individual to atmosphere is personal and . . . the individual's reaction to any combination of the factors [which influence atmosphere] can only be determined or controlled by rudimentary principles.' The problem lies in the essential paradox that customers need to feel 'at home' in their surroundings, without feeling that they are at home. Thus the decor of a restaurant must be different without undermining the sense of security of customers; it should provoke feelings of pleasure and relaxation rather than tension and anxiety. The decor must also play an integral part in the whole meal experience—if customers are paying a lot for a meal, then they will expect plush surroundings, whereas if customers want a quick, cheap meal, then they will expect functional rather than decorative decor.

Lighting

The lighting in a restaurant is determined in conjunction with the decor. In the same way that colours can affect moods, brightness or dimness can too. Generally, bright light will promote a sense of warmth and sociability, whereas dim lighting will have the reverse effect. Thus restaurants that aim to attract couples will have dim lighting which will make the partner appear to be more attractive and increase the sense of relaxation, whereas restaurants catering for groups of people will be bright to aid sociability. Lighting can also have the effect of distorting true colours, for instance, butchers have used a particular light bulb to enhance the redness of raw meat, while the effect of ultra-violet light on white is well known. The caterer must ensure that the lighting does not have an adverse effect upon the appearance of the food, decor and customers. Lighting should also reflect the time of day, so that at lunchtime it is more acceptable to eat in a bright environment than at dinner. Newell goes so far as to suggest that 'there may be a need in some premises for two separate lighting systems. The clientele and the staff are in a different mood at night and, when it is dark outside, are adjusted to softer lighting of lower brightness.' (1965 op. cit.) Finally, lighting in conjunction with turnover can help to establish a fast turnover of custom by creating a brisk atmosphere.

---

* Burt, T. in *Caterer & Hotelkeeper*, 30 August 1979.

Task 10.4

Describe the decor and lighting of a McDonald's or Wimpy restaurant. Do these units illustrate the impact of decor and lighting upon mood and turnover?

Air conditioning

In the United States, with their far greater extremes of heat and cold, air conditioning is found everywhere. This is not the case in Britain and generally the problems of heating and ventilation are dealt with separately. Restaurants are busy places, or should be, with customers coming in and going out and waiting staff to-ing and fro-ing, so that it is very difficult to maintain a constant temperature. Similarly, the proximity of the kitchen must give rise to cooking smells which may stimulate the appetite but can just as easily be off-putting. There are two aspects to heating the establishment—actual and psychological. Both the illumination and the colour scheme can affect the customer's sensation of warmth and other factors have a similar effect. For instance, a convected air curtain over the entrance gives an immediate sensation of warmth for people coming in off the street in winter, or of coolness in summer. Similarly, an obvious radiant source of heat like a coal fire also creates a feeling of warmth, even if its contribution to the actual room temperature is minimal. It can also have the undesired effect of making people feel too hot—customers have even been known to ask to be moved to another table because they are too hot from fake gas-fired 'coal' fires that give off no heat. As far as the actual temperature is concerned, the most pleasurable temperature for people sitting down is around 18°C (65°F). This will be affected by the number of people in the room since 'sitting ten customers in a room will produce about as much heat as a one kilowatt fire'.* In this respect, heating that is controlled by a thermostat is desirable, if not, a small thermometer placed in the room will give the caterer an indication of the room temperature.† Customers will also strongly object to sitting in a draught. The source of most draughts is doorways or windows. Screens near the service doors and entrance should help to eliminate draughts and likewise, windows should be checked and possibly double glazed, particularly those with an easterly or northerly aspect. At the same time, it is desirable that the air in the room be circulating and moving to remove unwanted smells and help maintain the ambient temperature. This must be done in a controlled way, using fans or extractors. In the kitchen too, extractor fans must be properly sited and maintained correctly to minimize cooking smells in the restaurant itself.

Furnishing

The functional design of restaurant furniture reflects greatly upon customers' enjoyment of meals and the length of time they will spend in the establishment. It will also affect the number of covers that can be accommodated in the food service area and thereby influence customers' sense of security and intimacy. This same factor will also

---

* Newell, M. (1965) op. cit.
† The Offices, Shops and Railway Premises Act 1963 also stipulates the temperatures to be maintained in certain catering establishments, but if temperatures were above or below these limits, it is very unlikely that there would be any customers anyway.

affect the profitability of the enterprise, so that a great deal of research has gone into the design of tables and chairs, to the extent that the Council for Industrial Design set up an Advisory Committee on Hotels and Restaurants which has made recommendations concerning restaurant furniture.

Consumers, of course, are not concerned with this detailed analysis; their only concern is comfort and well-being. Thus, if customers are in parties of four or six, they will prefer to sit at a round table which enhances personal contact and conversation, rather than at a rectangular table, which from the caterer's point of view will increase the seating capacity. Likewise, it was found in popular catering units that fitted booth seating, where there were places for four people, couples preferred to sit next to each other since it was difficult to talk to each other when facing each other across the table without addressing the people on either side. This meant that the seats had to be made sufficiently long and wide to allow people to turn inwards wihout discomfort. Customers too are fussy about where they sit in a restaurant. Many people, for instance, will insist on sitting so that they are facing into the room, partly so that they have something other than a wall to look at and partly because they feel more secure with a wall behind them. Finally, according to research by the Council for Industrial Design women seem to have different sitting habits to men. Men prefer to slump back or lean on their elbows in a relaxed position, whereas women can sit upright for longer periods without suffering the same amount of fatigue as men. Obviously it is impracticable to have two sorts of chairs, but if a restaurant wishes to encourage people to linger over their meal, it must provide chairs with arms.

Acoustics

Restaurants are noisy places, or they would be if care was not taken to reduce the level of noise. In fact, 'reducing the level of noise of movement and bustle is the first step taken by restaurateurs who want to upgrade their premises' (Newell, M. (1965) op. cit.). The most important point to note with regard to levels of acceptable noise is that age group rather than social class is the determining factor, young people being able and willing to accept much higher levels.

There are three contributory factors to noise in a restaurant (apart from outside or extraneous noise which presumably could be avoided if necessary).

Voices

Customers need to communicate with each other and with the staff. Therefore the general level of noise should not exceed that which makes ordinary conversation impossible. Obviously, the more people in the room, the more noise there is, but as one can hardly request customers to talk more quietly, the caterer must reduce the general level of noise by reducing the input from the two other factors.

Operational

Eating and serving food can be a fairly noisy business. To illustrate this very simply, place a joint plate on the following different table surfaces—formica, wood, table with a paper place mat, table laid with a cloth and a table covered in green baize and laid with a cloth. Compare the level of noise.

Apart from the noise derived from serving food, there is also noise caused by movement. Some floor surfaces are much noisier than others, for instance, tiling as opposed to carpeting. But in addition, the decor can contribute. A report in *Catering and Hotel Management** showed that carpeting and curtains reduced noise, while a textile wall fabric made in France called 'mur de silence' was credited with reducing noise from an adjacent room by up to 90 per cent. The same report states that if 'premises are carpeted, the electricity heating bill can be reduced by 12 per cent, according to research conducted in Japan'. The main factor contributing to this saving is pile height, irrespective of whether the carpet is wool, nylon, polyester or acrylic.

Music

Most experts agree that 'music has a direct and strong effect on the customer's mood' (Newell, M. (1965) op. cit.). It is used in many different environments—on Waterloo station or in supermarkets to speed up the flow of people, in factories and workshops as 'music while you work', and extensively as background music in hotels and restaurants. It can achieve many things for caterers so long as they are aware of one essential point—that background music is forced upon the customer whether they like it or not, and if they do not like it then the restaurant loses customers. Otherwise, music may be used to create an environment of bustle until the restaurant fills up and then be turned down to allow for conversation. It can reinforce the particular image of the restaurant by playing appropriate music: rock music in the Hard Rock Café, and chamber music in the Ritz. It has even been suggested that music can be used to overcome customers' prevailing moods of depression on a wet, rainy day by playing bright and cheerful tunes. Newell proposes the following points to consider:

No vocals because people listen to vocals.
No 'top ten' because they are fashions and become dated too quickly.
A balance of light pop, film themes, musicals and any music that will have lasting popularity.
Not mass produced but carefully considered for the particular style of restaurant.

Size and shape of the room

This factor will certainly affect the atmosphere of the eating environment by creating feelings of intimacy or spaciousness. As we have seen, the caterer can affect people's reactions to the room by careful use of colour, patterns and lighting. Unless the restaurant is purpose built, restaurateurs may have to resort to employing the skills of the interior designer to modify establishments where the ceiling is too high or too low, the room is too narrow, too small or whatever. Many High Street sites for instance are designed with shops in mind and therefore tend to be long and narrow (the wider the frontage onto the street, the greater the expense of buying or renting the site) which is why so many catering units in such sites have mirrors along one wall, in order to create an illusion of width.

---

* *Catering and Hotel Management*, January 1979.

Clientele

This factor is one over which the caterer only has limited control. Most certainly, however, customers' enjoyment of the meal will be affected by the other customers in the room. In general terms they will feel at home and reassured if the other customers are of a similar age, wearing similar clothes and behaving in a similar way. Whereas they will be upset if others are behaving too loudly (or too quietly), or if they are casually dressed when they are formal and vice versa. In most instances, however, the restaurant will reflect the socioeconomic and age group that will be attracted to it, as outlined above. A man who dines at the Savoy will expect to eat in formal, reserved surroundings with others of middle age and thick wallets, and someone eating in a Happy Eater will expect to see children.

The only control that caterers have over clientele is that of refusing to serve customers, which so long as the restaurant is not an inn as defined under the Hotel Proprietors Act 1956 (see Chapter 16), they are perfectly entitled to do. It was the practice in years gone by to refuse customers on the basis of their dress, and some places still insist that male customers must wear a tie, although this practice appears to be dying out.

Price

I have mentioned briefly the idea of service providing value for money but have not considered the impact that price has upon the customer's enjoyment of a meal. In the gloomier economic climate of the 1980s, many people would argue that this factor is *the* most important consideration in the mind of a potential customer. What is certain is that, in the catering industry, pricing has tended in the past to take little account of its effect upon customers. The traditional cost-plus method has recently been seen to be a poor policy in a consumer-oriented business, since it means that more expensive items such as steak, lobster and so on are priced higher still by adding a fixed percentage. This has led to suggestions that a fixed amount rather than a percentage should be added to all items, so that, irrespective of cost, all dishes on a menu would have, for example, £1 added to the cost. The question is a complex one and I do not intend to discuss it here. However, whatever pricing technique is adopted, it is important that caterers understand the implications of pricing policy. (See Chapter 15.)

10.6 CONCLUSION

In this chapter we have looked at eating out from the customer's point of view. All too often professional caterers or students of catering become too wrapped up with the techniques and mechanics of the trade to worry about the customer, and even when they dine out themselves, they tend to view the operation through the eyes of a professional. Although disliked by the trade, in general I believe that it would not do any caterer any harm to look through the *Good Food Guide* just to see what it is about restaurants that *customers* like and dislike. Likewise, how many restaurant managers have sat down for a couple of minutes at every single place setting in their unit just to see and feel what the customer experiences: Can you see straight into the kitchen? Is there a draught? Is it dusty behind the picture? And so on. Again, because the caterer is immersed in it, how many managers have stopped to listen to the noise output in their restaurant or bothered to adjust the level of background music according to how busy it is? The answer to these questions would be that good restaurant managers talk to their customers to find out if they have any complaints. But the British are renowed for their reluctance to make a fuss. They show their disapproval by never dining in that particular restaurant again. That is why it is so essential to look upon the meal as an *experience* and to examine very carefully every aspect of that experience in order to create an environment and occasion that will encourage the customer to return.

Exercise

Outline those factors that contribute to the customer's enjoyment of a meal. Discuss how one restaurant you are familiar with fulfils these requirements.

11 Marketing the Outlet

How to get the customers coming in and coming back

OBJECTIVES: to outline the media available to the caterer for sales promotion, advertising, merchandising and public relations . . . to examine the role of the menu in merchandising and marketing the outlet . . . to understand the concept of market.

There will be plenty of opportunities for the good businessman to make a fortune in hotels [and catering?] because . . . the marketing side of the industry remains for the most part very amateurish.

Taylor, D. & D. Bush (1974) op. cit.

11.1 INTRODUCTION

THE Institute of Marketing defines marketing as 'the management function responsible for identifying, anticipating and satisfying customer requirements at a profit.' Miles Quest wrote in an editorial in *Caterer & Hotelkeeper* (12 March 1981): 'Today, more than ever, it is a question of marketing accommodation, takeaway food and seats in restaurants rather than merely enthusiastic selling. No hotel or fast-food chain could survive in today's economic climate without knowing who they want to sell to, tailoring their service to their chosen markets . . .'

In the last chapter we examined the meal experience. This is the very basis of the marketing concept: to examine the public's needs and then to provide the right product at the right price. The problem with providing the 'right' product is that in food service, people's tastes and needs change quite quickly and it is relatively difficult to alter purpose-built buildings from one style of restaurant into another. The full range of marketing activities are outside the scale of this book. Nevertheless, the restaurant manager and catering supervisor are very much part of the marketing process (particularly with regard to satisfying customer needs) and it is they who will be responsible for implementing some of the sales promotion ideas introduced by their firms and their managers. For the owner-manager, though, sales, advertising and promotions are entirely his or her responsibility, and even in some large hotel companies, managers have a budget allowance for advertising in the local press. It is important to keep in mind that 'most staff should be involved in the marketing operation since it is the whole business rather than individual activity which will create the desirable impact.'*

Case study 11.1   As You Like It

After Britain joined the EEC in 1971, many British people moved to Brussels to work for the European Community or for British and US firms who had established their European headquarters in the city. By 1975, there were estimated to be over 30 000 British nationals resident there, many from socioeconomic groups AB, although there were also a large number of secretarial and computer staff (in the 20–30 age group) who could be identified as group C1. These were fairly conservative in their eating habits, but due to higher than average salaries, could afford to eat out at least two or three times a week. It was no exaggeration to say that upon their fairly frequent returns to Britain, most would have gone for a fish and chip supper and returned with tinned steak and kidney pies in their suitcases. Thus, although there was no *formal* market research undertaken, three entrepreneurs† collaborated to open a restaurant satisfying these middle-market British consumers. Called 'As You Like It', the restaurant served 'British' food, much to the amazement of the Belgian populace, but to the delight of the market at which the restaurant was aimed.

Menu items included fried fish in batter, steak and kidney pie, liver and onions, sherry trifle and other standard items, which were priced to compete with the average Belgian restaurant. The style of service, the decor and the 'atmosphere' were easy-going and relaxed to appeal to the youngish market. Most of the staff were English, the menu was printed in English and the background was 'imported' pop music in English. Since, with limited capital, the decor could not be made to appear British (even if such a style exists) the restaurant was situated in a seventeenth-century house with cobblestones in the road outside, so the 'olde Englishe' theme was developed around the name of 'As You Like It'. A portrait of Shakespeare was adopted as the restaurant's logo and appeared on place mats, tent cards and in most advertisements. Speciality evenings were introduced that developed this theme of medieval banquets with British minstrels, food and 'serving wenches'. Advertising was confined to mailings at British firms in the area, advertisements in the theatre programmes of the English Comedy Club and advertisements in the two English-speaking weekly publications—the *Brussels Times* and the *Bulletin*—with a combined circulation of more than 12 000.

11.2 MARKETING PRINCIPLES

The above case study illustrates some of the basics of marketing. First, identify the customers, their needs, how much they are prepared to spend, how often they will

---

* *Marketing for Independent Hoteliers* (1980) London: HCITB.
† John Hickey, Peter Moore and the author.

want to eat out, and so on. Second, design an outlet that will satisfy these needs, taking into account all aspects of the meal experience that will affect the customers' view of the operation. Third, tell the potential customers that the unit exists. Fourth, make sure that in a changing market the product is flexible enough to adapt to new tastes and trends among its customers if need be. Last, encourage customers to spend their money while in your establishment. This may appear to be relatively simple, but marketing and sales in the food service industry could have entire books written about them. For this reason, we shall confine our discussion to those marketing activities that the manager/supervisor may become involved in.

11.3 MARKET RESEARCH

In 1977, £55 million was spent on commissioned research, and the science of market research has become very sophisticated. It is not just confined to stopping people in the street with a questionnaire but may be carried out by telephone or direct mailing, be confined to observation or counting, or may not take place in the 'field' at all—desk research involves looking into sources such as the *Statistical Yearbook*, food consumption statistics, NEDO reports and so on. But as we have seen from the case study, market research need not be sophisticated. Many successful restaurants have originated without any formal research. The advantage of research, however, is that it clarifies everyone's view of the customers' wants, for whatever form the research takes, it is essential to know the type of customer that the unit appeals to. The HCITB provides a checklist* of factors that identify different types of customer:

Age group
Occupation
Prosperity/willingness to spend
Type of home and life style
Familiarity with hotels (or eating out)
Attitudes to other guests
Why they are staying (or eating out)

Although designed for independent hoteliers, this checklist is appropriate for caterers too (as indicated in brackets). Much of this information can be obtained by observation of customers or potential customers. McDonald's, for instance, do not select a site at random for one of their restaurants. As we have seen, their operations depend upon a throughput of 500 customers per hour. Their site, therefore, is chosen where the number of passers-by and people working in offices and shops during the day is sufficient to achieve this figure. For existing operations, a scrutiny of the regular clientele quickly identifies age group, life-style and willingness to pay. In addition, further information can be obtained either by talking to customers or by asking them to complete a questionnaire. The former is a less systematic research method, but in most circumstances is preferable to a questionnaire which paying customers may resent. None the less, questionnaires have been very successful in obtaining information from customers, particularly in the institutional and industrial sectors where customer relations are slightly different to the profit-motivated operations.

---

* HCITB (1980) op. cit.

How do customers choose which restaurant to eat at?

The decision to eat out is a two-fold process. First, the potential customer decides what type of restaurant to eat at—popular, fast food, gourmet, speciality, or whatever. Such a decision will be based on factors mainly outside the caterer's control—the amount of money the customer has to spend, whether he or she is dining alone, or with the family or a business colleague, and how much time he or she has available. The second process is the decision to patronize a particular restaurant of the type selected, i.e. whether to eat at McDonald's, Wimpy or Burger King; to dine at Leith's, Carriers or Taj Mahal. It is here that the caterer's marketing and sales skill can have the most influence. A survey printed in the *Cornell Catering and HRA Quarterly* in November 1980 suggested that there are three models of consumer choice and although only tentative conclusions may be drawn from the report, the results are thought-provoking.

1. Disjunctive model

In this case, the consumer chooses between restaurants on the basis of one or more particular attributes. For instance, the most significant factor affecting choice between alternative gourmet restaurants is the quality of the food and to a lesser extent menu variety, and the customer will not consider relatively other factors such as price, convenience and atmosphere. The implications of this are that the best way to advertise or promote a gourmet restaurant is to stress how good the food is and the choice of dishes available.

2. Conjunctive model

This view of consumer behaviour rates all the factors affecting choice more or less equally. A restaurant must meet or exceed a minimum level or standard in each of these areas to attract custom. Consumers using family-popular restaurants are predicted to behave in this way, so that restaurateurs in this sector must ensure that factors such as price, food quality, atmosphere, convenience and menu variety are well-balanced and no single factor should be promoted.

3. Compensatory expectancy value model

The consumer in this third model weighs up the good points and bad points about a number of restaurants and selects that restaurant where the good points most outweigh the bad points. This is probably the view of consumer behaviour that most caterers have and is the basis for most of their promotional efforts, i.e. to advertise those factors that are the main selling points.

Task 11.1

Although the research reported here involved very sophisticated statistical techniques, conduct your own survey of customers at a particular unit, perhaps in your own college cafeteria. Find out what the alternatives are to eating in the particular unit* and ask why the customers have chosen to eat there. Find out from this what the caterer could do to improve sales.

Case study 11.2   Happy Eater

In the summer of 1978, the Happy Eater chain of restaurants conducted a market survey in order to establish clearly their market appeal. In other words, the survey aimed to identify what sector of the population (i.e. market segment) used their units. The questionnaire then went on to determine the reason for the customer choosing to eat in a Happy Eater and to identify any aspects of the operation that may be causing customers dissatisfaction. The survey was conducted at three different units meant to represent typical Happy Eaters during the period 3 to 9 July. Customers were requested to complete the questionnaire while in the units and in most cases they did so; the sample size was therefore large and the results can be regarded as an accurate representation of customer opinion.

The following tables indicate the form of questionnaire and show the actual results of this particular survey.

	(1) %	(2) %	(3) %	All %
(1) *Number in group*				
Individual	25	23	21	23
Group of 2	47	41	43	43
Group 3–4	23	31	28	27
Group over 4	6	8	8	7
(2) *Customer status*				
Business	30	31	32	31
Family group	26	37	30	31
Husbands and wife/couples	35	27	29	30
Group of friends (over two in number)	9	5	10	8
(3) *Age of customer*				
0–6	6	9	8	8
6–12	9	7	8	8
Teenage	7	5	12	8
20–30	18	14	26	19
30–50	40	44	29	38
Over 50	21	21	17	19

---

* There must be alternatives otherwise the investigation will have little worth.

	(1) %	(2) %	(3) %	All %
(4) *Have your children asked to come?*				
Yes	26	20	40	28
Because of the play area	20	18	5	14
Badge and lollipop	26	32	20	26
Children's menu	22	26	35	28
Happy club/happenings	6	4	—	3
Other	—	—	—	1
(5) *Do you like our decorations/furniture/colour scheme?*				
Yes	92	86	88	88
No	8	14	12	12
(6) *Is the liquor licence an attraction to visit Happy Eater?*				
Yes	53	36	40	43
No	47	64	60	57
(7) *Do you feel Happy Eater gives good value for money?*				
Yes	94	90	88	90
No	6	10	12	10
(8) *Are you satisfied with our style of cleanliness and service?*				
Yes	86	84	87	85
No	14	16	13	15
(9) *Have you ever bought any puzzles, T-shirts, flasks or other sundries?*				
Yes	40	43	27	37
No	60	57	73	63
(10) *How did you hear of us?*				
Recommended by individual	22	6	6	11
Recommended by business house	6	3	—	3
Spotted sign for first time	25	29	64	39
Do you look out for our signs?	35	61	22	39
Do you carry company leaflets/menus, etc. in the car?	2	1	2	2
Did you see us advertised in the local newspaper/national newspaper/magazine?	10	1	6	6

11.4 MARKETING AND SALES

It would be foolish to believe that once a unit is in operation then customers will flock to it without some form of communication between the two parties. Furthermore, once customers are through the door for the first time, the caterer wants them to spend as much as they are prepared to and to come back again as frequently as possible. If the unit provides the meal experience that the customers expect, then they should come back again. For the rest of this chapter then, we will consider three main questions: how to get the customer through the door for the first time, how to maximize the spend per head without deterring a return visit and how to achieve a satisfactory turnover of customers.

There are four marketing tools available to the caterer, namely advertising, sales promotion techniques, merchandising and public relations, and while these will be discussed separately, they do overlap to a great extent. Moreover, it is important that each of these is part of a complete strategy (or marketing mix) and closely related to marketing the meal experience.

Advertising

Advertising has been defined by the American Marketing Association as 'Any paid form of non-personal presentation and promotion of goods or services by an identifiable sponsor'. This definition emphasizes four points. First, advertising has to be paid for and therefore has to be effective by at least bringing in enough new customers to cover the cost of advertising. Second, there is no personal contact between advertiser and consumer. This is significant in the food service industry since personal contact should be one of the skills caterers are good at, but they may be less capable of non-personal communication. In September 1979, judges of the 11th Catering and Hotelkeeper's Marketing awards found that 'caterers have much to learn on the subject of how to sell themselves effectively'. Third, the customer has to be given information about the product or service, and lastly, information about the firm promoting the product, preferably identifying a brand image that will stay in the consumer's mind. The scope of media available for advertising is very wide, including television, radio, national and local press, posters and guides. It is extremely unlikely that individual catering managers will be responsible for a national advertising campaign, although they may well work for a company that conducts such a campaign and as such need to be very aware of what the advertising is attempting to do. For instance, McDonald's promoted a litter-free image with a television advertisement featuring eight litter-bins singing a jingle. During this campaign, therefore, McDonald's operators should have paid particular attention to the provision of litter-bins at their outlets, lest a campaign that cost thousands was to prove a failure.

The HCITB* discuss the content of advertising and give four basic hints as to how to create effective advertising.

Target audience

As we have seen, a restaurant usually appeals to a particular type of customer or market segment. Therefore the advertising media must be chosen to reach that particular audience. This is partly why independent operators do not advertise in the national press, since their target audience is likely to live in the area. People going out for a meal in the evening are unlikely to drive many miles, especially in view of Britain's drink and drive laws.

Task 11.2

Look in as many national and local papers as you can obtain and compare their advertisements for restaurants. Try to identify the particular target audience of the advertisement.

Image

The advertisement must reflect the style of the restaurant itself. For instance, advertisements for up-market, expensive restaurants should be glamorous and glossy, but if

---

* HCITB (1980) op. cit.

the restaurant is bright and breezy, the advertisement should reflect this. Furthermore, this image should be consistent in all aspects of the operation.

Benefits

The advertisement should sell the product in such a way as to make it different from all the other similar products on the market. 'It is the benefit which the customer will receive by being with *you* that he is buying.'* For instance, a recent national campaign by Trusthouse Forte in the press had pictures of the group's hotel staff smiling, without illustrations of the hotels at all. The campaign was selling the idea that what made THF's hotels better than anyone else's was the friendliness of the staff.

Dominance

The advertisement must attract potential consumers and claim their attention. This is not easy for the non-expert and advertising experts have become very esoteric in their attempts to capture consumer's attention: advertisements for Smirnoff, Benson and Hedges, and so on. Advertisements for the catering industry tend to be a lot more prosaic but they must none the less be effective.

Case study 11.3   Worplesdon Place Hotel

The Worplesdon Place Hotel is a small 15 bedroom hotel situated approximately 4 miles from Guildford and Woking, and 7 miles from Aldershot. It has an à la carte restaurant seating 36 covers, with a separate lounge bar, and two small function rooms suitable for meetings, receptions and buffets. The manager (in 1980) wished to develop in particular the food sales through the restaurant and decided to advertise in the local press. However, to establish which of the local papers was the most effective means of reaching his prospective clientele, he ran an advertisement offering a free bottle of wine with a meal for four that necessitated cutting a coupon from the paper. In this way, by making each advertisement in each paper slightly different, it was possible to establish which paper had been more effective in promoting sales. The promotion also helped to identify if business was derived from one particular area, primarily Guildford, Woking or Aldershot.

The advertisements were placed in the *Surrey Advertiser*, *Guildford Times*, *Woking Review*, *Woking News and Mail*, *Aldershot Star* and *Aldershot News*. Table 11.1 shows the response to the campaign.

Table 11.1 *Response to Worplesdon Place Hotel's local advertisements.*

Newspaper	Coupons redeemed	Average spend per head
Surrey Advertiser	21	£7.86
Guildford Times	4	£6.99
Woking Review	7	£7.32
Woking News and Mail	15	£7.57
Aldershot Star	3	£6.86
Aldershot News	4	£7.31

* HCITB (1980) op. cit.

Sales promotion

The Worplesdon Place case study also illustrates another aspect of marketing, namely, sales promotions. In this context, promotion refers to those activities designed to promote sales in two main ways: temporal sales and product sales.

Temporal sales promotion

Many businesses in the catering industry are subject to weekly and seasonal fluctuations in trade. This depends where the restaurant is sited but an analysis of daily and monthly sales will soon identify those times when business is slack. There are many promotional strategies available to operators to increase business during these times. First, the advertising effort may be increased to bring the restaurant to people's attention more often. Second, the restaurant may promote special offers, such as in the previous case study. These offers may take the form of reducing the prices of items or to make a combination offer—a customer who buys one menu item gets another menu item free. Such promotions may be made through cut-out slips in the local press, by vouchers and by in-house promotional material. The advantage of vouchers is their flexibility. They can be distributed door-to-door, handed out on the street, offered as prizes for raffles to local organizations and given away in the outlet itself. Among the in-house promotional material that may be used are such ideas as special offers on the menu card itself, tent cards on tables and posters explaining the special offer.

Case study 11.4   Viking Restaurants

The following report appeared in *Caterer & Hotelkeeper*:

> One British restaurant group which applies various special price offers to good effect is Fry Fare. For customers at the company's 84-cover Viking fish and steak restaurant in Staines, the menu features a shoppers' special, designed to boost trade in the pre-lunch lull by giving free soup or fruit juice and free tea or coffee with any meal ordered between 11.30 a.m. and 12.30 p.m. Monday to Friday. A similar offer operates on Sundays. This offer amounts, on menu prices, to a discount of 50 pence, although the actual cost, bearing in mind that the items given away are high mark-up lines, is obviously much less.

Product sales promotions

Rather than promote the entire business, it may be desirable to increase sales by promoting a particular product. Wines and spirits promotions are particularly common in the trade, and caterers receive a great deal of promotional help from the supplier if they take part in such a promotion. The reasons for promoting a product rather than the restaurant (although obviously the restaurant must be mentioned in the promotion) are threefold. First, such a promotion may attempt to reach a new market, such as promoting children's portions being available, a 'dieter's special', and so on. Second, it may promote a product to take advantage of a supplier's special offer, such as wines and spirit promotions or the seasonal lowering of the price of a meat item. Third, the product promotion may be used as a means of identifying the 'unique' nature of the operation that distinguishes it from other food service units in the locality. An essential feature of this type of promotion is the involvement of the food service staff. In addition to the written material, it is essential to involve the staff to draw customers' attention to the offer. They should be aware of the fact that an increase in sales is good for the business and consequently good for them, but a further incentive may be given by offering a small bonus to the one who sells the most of the product during its promotional campaign.

Case study 11.5   Mandarine Napoleon

Following a pilot launch in the north-west of England, Hedges and Butler have been heavily promoting their liqueur Mandarine Napoleon. This promotion has included discounts on the product for caterers, a competition for bar staff to develop a cocktail containing the liqueur, the development of a recipe booklet, given free to caterers, containing more than 100 savoury and sweet recipes, and a 'Grand Prix Internationale' which in 1980 offered prizes totalling £6500 to competitors inventing and preparing a dish containing the liqueur.

Case study 11.6   Wine sales

In 1981, Gilbey Vintners prepared a merchandising and presentation package that helped caterers to promote wine sales at special themed evenings or as a 'wine of the month'. With the slogan 'Make time for wine', the package included menu cards, table tent cards, coasters, posters and till stickers.

Merchandising

This refers to creating a favourable image of the restaurant and persuading the customer to buy using less direct means than those discussed previously. This is best exemplified by the impact that display can have upon the customer. As we shall see (p. 166) how the way in which the menu is displayed can play a significant role in the sales effort, but the display, or 'visual merchandising' of foodstuffs is also important (Fig. 11.1). Such displays may be seen on hors d'œuvre or sweet trolleys, beverage displays, buffets, and window displays. The trolley can achieve sales, particularly of sweet items since by taking a selection of attractive and colourful sweet items to the customers' table, they may be tempted to buy even when satisfied by two previous courses. Beverage displays (such as racked wines in the restaurant or on display on a side table) have the advantage that, unlike fresh foodstuffs, the product does not deteriorate quickly when put on display. Buffet or self-serve displays in particular promote sales. In cafeterias, customers who may only want a beverage are encouraged to purchase a snack item when they have to pass along a counter displaying such items. Other display ideas include allowing the customer to select fresh trout or lobster from a tank, a self-serve salad bar or smorgasbord, the carvery operation and fresh food may also be put on display just for decorative purposes.

Finally, window displays used extensively in retailing may also be used in food service. Since foodstuffs will deteriorate in displays in the window, such displays may consist of a view of satisfied customers or pictorial presentations of the food to be found inside. As fast-food companies have demonstrated, well-photographed meals

FOOD FESTIVAL PROMOTIONS

A growing trend in food and drink promotions is food festivals, promoting the cuisine and beverages of a particular region or country for anything between a weekend and a fortnight. Holiday Inns International, for example, has a central policy for co-ordinating such events, so that in 1980 every one of their British hotels had a one- or two-week food promotion each month, either promoting a national or regional cuisine or a particular food item.

A themed promotion may help the business and promote sales in a variety of ways to:

1. Increase sales during off-peak periods by attracting new customers.
2. Gain publicity in the local press and radio.
3. Stimulate and interest regular customers.
4. Provide a challenge and rekindle staff enthusiasm.

But in order for the themed festival to work successfully, planning and organization must be done in great detail. Each promotion will be different but the following guidelines indicate some of the points of importance.

1. Involve other organizations with an interest in the theme such as wine and spirit merchants, food importers, tourist organizations, travel firms, airlines and cultural organizations. *clval*.
2. Research and prepare the theme to achieve the greatest possible degree of authenticity, especially with regard to the menu dishes, and ensure that all ingredients will be available at the time the promotion is planned.
3. Plan well in advance to achieve the maximum publicity and promotional impact.
4. Ensure that the event does not coincide with a major function.
5. Use the expertise of your staff to stimulate ideas. For instance, the success of the Grosvenor Hotel's 'Taste of Sri Lanka' promotion was partly due to the energy and expertise of their Sri Lankan sous-chef.
6. Use the opportunity to show new customers the normal table d'hôte and à la carte menus to promote sales at times other than during the festival.

Task 11.3

Following your investigation of foreign cuisines (see page 142, Task 10.2) select a country or a region and plan a promotional package. Keep in mind the points listed above and indicate the other organizations you would approach for promotional purposes.

Figure 11.1 *Display and merchandising (Hilton Hotel, London).*

presented in the form of full-colour posters or transparencies illuminated in light boxes have a big impact. It is even possible to obtain moulded and coloured plastic replicas of food items for display in windows.

Apart from display, merchandising includes the provision of promotional material such as book matches, give-away menus, badges (such as the Kentucky Fried Chicken badge), T-shirts, jigsaws (used by Wimpy in a promotion), hats and caps (such as McDonald's 'Happy Hat' used in the children's promotions), pendants and key fobs, which are meant to be taken away by satisfied customers. Apart from promoting a sense of well-being in customers as a result of being given something free, such material reminds customers of the restaurant perhaps for some days after eating there and can also be used by them to reinforce personal recommendations to friends or colleagues. For instance, the telephone number of the restaurant may be quickly to hand because it is on book matches or on a card in a wallet or handbag. Such items are particularly useful if opening a new restaurant which needs to reach people quickly and may not be listed in the telephone directory to begin with.

Public relations

Large companies spend a great deal of money on public relations. The oil companies, for instance, advertise on television and in magazines not only their products but also their contribution to British success, or their care of the environment and so on. The litter-bin campaign by McDonald's was also partly public relations as well as advertising, since one of the objections to their operations by people working and living near their outlets was the potential amount of litter in the streets created by their exclusive use of disposables. But PR need not cost money, and publicity may result from cultivating a good relationship with the media.

The old adage that any publicity is good publicity does not apply in food service. A local newspaper report about a restaurant which was taken to court by the Public Health Authorities and fined for malpractice will not be good for business. None the less, the local press will always be pleased to print a favourable story about the restaurant if it is newsworthy and if they are told about it. The caterer should regularly prepare and mail information about the operation to the press, provide hospitality to travel writers and local reporters, participate in tourist board and other press conferences and workshops and devise new publicity ideas.

Most newspapers also have an eating-out column and my own experience is that a restaurant is more likely to be mentioned in such a column if it advertises in that paper, but it is up to the restaurateur to make sure that the report is favourable.

Case study 11.7   Routine mailing

The Happy Eater chain regularly mail public relations material to the media. It expects a limited response, but these can be invaluable. In one case, Plymouth Sound Radio invited the Chairman of Happy Eater onto a two-hour phone-in programme following a routine mailing. This led to 'considerable exposure for the company's new roadside units in the area'. (*Caterer & Hotelkeeper*, 8 February 1979.)

Case study 11.8   Original ideas

Original ideas reported in the local press can also lead to national coverage. The proprietors of a small hotel in Teignmouth marketed the idea of holidays for couples called 'Mr and Mrs Smith'. This was reported in the local paper and led to the *Sunday People* and *Daily Mail* covering the story, 19 interviews on radio stations and an appearance on the BBC *Nationwide* programme. The cost of this publicity was negligible, the increase in sales considerable. (*Caterer & Hotelkeeper*, 6 December 1979.)

11.5 THE ROLE OF THE MENU

The menu is *the* most significant factor in a food service operation. As we saw in discussing the meal experience, although people are motivated to eat away from home, for many reasons the food that they eat has the greatest and most significant impact upon their enjoyment of the experience. Therefore, the menu which proclaims to the customer the choice of food items available will be a major factor in selling the restaurant and promoting food (and drink) sales.

The menu has five functions:

1. Information. It satisfies the customer's need for information about what food is available, how it is cooked and presented and at what price.

2. Order. It presents the information in a logical order, usually listing food items under course headings according to standard practice and conventions. This enables the customer to comprehend the menu more easily and presents the items in a way that should stimulate the appetite.

3. Choice. It determines the freedom of choice that a customer may have. By grouping food items into courses the alternative meals that can be chosen are limited. For instance, on a simple table d'hôte menu of two starters, ten main dishes and two sweets there are 14 different dishes but only 40 different meal possibilities, whereas a menu comprising four starters, five main dishes and five sweets has the same number of dishes in total but the customer has the choice of 100 different meal combinations.

4. Image. The menu helps to present in printed form the overall style or image of the restaurant. For instance, a bright, colourful card in a coffee shop or a large, extensive à la carte menu in a top-class establishment. A. B. Seaburg believes that the menu 'must look attractive, that it is colourful and reflective of the style and general appearance of the establishment'.*

5. Sales. Lastly, the menu is a means of promoting sales by describing the dishes in an appetising way, presenting dishes pictorially, promoting 'specials' or 'dishes of the day', promoting speciality evenings or weekends and so on.

In order for the menu to achieve all of these functions successfully, it must be informative, accurate, understandable, inspire confidence and be well-designed. From the point of view of accuracy, the caterer must ensure that items are not 'off' since there is nothing more frustrating for the customer than making a decision only to be told that a dish is unavailable; the dish must conform with the description of that dish on the menu to ensure customer satisfaction and comply with the Trades Descriptions Act; and lastly, pricing must be clear and accurate. Understanding a menu improves confidence, so the menu must be well-written, easily read, and if dishes are described in a foreign language, an English description underneath is desirable. Most menus are printed which aids clarity but hand-written cards have the advantage on cost and adaptability. Very often inserts for the dish of the day are handwritten and can be very effective. J. Langdon cites the example of the Dorchester Hotel where 'in the middle of a fastidiously printed menu, the eye lights on an apparently hand-written section in that violent ink so dear to French chefs and restaurateurs, and this section is devoted to the day's specialities. The contrasting informality of this section conveys something fresh, topical and personal. This is really hard, effective selling effected by the most ingenious of devices.' Finally, the menu card should be kept simple. A single menu card which attempts in one format to convey the à la carte, table d'hôte, chef's specialities and business lunch will not attract custom. In conclusion, thought must be given to the cover art and design; size and style of type used; size, weight and colour of the paper or card and inks to be used. Technical expertise is invaluable here. It need not be the conventional rectangular card. The menu may be presented on a blackboard, or on the place mat, or on cards shaped in the form of fish, the Eiffel Tower or the Pyramids. But whatever the format of the menu card, the restaurant manager or catering supervisor must have two things in mind—if the card is torn, stained or scruffy throw it away, and never present a card where the prices have been modified by crossing out or placing gummed labels over the old prices.

---

* Seaburg, A. B. (1973) *Menu Design, Merchandising and Marketing,* London: CBI.

Task 11.4

Compare the two menus (Figs. 11.2 and 11.3). Try to evaluate to what extent they are informative, accurate, understandable and well-designed. You may wish to do this with other menus you have come across.

Figure 11.2 *Traditional menu (pre-decimalization) (the Chelsea Room).*

11.6 THE ROLE OF THE STAFF

So far little mention has been made of the role of the staff and their importance. The role of employees selling to the public is the subject of much debate in the industry at the present (*Hospitality*, May 1981 and August 1981). Many people have found disturbing the emphasis upon food service staff as sales people and dislike some of the techniques used to promote sales by employees. Such techniques often originate in the

Figure 11.3 *Contemporary menu (Rockgarden).*

USA where the attitude to this question is expressed very well by Richard Lynch*—
'The owner of a food service operation may have the right merchandise, at the right
place, at the right time and at the right price, but that is not enough. The owner must
also employ sales people who can persuade customers to buy the dinner.'

The author takes the view that so long as the employee is made aware first of the

---

* Lynch, R. & W. O. Smith (1979) *Food Services*, New York: McGraw-Hill.

importance of pleasing the customer so that they return and also recommend it to their friends, and second that it is desirable to encourage customers to spend a little more than otherwise they might have done, then much of what is sometimes called 'selling' is really good public relations. For example, a US writer emphasizes the importance of greeting the customer and identifies three types of approach which should contribute to increased sales:

1. *The customer approach.* A 'customer is greeted with a statement or a casual question such as "Good morning, Mr Ericson. How are you?"'
2. *The service approach.* The salesperson offers to be of assistance to the customer, 'Good evening. May I help you?'
3. *The merchandise approach.* The customer's attention is called to a particular item. For example 'Hello. Here is our menu. You might be interested in our luncheon special today.' This approach 'is a proven advantage in selling'.

Several operators prescribe exactly how their staff would greet a customer and also train them to ask at some point during the meal if the customer finds everything to his satisfaction. The danger with this approach is that the employee may find it reduces his job satisfaction and that stereotyped interactions such as this may lack sincerity on the part of the employee. An alternative policy would be to employ staff with the ability to communicate well and leave it to their discretion how to greet the customer. The disadvantage here is that such staff are difficult to find and may expect a relatively high wage.

Whatever approach is adopted, the key to good selling is good listening. Although the restaurant is aimed at a particular market segment, customers will still have many differences—they may be in a hurry, on a diet, unable to eat certain food items, on a restricted budget. Staff should be encouraged to identify particular customer needs so that they may make helpful suggestions. Thirty years ago, Walter Bachman wrote

> It is a great error to try to force expensive dishes on undecided guests or those who order without looking at the menu. [But]—if a guest sees that a waiter speaks expertly about the food and wine, if he can give interesting information about the specialities of the house, he feels that he can rely on his advice. That it is then easier to sell more expensive goods is obvious. (Bachman, W. (1952) op. cit.)

Case study 11.9   The Mr Grub campaign

It is easy to believe that advertising and sales promotion belong only in the private sector, but as the Somerset schools' Mr Grub campaign illustrates, marketing also has a role in public sector catering. The promotion is almost a classic example of how all aspects of sales and marketing should be co-ordinated into a specific campaign with identifiable objectives. In this particular case the targets were exceeded, as the number of school meals increased by 15 per cent (see Case study 7.4). Aspects of the campaign included the following.

A tape–slide presentation was shown to parents at PTA meetings to show them how Somerset feeds school children and to introduce them to 'Mr Grub'. At the same meetings parents were provided with sample meals. Regular articles about Mr Grub appear in the Somerset Education Authority's newsletter which is circulated to all heads and teachers in the county.

Complimentary meals are given to all children when they first start at primary and secondary school, and badges and stickers as shown in Fig. 11.4 are given away,

Figure 11.4 *Marketing school meals (Mr Grub campaign in Somerset).*

usually in conjunction with a specific product sale, e.g. a free badge with every yogurt. Menus are printed on the 'Mr Grub's Lunch Club Menu'.

The campaign has caught the imagination of not only the local press and radio, but has been reported nationally. For instance, the authority included children on the tasting panel to decide which luncheon meat should be awarded a supply contract and this was reported on the BBC and ITV networks. Other firms and organizations have been encouraged to participate in the campaign, and sponsorship has been received from the Milk Marketing Board, a vending company and a major meat supplier.

Task 11.5

In what ways does this campaign differ from that which might be launched in the private sector?

11.7 CONCLUSION

The successful restaurateurs—like Ritz, Prunier, Quaglino, Carrier—have all been marketing men or women. They may not have had any formal training in marketing skills at all, but their knowledge of their customers has resulted in providing meal experiences that have established and maintained custom. The catering industry is an extremely competitive business and is likely to remain so. Good caterers should be aware of the opportunities for selling to their customers, as well as how to serve food.

In looking at marketing in this chapter, much of the jargon and technicality of the field has been avoided. But, in conclusion, it is probably worth mentioning two marketing concepts that identify clearly the role marketing has to play. The first of these is the 'unique selling proposition'. This quite simply means the way in which a business hopes to differentiate itself or its product from its competitors. In other words, it goes out to sell itself as unique in some way from all the other firms supplying the same product. This quality is often captured in the slogans used by firms, for instance, 'You're better off at a Berni', implying that Berni Inns provide better value for money than comparable steakhouses; 'There's a difference at McDonald's you'll enjoy' speaks for itself; and 'Wimpy—the home of the hamburger' is an attempt to regain customer loyalty in the face of US opposition.

The second concept used by marketing experts is that of the 'critical success variable'. This refers to the idea that any business has certain features upon which the success of the venture is absolutely reliant. For instance, fast-food operators' critical success variables might be a product that does not deteriorate quickly and may be consumed in or away from the outlet, a very high level of turnover and very competitive pricing strategy. The value of identifying these variables is that it enables the operator to be constantly aware of those areas of the operation which must be maintained at all cost.

Task 11.5

Identify the critical success variables for catering on aeroplanes, at motorway service areas, and in factories.

Exercise

Read the following extracts from reports in the *Sunday Times* and *Catering & Hotel-keeper* about the Surprise restaurant and answer the questions that follow it.

You've seen the fast food; here comes the good food

THE GREAT AMERICAN SURPRISE

AMERICAN food has become a culinary phenomenon. It is a phenomenon because of the speed with which the habit has spread. . . . [Kentucky Fried Chicken, McDonald's and the Pizza Hut are all] common in London; and the assault on the provinces is about to begin. This is the fast-food business. It is the cheap end of the market in which profit is based on a high turnover. But class is not among its qualities, so a process known to business . . . as 'market segmentation' has begun. The gaps in the market are being filled.

Joe Allen's occupies the middle ground of the market for American food, known in New York as the bare-brick-and-spinach-salad trade. Here, there are spare ribs and bowls of chilli with black-eye beans, as well as the hamburgers and fried chicken. . . . The London version opened in 1977 in a converted flower warehouse in Covent Garden, by the side of the Lyceum Theatre. The investment was £140 000, and Richard Polo, the restaurant's manager, reports Joe Allen is 'very, very happy with it'.

There is only one segment in the market place to go from Joe Allen's—where two people can eat simply and drink moderately for about £15—and that is up-market, which is exactly where five American entrepreneurs

living in London propose to take the American restaurant business. In June [1980], they opened Surprise, in Great Marlborough Street, just down the road from the Palladium and the Police Station. And it ain't cheap. The original investment was precisely $857 000, or, at the sterling rate of exchange they used to plan their budget, £372 565.21.

Surprise is not quite chic, but it is smart: brown felt lines the walls, and there is tan suedette on the banquette seats. The bar sparkles with glass, and the menu has Reuben sandwiches made with fresh salt beef, cheese blintzes, cottage fries, corned beef hash, spare ribs—everything a returning visitor or an American tourist remembers fondly, in fact, except perhaps catfish and soft-shell crabs.

The three men who originated the idea . . . are expatriates and nostalgics, and each is expert in a different area of management: one a public relations man, another a financial consultant, and the third a property developer. They were joined by a wine-loving advertising executive, and—finally—a restaurateur. I talked to four of the begetters (the property man was away developing another site) to discover what facet of the concept they proposed to phenomenalise.

Bob Leaf is president of the second largest

public relations company in the world, Marsteller International . . . —'It began in the summer of 1978 when I was thinking about market segmentation. We wanted an American restaurant that was smarter than the fast-food and saloon type, but with simple main dishes of the right quality and the right size portions. We were never looking for fancy recipes; our only sauces are hollandaise on the eggs benedict and barbeque sauce on the spare-ribs. Presentation and the whole concept of service are just as important as the cooking. A shrimp cocktail doesn't need the world's greatest genius; all you need is the best shrimps.

But it needed another element, therefore we came up with the concept of surprise. We started with the name, which is super because it's the same in French, and it's a base from which to structure everything. The surprise element gives you every kind of merchandising possibility.

The idea was based on a series of surprises. At first we thought we'd ask the name, nationality, and occupation of all our guests and the customer who came up with the right combination would get a surprise, but my partners thought that some of our business guests would find that intrusive. You don't want to have a customer angry with you from the start. The idea of a secret word which patrons would guess was dropped too. But we've kept the idea of a Surprise Poll. Dieters are given cards where they write down their views on issues of the day—the American Presidential election for example—and we keep an up-to-date scoreboard.

Then we found our restaurant man, Bob Cooper, who told us: "Look you have no idea what it entails, you don't understand. It's going to take longer than you think and it's going to cost more." He said that even if you manage correctly and market correctly, marketing will only get people in through the door once. So we decided that the concept of a restaurant based on food would be better accepted.

We haven't removed the risk factor but what we've done is as much as you can to remove the possibility of failure. I doubt whether as much thought has ever gone into a restaurant.'

Restaurateur Bob Cooper had retired to London from Chicago . . . he agreed to manage Surprise.

'You have to start with quality, and that has a different connotation in England. Take meat, for example. In the United States we have pre-cut graded meat, prime and aged. I went to meat suppliers and asked if they butchered their meat into similarly sized steaks, chops and ribs; and most of them looked at me as though I'm barmy. I didn't want a whole animal because that means having a long menu. When you order specific cuts, the menu gets smaller. They cost more, but you get more turnover and less waste.

. . . Here beef is grass-fed rather than corn-fed, which is what gives American beef the marbling of fat that makes it tender. The real trouble with grass-fed beef is that it can't be aged for as long as the corn-fed beef because it shrinks more while it's hanging, and you lose too much.

Another thing I can't believe in England is that you can't get a real American-style sandwich with enough meat in it to make a meal. Our corned-beef sandwich is made of brisket properly carved, because the grain changes half-way down the brisket. These sandwiches aren't cheap; we can't sell them cheap.

The salad bar is our main feature, with 12 to 15 fresh vegetables, and to me it's one of the most beautiful things that can happen to a person. Omelettes are made with three large eggs, and our English muffins are specially made, because you can't buy English muffins in England.

We have 12 to 15 pastries too, including a deep-dish apple pie and a chocolate fudge brownie à la mode, and a real fresh fruit salad. The fish we get from a man in Shepherd's Market. The only item we have to buy frozen is the jumbo shrimp. You can't buy them fresh here. But there are no convenience foods of any kind; no frozen pre-breaded onion rings. We think the average lunch is about £5 to £6 a head and double that at dinner, plus VAT and service. [My own experience suggests it is 50 per cent more than that.] As for the staff, I want youth in there. I want fun. We have a very, very stringent training programme, a four-day seminar with a lot of films and lectures and role-playing, teaching the girls [sic] how to deal with a rude customer, for example. But I don't want professional waiters. This is not haute cuisine; it's plate service out of the kitchen. We want people who like people, as long as they haven't got two left feet.'

Up-market American formula takes London by storm

Within days of opening, Surprise had a daily turnover of £1300 instead of the expected £500; within weeks it was serving 140 lunches and 120 dinners a day. EVE JONES asked Bob Cooper why the restaurant has been so successful so quickly.

IF running a successful restaurant depends on getting your initial sums right, then a group of expatriate Americans in London can look forward to a secure future . . . During the 14 months it took to put the package together, the group raised over £370 000, mainly from friends and personal contacts. It was around 20 per cent more than they reckoned they would need.

They commissioned a feasibility study from a firm of management consultants; hired an interior designer who had worked on the Carlton Tower Hotel in London and the Plaza in New York; and spent several months whittling down their choice of meat suppliers from 25 to just two.

Research into the location, the menu, the interior decor and ways of retaining the element of 'Surprise' (which was to be the restaurant's hallmark) was extensive. And Bob Leaf, president of the international public relations company Burson Marsteller, used all his marketing and public relations know-how to launch the venture on May 19 [1980].

Within weeks there were queues outside every lunchtime. Within months Surprise, near the London Palladium stage door, was serving 140 lunches and an average of 120 dinners a day.

Finance man Bob Lund budgeted on daily turnover rising from £500 to £1500 in six months. Instead, within days it rose to £1300, and now Bob Leaf admits they are 'Months ahead of schedule', although he is not yet prepared to release more detailed figures. Whole-

some as blueberry pie, the restaurant is air-conditioned and beautifully decorated in cool, relaxing browns with a mirrored cocktail bar and suedette-covered banquettes. It seats 120, and the average spend is around £7 at lunchtime, including drinks, rising to about £11.50 in the evening. There is staff of nearly 40, including seven in the kitchen.

Bob Cooper, the operations director, [explained] 'We had to devise a total scheme . . . You cannot put in bits of this and bits of that, taken from restaurants you have admired, and hope the bits will blend together. We had to work out who we were trying to attract—the young crowd of the jet set, older wealthier people or families with children. Then the menu, which had to be specialised and not long-winded. There was the production of the food—how and what. And finally, the type of service . . .'

Everything about Surprise seems clean-cut, clear and simple. Its lunchtime menu features authentic American sandwiches, interesting salads, main courses like Corned Beef Hash and Broiled Pork Chops, and specialities like Potato Pancakes and Cheese Blintzes. In the evening there are Barbecued Spare Ribs and Southern Fried Chicken, T-bone and Carpetbagger Steaks, Lobster Tails and Deep Sea Scallops.

The price of the main courses includes a self-service selection from the salad bar, with up to 20 fresh vegetables and five dressings to choose from; baked jacket potato or french fries; and an individual loaf of fresh-baked granary bread, served on a wooden platter with a bread knife.

Later this month, Bob Cooper says they will incorporate some of the most popular lunch-time specialities, such as Eggs Benedict and Corned Beef Hash with Poached Eggs, into the evening menu as well.

The menu will, however, be kept simple and relatively short, and, except for the jumbo shrimps, nothing is frozen or convenience.

'American cooking is basically honest.' Mr Cooper declares. 'You buy in the best quality ingredients and you prepare them in the simplest fashion. You just let the quality of the food come out.'

Service too, is kept simple and wholesome. Waiting staff are young people—largely American university students. 'I wanted enthusiastic young people here, not professional waiters,' Mr Cooper explained.

'If a kid comes up to you with a smile and says, "Hello, my name's John and I'm your waiter for this evening—I hope you enjoy your meal," then you'll be more ready to for-give him if he spills some water over you. Too many professional waiters and waitresses just don't like people.'

The staff are dressed in a 'uniform' of Levis and shirts. There are joke awards for all kinds of things—for instance, the young man who worked the most shifts (eight nine-hour shifts in one week). Then there are more serious rewards for the boy or girl who sells, for example, the most Surprise cocktails in one evening—25 is the record so far.

Staff are trained for up to four days when they arrive—role-playing, watching training films, listening to lectures, and studying the detailed and comprehensive training manual . . . All this will stand the firm in good stead when, eventually, Surprise branches into the franchise or partnership operation it intends for the near future. 'Possibly it will be in the U.K.,' says Mr Cooper, 'but more likely in Europe or further afield. Definitely not in the U.S. though. Although Surprise is new to this country, it is quite like a lot of other good American restaurants.'

Questions

1. To what extent did the proprietors undertake market research?
2. Can you identify a particular market segment at which the restaurant is aimed?
3. What is it about the restaurant that distinguishes it from other restaurants?
4. What form has sales promotion taken?
5. How effective is their PR (public relations)?

12 Planning and Design

How to make the customer feel at home and still make a profit

---

OBJECTIVES: to outline the role of ergonomics and interior design in the catering industry . . . to understand the principles of restaurant seating in order to maximize capacity within the limits of the food service style . . . to understand the advantages and disadvantages of different floor, wall and furniture coverings in food service operations . . . to describe adequate lighting levels.

Service occurs during the span of time between completion of production and presentation of food to the customers. Its quality is likely to be at its most fragile point of excellence . . . The effective functioning of the service area will depend on [planning], selection of equipment to meet specific needs and a good flow of travel from customer order to service of food.

Kotschevar, L. H. & M. E. Terrel (1977) *Food Service Planning*, New York: Wiley

12.1 INTRODUCTION

IN the same way that the caterer was not expected to be a public relations or marketing expert in the last chapter, in this chapter he or she is not expected to become an expert ergonomicist or interior designer. Probably every major catering firm and many small ones have employed experts in these fields to design the layout and decor of their service facilities, recognizing the importance of these two factors upon operational success. Furthermore, caterers who may become involved in the planning or designing process rarely have a completely free hand in the choice of equipment, fittings and furniture. To a great extent they are limited by what is available from manufacturers and suppliers. None the less, one can imagine many situations where the caterer is asked to participate in this process, particularly where changes in consumer trends or operating policy necessitate altering an existing operation. For instance, we have already seen the importance of understanding design considerations in the operation of a cafeteria counter, as well-planned counters help to speed decisions as to what to select, thereby doing much to reduce costs and please customers. This chapter will consider three broad areas: layout and seating arrangements; furniture and large equipment; and decor and interior design.

12.2 LAYOUT AND SEATING ARRANGEMENTS

As we have seen from our consideration of the different sectors of the industry, much of the difference between styles of service depends upon the alternative configurations of the service area and seating within the unit. But irrespective of the style of service, there is a *minimum* area that a customer needs in order to consume a meal when seated: about 0.8 square metres. This does not mean that 0.8 square metres is the desirable amount of seated space that should be provided in all operations. Consideration must also be given to spacing between tables. For access, 0.25 m is regarded as the minimum distance between adjacent seated customers, while for service to take place, 0.9 m is recommended. Generally speaking the higher the turnover, and lower the profit margin, then the smaller the allocation of space per customer. This is reflected in the styles of service—self-service requires little space between customers seated side by side, whereas silver service requires a gap to enable the waiter to serve, and gueridon service requires a larger amount of space to enable the passage of service trolleys. But as we have seen in Chapter 10, we must also consider the impact of seating upon consumer satisfaction; increasing the seating capacity of a unit may actually reduce turnover rather than increase it as expected.

Case study 12.1   British Home Stores

Catering and Hotel Management (May 1981) reports,

> At Doncaster, and more recently Maidstone, British Home Stores have passed through a three-stage phase in reducing the seating in their restaurants by 15 per cent but at the same time increasing total seat usage at peak hours by 30 per cent. This has been mainly accomplished through installing a higher proportion of two-seater, rather than four-seater, units. Attention has also been paid to banquettes and the width of the aisles. Originally, the restaurant at Doncaster had 214 seats with about 60 per cent four-seater tables and 20 per cent two-seaters. The remaining places were accounted for by a few larger units, but for the most part they were wall-sited banquettes. What with the 'habit' of shoppers using a further seat as a stand for their parcels and the natural reluctance of anyone newly arriving to share a table, it was found that the majority of four-seater tables were used by two or even only one person. So, when the premises were being renovated, the proportions were reversed with now 60 per cent two-seater tables and 40 per cent four-seaters. Almost immediately, the seat usage at peak hours rose from 50 to between 60 and 70 per cent. Of course, a number of these tables for two are, in fact, set a mere six inches apart [0.15 m], which seems perfectly sufficient for one pair of customers to feel that they are sitting completely separated from the next. But this is only effective when access to both sides of the tables is equally easy.

Restaurant seating

Table 12.1 *Sizes of tables to seat various numbers.*

Number of covers	Shape of table		
	Round (diameter)	Square	Rectangular
2	0.8 m	0.75 m × 0.75 m	0.6 m × 0.7 m
3	0.9 m		1.0 m × 0.75 m
4	1.0 m	1.0 m × 1.0 m	1.2 m × 0.75 m
6	1.2 m	not advisable	1.5 m × 0.75 m
8	1.5 m	not advisable	2.4 m × 0.75 m

Table 12.1 indicates the sizes of tables needed to seat between 2 and 8 customers. This is based on the requirement that a person needs a minimum of 0.6 m to avoid touching people on either side and a table will need to be 0.7 m deep to avoid two people's knees touching when seated opposite each other. Although for four customers the round table appears to require less room than the square, both take up the same amount of floor space, whereas the rectangular effectively takes up only slightly less but can be arranged in combination with other tables more effectively than either the square or the round table.

There is also the need for flexibility in the layout to accommodate larger parties which round tables cannot provide and for which square tables tend to take up more space and be less comfortable. For instance, two square tables of 0.75 m × 0.75 m provide seating for four customers when pushed together but for six, it would be very crowded, whereas rectangular tables of 0.6 m × 0.7 m can be pushed together to

Figure 12.1 *Restaurant interior showing different types of seating.*

make up a table of four using two tables and of six using three tables, and in the latter case, six are seated comfortably in an area only 10 per cent larger than that taken up by two square tables of 0.75 m × 0.75 m (see also Figs. 12.2 and 12.3). The seating plan shows that 20 covers can be sited in a room of this size using rectangular tables.

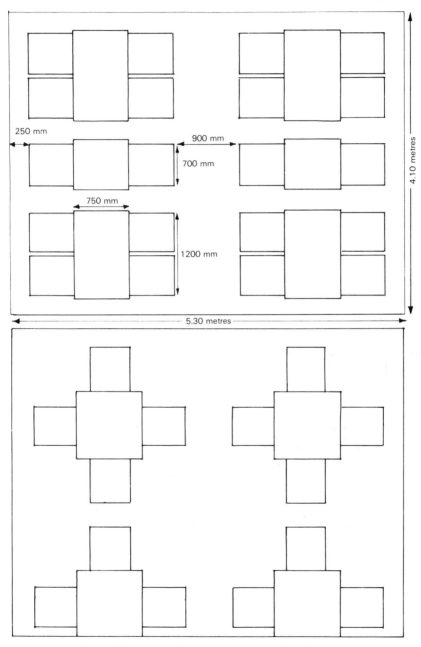

Figure 12.2 *Seating plan using rectangular tables. (Top).*
Figure 12.3 *Seating plan using square tables. (Bottom).*

Although each cover has slightly less 'elbow space' than those shown in Fig. 12.3, there is adequate access for customers and a clear central passageway for service staff. Using square tables, as shown in Fig. 12.3, only 14 covers can be sited in the same amount of space, and the distance between tables is not really wide enough for service staff to pass through with comfort. Lastly, if round tables are employed, it is impossible to locate them as in Fig. 12.3 (see Table 12.1) so that the number of covers possible is reduced to no more than 12. Quite obviously the caterer must weigh up very carefully the conviviality of round tables with the practicalities of rectangular ones. In addition, a flow pattern must be established within the unit. Whether it is self service or waiter service, it is undesirable for customers or staff to thread their way through a maze of tables, especially while carrying trays of food. Aisles between tables should be 0.9 m to 1.5 m wide depending on the amount of use.

Planning the seating in a restaurant must also take into account the type of customer using the unit. Research has shown that customers prefer a certain amount of seclusion when eating out and choose tables near walls, or in booths, or near windows if these are not on view to passers-by. Partitions, screens and other forms of divider may therefore be needed to break up the space, particularly in larger units.

As there is now considerable emphasis placed on providing for the needs of the disabled, facilities should be made available for accommodating wheelchairs. Wheelchairs come in certain standard sizes, although dimensions vary slightly from one manufacturer to another. The overall width of a 'standard adult' chair is 0.61–0.66 m.

Cafeteria seating

Cafeteria seating, operating on a self-service basis, requires less space per customer than restaurants operating with waiter service. It is usual to assume that 25 to 30 per cent of an establishment's total workforce will use the catering facilities on average and dining rooms are planned accordingly. Since, however, it is usually undesirable to have the entire workforce eating simultaneously, the total seating capacity need only be half of the expected turnover, so that meals are served over two sittings. Once the seating capacity has been determined, the caterer must ensure that the speed of service is fast enough to achieve the required seat turnover. Thus if the cafeteria became more popular, since the size of the dining room is not easily altered, the variable factors affecting the availability of seats is the speed of the service, the length of the dining period and the time customers take over their meals. For example, if six customers per minute are served, then for every minute of the service, six seats must be made available. If the average customer spends 20 minutes eating, then there must be seating for 120 customers before a seat may be used a second time. And if the average meal time is 25 minutes, then 150 seats are needed. If the service speed increases to eight customers per minute, then the seating capacity must increase to 160 seats and 200 seats respectively. Where a large number of customers are expected and only a short time available in which to serve them, the service speed must be kept high and the average meal time for each customer must be kept short. Many establishments provide coffee lounges or similar to encourage quick vacating of tables in the main dining area.

Function seating

In Chapter 2 we saw that most operators have well-established floor plans for their function rooms. Seating arrangements can be either *informal* (Fig. 12.4) or *formal*, i.e. top table with sprigs (Fig. 12.5). The type of function will determine the particular style adopted.

Figure 12.4 *Informal table layout (Hilton Hotel, London).*

Task 12.1

Using the banqueting memorandum from Chapter 2 (Fig. 2.9) decide which type of table plan would be the most appropriate. Draw a sketch diagram of a possible seating plan assuming that the function room is 10 m wide by 18 m long.

12.3 ERGONOMICS

R. H. D. Strank, in a pioneering booklet published in 1971 and sponsored by the Luncheon Voucher Catering Education Research Institute,* described ergonomics as 'a

---

* Strank, R. H. D. (1971) *Ergonomics: Functional Design for the Catering Industry*, London: Edward Arnold.

Figure 12.5 *Formal table layout (Cavendish Hotel, Eastbourne).*

comparatively new science that deals with the way that people are affected by their environment. It studies the way that efficiency and comfort are affected by such things as temperature, lighting and the size, shape and layout of equipment of all types.' It also examines the role of people and machines and attempts to identify in a catering context those activities that are best performed by staff and those that are suited to machines. We have seen, for instance, that automatic vending can sometimes provide a better service than a more labour-intensive style of operation, and Strank illustrated this people/machine interaction by discussing the task of a cash-till operator in a self-service cafeteria. Case study 12.2 is based on Strank's study and brought up to date.

Case study 12.2   Cashiering duties

The cashier's job can be analysed into the following tasks (1–10).

(1) Identify items on tray. This is best allocated to the human operator in view of the 'special sensory abilities'. Note, however, that in a similar situation, at supermarket check-outs, this identification process is being done more efficiently now by machine. Products are marked with vertical black and white stripes which are read by a light pencil moving across them, which effectively carries out tasks (1), (2), (3), (4) and (10) simultaneously.

(2) Price items. This may be achieved by the operator, i.e. by converting the identity of the item into a price, or by machine i.e. the operator presses a key marked with the dish name and the till prices the item according to its program. The former is best

when there is a limited choice menu and little price variation, whilst the latter allows frequent changes in price and menu item.

(3) Add prices. Machines are much better than people at this task.

(4) Store and total price. This is also a machine operation.

(5) Obtain cash from customer. Have you noticed how customers in a supermarket or cafeteria often do not listen to the cashier but look at the total displayed on the till when paying their bill?

(6) Identify cash received. This is possible mechanically but a person is probably more effective at this task.

(7) Calculate change. This is 'better performed by a machine due to its superior speed and accuracy'.

(8) Store cash received. Done better by machine.

(9) Give change. This is incorporated in some till operations with task (7).

(10) Keep records. Done better by machine.

This exercise has many implications, especially in view of the robot-serve restaurant (see page 9) and the electronic cafeteria (see page 9) mentioned previously.

Task 12.2

List those factors that must be considered (in view of the above) when designing and siting a cash desk for a cafeteria.

12.4 SIDEBOARDS AND TROLLEYS

So far we have concentrated on the arrangement of tables and chairs but we must also consider integrating into the seating plan the position of service points in waiter-service restaurants and the position of clearing trolleys in self-service units.

Siting of service points. Wall locations are usually at a premium from the customer's point of view, so that it is preferable to place sideboards on island sites, particularly if there are columns in the room. This has the advantage that staff must take greater care to maintain the sideboards in a clean and orderly manner, since they are not in a secluded position.

Siting of clearing trolleys. Where customers clear dirties themselves, trolleys must be situated away from the service counter, near to the exit to avoid congestion between customers about to eat and those about to leave.

Establishing stations

In those restaurants where staff work from a sideboard, care must be taken to ensure that the allocation of covers per station is equitable, so that all staff serve approximately the same number of covers. This is desirable since they will be paid more or less the same wage (unless this is based upon a service charge that can be accredited to particular members of staff) so that resentment, poor morale and low job satisfaction may result if some staff feel they are working harder than their colleagues. It should be remembered that by allocating the same number of tables to each station, the restaurant manager cannot be sure that each station waiter will serve the same number of customers. As we have seen, customers prefer to sit at some tables (near windows or with their backs to the wall) rather than at other tables.

Task 12.3

List alternative policies for the restaurant manager to adopt to create an equitable situation.

12.5 FURNITURE

The Council of Industrial Design, following reports by the Advisory Committee on Hotels and Restaurants, has made recommendations concerning the size, and shape of tables and chairs. These are of less importance to the caterer than may at first appear since the caterer must purchase furniture from manufacturers and it is they who are most interested in these ergonomic considerations. Thus it is unlikely that chairs and tables will be put on the market if they are not made in accordance with these guidelines. The most important criteria are:

Height of table from floor—0.7 m
Height of chair seat from floor—0.41 to 0.43 m
Width of chair seat—0.5 m
Depth of chair seat—0.4 to 0.45 m
Clearance between chair and underside of table—0.2 to 0.23 m.

This last point emphasizes the importance of purchasing tables and chairs that have been designed as one unit.

If we presume that furniture has been well-designed ergonomically, the caterer will select tables and chairs according to their appropriateness for the type of operation, cost, ease of cleaning and maintenance, durability and appearance. The caterer may select two basic modes of seating, free standing or fixed.

Free standing

This means tables and individual chairs. The advantages of this type of furniture are customer preference (freedom of movement), ease of replacement (worn or broken seats can be removed) and it is easier to clean.

Fixed

This may be banquette seating, purpose built for a particular restaurant or mass-produced units for cafeteria operations (Fig. 12.6). The caterer may select this style of furniture because less floor space is needed per cover, well-designed units minimize obstruction which makes cleaning quicker.

Generally an up-market unit will select furniture that is comfortable, e.g. chairs

Figure 12.6 *Fixed seating layout (the Bridge Buffet, Birmingham New Street Station). British Railways.*

with arms, upholstered, and so on and aesthetically pleasing (made from expensive woods, classic designs). A self-serve operation, however, will consider functional design, durability and ease of cleaning the more important criteria. But whatever the unit, tables and chairs should comply with the following recommendations.

1. The foot of the chair or table should be fairly broad to spread the load, so avoiding damage to the floor surface.
2. Tables and chairs should offer minimum resistance when moved on carpet but at the same time be slip-proof on most types of floor surface.
3. Upholstered chairs should be made of easy-to-clean materials, and where possible upholstery covers should be easily removed for cleaning and repairs.
4. Upholstered chairs should have a gap between the seat and the back for ease of cleaning.
5. Chairs with arms should have the arms low enough to allow the chair to be pulled up to the table.
6. Table legs should have no sharp edges or protruding fixtures to avoid damaging shoes or stockings.
7. Table tops should be non-slip (or covered in green baize) where table cloths are used.
8. Tables with removable legs to facilitate movement and storage should be easily dismantled and parts should be fully interchangeable.

Furthermore the Design Council has made recommendations with regard to the suitability of upholstery: resistance to abrasive wear; resistance to burning; and colour fastness in light, rubbing and cleaning. The second of these factors is particularly important in catering. Foam filled cushions and upholstery are generally preferred to spring seats in modern furniture, but foam is susceptible to fire. High density foam is more fire resistant but smokes a great deal more than the more inflammable low density foams.

Table 12.2 compares the suitability of the different materials used in furniture manufacture for the catering industry and outlines the correct cleaning methods for each material.

Table 12.2 *Materials used in the manufacture of furniture.*

Material	Advantages	Disadvantages	Method of cleaning
Wood	Wide variety of woods and wood finishes available. Hardwearing, especially if solid wood. Relatively easy to clean.	May be easily chipped or scratched. Possibility of woodworm. Heavy to move around especially solid wood furniture.	Depends upon finish applied, e.g. wax, nitrocellulose, melamine, polyurethane, paint. Generally dust or wipe with damp cloth, avoid abrasives and for paintwork alkali-based cleaning agents.
Metal	Strong and hard wearing.	May be heavy to carry. May tarnish if not protected by lacquer or some other finish. Shows fingermarks and may give you a shock through static electricity.	Dust and wipe only if an alloy of stainless steel, aluminium or chrome. Use appropriate metal polish if not lacquered brass or copper.
Plastics	Stain resistant and hard wearing. Wide variety of colours and finishes. May be moulded into many shapes.	May be scratched or chipped.	Dust or wipe with damp cloth. Avoid abrasives.
Upholstery	May be textiles, leather or plastic. Adds warmth and comfort to decor.	Subject to wear and tear. May hold dust and stain. May take additional time to clean and maintain.	Brush or wipe with damp cloth. Leather must be polished.

Task 12.4

Measure the dimensions of a variety of tables and chairs at home, in cafeterias and restaurants. Try to evaluate, if there is variation between dining sets, which you find the most comfortable. If the most comfortable proportions for you are different to the recommendations, why might this be?

12.6 INTERIOR DESIGN

The question of interior design is that of creating the most effective interior at a reasonable cost. In this respect, as for any investment, the interior design of a unit has both capital and running costs, although all too often the latter cost element is ignored.

Capital cost

The investment in creating the right interior must be such that a satisfactory return on capital will be achieved within a prescribed period of time. For instance, Wimpy International was reputed to have spent £1 million on redesigning their Oxford Street branch. Such investment is only justified if sales and turnover consequently increase substantially in order to pay back this investment. In fact, Wimpy International used their Notting Hill branch as a testing ground for their new 'image' and in 1979 estimated that turnover in that branch trebled in one year following redesign and refurbishment.

Running costs

The design of the interior will also affect the running costs of the operation. Some of these can easily be established:

Energy use, i.e. heating and lighting.
Cleaning costs of floors, wall surfaces, etc.
Replacement costs and depreciation.

But the interior design may increase running costs in a more intangible way. The best example of this is increasing staff turnover. A restaurant that is uncomfortable to work in, either due to the type of lighting or floor surface or whatever, may in fact deter staff from staying with the operation, so that the ergonomic considerations of staff must be considered equally with those of the customer.

Case study 12.3   Energy efficient lighting

David Butler,* a lighting specialist, has this to say about lighting: 'The dining room functions for all meals . . . Breakfast/lunch require a high general level of illumination whilst intimate, low key lighting is required for dinner/functions. Flexibility with lighting is required.' Dimmer controls can effectively achieve these requirements, and tungsten lamps can be dimmed easily and inexpensively. A US study has estimated that lighting constitutes 25 per cent of a hotel's energy charges.† It is therefore very important to look at lighting levels and to investigate ways of reducing energy consumption. Action that can be taken to achieve this reduction include switching off lights when they are not needed; using lower wattage lamps, although this reduces the amount of light; using long-life bulbs, which reduces the frequency of replacement and the time needed to carry this out; using fluorescent lamps which are more efficient; fitting anti-theft locking devices to prevent theft of light bulbs.

Factors affecting decor

Five factors have been identified by the Richmond Design Group (who work in the catering industry) as affecting decor in restaurants:

---

* *Hotel & Catering Review*, January 1981.
† *Lodging Hospitality*, December 1980.

1. Market profile. The type of customer using the establishment according to such criteria as age, income level, frequency of visit, and so on (see Figs 12.7 and 12.8).
2. Operational planning. The maximizing of operational efficiency by the 'accurate positioning of every element in the design'.
3. Maintenance. The incorporation of features that will reduce running costs and minimize maintenance.
4. Style of restaurant. Design will reflect the function and style of the unit, as well as the menu or specialities of the operation.
5. Life expectancy. The length of time that the decor will be expected to last until it is replaced.

When these five factors have been considered, most units have identified a theme around which the restaurant will operate. In this respect, the only difference between independent restaurateurs and chain operators is that the latter repeat their theme throughout all their units. The essential difference is that independent operators hope to appeal to customers by being different, whereas chain operators hope to establish a theme that will attract custom throughout their chain.

Figure 12.7 *Very formal decor in a restaurant.*

Figure 12.8 *Informal decor from a fast-food outlet.*

Case study 12.4   Pub interiors

Pub operators and brewers have, during the 1970s, spent a great deal of money in redesigning the interiors of their public houses. Many pubs built in the early years of this century had several rooms—a saloon bar, public bar, snug, games room and so on—each with their own serving area. This was satisfactory at a time when staff were relatively cheap and pub customers were more class conscious than they are today. Today, however, with the increase in staff wages and the need to maximize the income from a property, pubs have been redesigned with circular bars in the middle of the pub allowing free movement all around it, so that fewer staff can serve a larger number of customers. At the same time, it is recognized that a degree of intimacy may be desirable so that alcoves, room dividers and partitions may be incorporated for the less gregarious.

Elements of interior design

As far as decor is concerned, there are three general considerations.

Colour

The colours used in the decor of the room can have several effects—dark colours make a room appear smaller than it is, while bright colours expand it.

Blue is a 'cold' colour, while red is 'warm'. Research has shown that people placed in a room painted blue record that it feels colder than a room painted red, even though the actual temperature was the same in both rooms. Similarly, it has been established that the blue end of the spectrum will produce in people a desire to 'withdraw', whereas the red end of the spectrum induces feelings of 'expansion' and sociability.

Generally speaking, a clash of colours increases tension, although this appears to be more acceptable at the lower end of the market. Also, it 'has been established medically that . . . the red end of the spectrum increases blood circulation and increases muscular activity, which in turn assists digestion' (Campbell-Smith, G. (1967) op. cit.).

Patterns

Patterns too can affect people and great care must be taken to ensure that patterns are well-established. First, everything must blend together to form a whole. People have an instinctive desire for conformity and uniformity, for instance most people will straighten a picture if it is crooked or will straighten the cutlery on a table in a restaurant. Second, too many patterns on wallpaper can be distracting, rather like sitting inside a kaleidoscope. Lastly, patterned wallpaper can make a room seem smaller with large patterns, taller with striped patterns, and so on.

Texture

The texture of wallhangings, curtains, floors and furnishings also contribute to the customer's sense of security. 'The use of fabrics in relation to the other decorative features is one of the basic principles of design and is important to the customer, not only because of its visual impression, but because he finds it more pleasurable to touch than hard walls or wood surfaces.'* And as have seen, texture can play an essential role in the acoustics of a restaurant, and even in its heating.

12.7 MAINTENANCE AND CLEANING

One of the most important functions of the catering manager is that of maintaining the standard of hygiene and cleanliness in the establishment. A major problem is that food service personnel often do not regard themselves employed as cleaners, nor are they necessarily trained to vacuum clean carpets, polish furniture and dust fittings efficiently. There are two broad policies that may be adopted—either food service staff are entirely responsible for cleaning the unit or they do no cleaning at all and specialist cleaners are employed, either directly or on a contract basis. The latter has the advantage that these specialists should provide a high standard of cleanliness and may cost less to employ than an expert waiter or waitress. However, the unit may be too small to justify employing cleaning firms, or alternatively, if a cleaner is employed all

---

* Newell, M. (1965) op. cit.

too often because of their low rates of pay, such personnel are not very expert at their job. This means that the catering manager must lay down very clearly to cleaning staff the standards that are expected. A common way of doing this is in the form of a work schedule which details the cleaning activities on a daily, weekly or monthly basis. Although the schedule lays down what should be done, the manager must ensure that it *is* done to a satisfactory standard. For instance, it is all very well for the schedule to lay down that the carpet will be vacuumed clean every day, but it is up to the manager to see that the waiter or cleaner does not only do the visible areas between tables and chairs.

The caterer must therefore take three steps to ensure standards are maintained. (1) The cleaning duties of staff should be made clear to each member of staff when they are employed and if necessary this should be incorporated in their contract of employment. They should be reminded of their responsibilities when the need arises. (2) Staff should be provided with the products and equipment needed to achieve a good standard of cleanliness. (3) Staff should be trained in the proper methods of cleaning, the use of cleaning agents and the procedures to be adopted in the event of maintenance being required. It is essential that the unit has a clear policy with regard to safety and hygiene and that all employees are aware of and participate in this policy.

Tables 12.3 and 12.4 analyse the alternative floor and wall surfaces that may be found in catering operations and outline the most suitable method of cleaning and maintaining the surfaces.

Table 12.3 *Wall surfaces—types and cleaning procedures.*

Type	Advantages	Disadvantages	Cleaning method
Paintwork	Relatively cheap, long-lasting, easily cleaned. Emulsions easily 'repaired' if bumped or scraped.	Not suitable for up-market decor style.	Dust with duster, then wash walls with water and detergent using a sponge. Rinse with clean water.
Wallpaper	May be used to 'change' dimensions of a room	More costly. May become dated in appearance.	Dust with duster or brush. If washable sponge down.
Tiles	Hygienic	Can only be used to a limited extent due to cold appearance.	Cleans easily.

Table 12.4 *Floor surface.*

Type	Advantages	Disadvantages	Cleaning method
Wooden—block, —parquet, etc.	Quite durable, fairly warm.	Not resistant to water. Limited colour range.	Polish using floor polisher. Do *not* use water.
Thermoplastic tile	Non-slip. Resilient.	Noisy. Not as resistant to wear as ceramic tiles. Cold.	Wet mop with detergent and water.
PVC.	Quiet. Warm.	Reasonably durable.	Sweep, mop, polish.
Ceramic tiles	Highly durable.	Cold. Noisy. Unsuitable for areas where staff are standing/walking all day. Can be very slippery if wet.	Sweep with brush and wet mop with neutral detergent.
Carpet	Warm. Quiet. Non-slip	Not as resilient as other floor surfaces. May be expensive.	Vacuum and shampoo regularly.

12.8 CONCLUSION

There is no doubt that the atmosphere created by a well-integrated interior will contribute greatly to the success of a food service outlet. In all the sectors discussed, an important part of the catering operation has been the role of design, furniture and decor in creating the right image for the establishment and ensuring its smooth operation.

Food service managers must do their part in maintaining this image by ensuring that the intentions of the designer are recognized and the maintenance of furnishings and fittings is carried out regularly. Relatively small points, such as replacing light bulbs as soon as they wear out with a bulb of an identical design and wattage may appear trivial, but if the organization has paid a designer a considerable sum of money to develop the decor, then the operators must be prepared to accept this expert advice. Likewise, a shabby or scruffy interior will not attract custom. The restaurant manager must supervise the regular cleaning of all furnishings and furniture, making sure that the cleaning operatives are using the correct cleaning agents and materials.

Exercise

List the circumstances in which the caterer's knowledge of ergonomics, design and furnishings may contribute to lower operating costs.

13 Food Service Equipment

How to provide staff with what they need to give customers what they want

---

OBJECTIVES: to identify the alternative means of equipping a food service unit . . . to outline requisite stock levels of equipment . . . to describe the alternative methods of cleaning equipment . . . to identify the necessary qualities required for items of equipment used in the hotel and catering industry.

Nowadays all hotels, better class restaurants and catering establishments of all kinds use silver-plate . . . Porcelain looks well on the table and helps to cheer the guest and put him in a comfortable mood . . . Noble wines demand noble glasses of the proper shape . . .

Bachman, W. op cit.

13.1 INTRODUCTION

THE equipment needs of a food service facility are the same throughout the industry. This basic equipment is perhaps best described as (1) equipment for transporting food—trays, plates, glasses, cartons; (2) utensils for eating food—knives, forks, spoons, and so on; and (3) materials for protecting against spillage—tablecloths and napkins.

Many years ago, one could be far more specific about food service equipment. Walter Bachman, in his book *Professional Knowledge*, has sections on linen, silver, china and glass; for these materials were the only materials considered suitable for use in restaurants. Today, however, there are numerous alternatives including, as we shall see plastic and paper 'disposables'. In this chapter we consider how to purchase equipment and maintain it efficiently.

13.2 SOURCES OF SUPPLY

Equipment is an expensive item, a high capital cost, so that it is essential to obtain the equipment in the most cost-effective way. There are basically three sources of supply:

Manufacturer

The advantage of dealing directly with the manufacturer of equipment is that the cost of items should be at their lowest. However, this may be offset by the manufacturer's vested interest in supplying the equipment.

Catering supplier or wholesaler

Wholesalers, unless they are an agent for only one manufacturer, have no vested interest in supplying one particular brand. They can advise the caterer as to the most suitable type of equipment for the particular operation.

Leasing company

Nearly all catering equipment need not be purchased at all, as practically every item may be hired from a leasing company. The main advantage of leasing is that investment costs are reduced and equipment becomes an overhead. Also included in the hire contract are arrangements for maintenance and replacement of used equipment.

13.3 EQUIPMENT STOCKS

The stock level of equipment required to operate a unit efficiently will depend upon a variety of factors. Table 13.1 outlines this in broad terms.

Table 13.1 *Equipment stocks in different operations.*

Equipment	Self-service operations	Tray-service operations	Waiter-service operations
Variety of table layouts	Low	Low	High
Specialist items of service equipment	Low	Low (excluding tray itself)	High
Use of table linen	Low	N/A	High
Cost of service equipment	Medium	Medium	High
Use of disposables	Medium/high	Low/Medium	Low

The caterer must hold the stock level that will ensure a smooth-running and efficient operation with the minimum of capital investment. Minimizing the total amount of equipment and the variety of different items, also helps to reduce the amount of storage space required and reduce the time needed to take stock. In this respect, the caterer will probably require at least twice as many of each item of equipment as there are covers in the unit, although as the operation increases in size, the proportion of spare items can be reduced. There will also be differences in the loss and breakage rates of items—among cutlery items, teaspoons are usually high on the list, while teacups are also vulnerable. In the old days, and even today, very large hotels employed someone on a full-time basis to search through all the swill bins to look for items of equipment, and the cost of the equipment recovered in this way more than paid for that person's wages.

13.4 PURCHASE OF EQUIPMENT

In considering the purchase of items of equipment, the following points should be taken into consideration:

1. Fitness for purpose, both in shape and materials used.
2. Cost and value for money.
3. Durability and expected life.
4. Ease of storage or stacking.
5. Hygienic design and ease of cleaning.
6. Compatibility with the style and image of the unit.
7. Established pattern range for ease of replacement or enlargement.

We shall consider all of these points in looking at all the main types of equipment required in the food service industry.

Tableware

Crockery

All crockery items, such as plates, cups, bowls and so on are either earthenware, china or various ceramics that are midway between earthenware and bone china. The advantage of earthenware is that it is cheap since its constituents are:

25 per cent ball clay
25 per cent clay or kaolin
15 per cent china stone
35 per cent flint.

However, the low cost means that compared with other materials, earthenware is easily chipped or cracked, liable to stain and much heavier than bone china. Bone china is on the other hand extremely robust, hard wearing and finer in appearance, being translucent. Its constituents are:

25 per cent china clay
25 per cent china stone
50 per cent bone (calcium phosphate).

This high quality, however, makes bone china very expensive, so that crockery manufacturers have attempted to produce a product that is much less expensive than bone china but has all its good qualities. They market such crockery under a variety of trade names such as Steelite, Vitrex, Vitrock, etc. Such vitrified tableware complies with British Standard 4034 specification which outlines the durability and strength needed by crockery to meet the demands of the industry.

In particular, crockery items should have the following features. Items should be designed so that they are multi-purpose, e.g. bowls suitable for use as cereal or sweet bowls, plates sized for use with fish or sweet, and so on. This reduces the amount of capital investment in equipment and the amount of storage space required. Crockery should be capable of being handwashed and machine washed and therefore should be resistant to high temperatures (up to 85°C), impervious to water, chip and crack resistant, and must neither stain nor 'blotch'. Design of items should facilitate cleaning or polishing so that there are no recesses or protrustions that are difficult to get at. Items should be stackable, up to 30 plates or saucers in one pile, and cups in particular should be designed so that the base of one fits inside the rim of another, thus avoiding stress on the weakest point of the cup—the handle. Plates should have a rolled edge to prevent chipping, although this makes the edge of the plate slightly thicker. Items should be light in weight and retain heat if need be, although handles of cups and pots should be poor conductors of heat.

The hotel and catering industry tends to select crockery that is standard in appearance so that it does not become out-dated too quickly and that can be replaced easily. Manufacturers are likely to produce a successful pattern for at least three years if it is earthenweare and ten years if china. There are two types of decoration, *underglaze* and *on-glaze.*

Underglaze is used mainly on earthenware; the piece is printed or painted after one firing, then glazed and fired for a second time. This process means that the pattern is completely protected and will not wear, but the range of colours that can be used is restricted.

The on-glaze method applies the decoration after glazing and then an enamel firing fixes the design. This method is less resistant to wear than underglaze decoration, but modern research has resulted in more durable colours being available.

In most cases, the most widely used decoration is the transfer which is printed by silk screen or lithograph and can be applied by either of the methods above. Transfers make possible virtually any design in any number of colours. Another popular type of decoration is a simple band of gold or colour, applied to the rim, either by hand or machine. Finally, caterers can choose to have a plain item emblazoned with their logo or crest to identify the unit. For instance, a bistro in London had printed around the rim of all its crockery 'This plate was stolen from Bortsch "n" Tears'. In most cases, however, the cost is such that only the larger operators can afford to have items made with their own design. This crested design is also only suitable for restaurants where the waiting staff have time to place the plate so that the crest is at the top of the place setting—for banquet service where time is short, plates should be capable of being placed so that their orientation does not matter.

Case study 13.1   Royal Doulton Hotelware

The selection of plates, cups, saucers and other pieces of crockery available in the Country Club range outlines some of the essential criteria concerning tableware (see

Fig. 13.1). Certain items illustrate the versatility that is desirable, notably the double well saucer, which may be used for teacups, coffee mugs, soup cups and creamer. At the same time, the Atlanta range of plates is available in ten different sizes, all of which could be used in one establishment, for the different dishes and courses available.

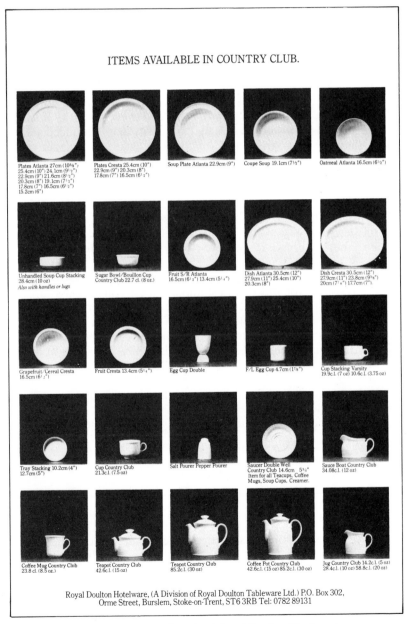

Figure 13.1 *Types of crockery (Royal Doulton Hotelware).*

However, from the point of view of rationalization, the caterer may well consider only stocking the 25.5 cm (10 inch), 20.3 cm (8 inch) and 15.2 cm (6 inch) diameter plates. Likewise, there are alternative bowls available for soup, cereal, fruit and so on which could also be rationalized. The illustration also shows the two main types of cup available—the stacking variety and the 'Cup Country Club'. This theme is repeated with regard to egg cups and soup bowls, which also are available in stacking and non-stacking designs.

Glassware

There are two main types of glass—lead crystal and soda-lime. Lead crystal is the best quality and has a brilliant finish that enables it to be engraved or cut and polished. It is, however, expensive, so that most glassware used in the catering industry is soda-lime glass. There are a variety of grades that depend upon the ratio of lead oxide to soda-lime. The advantage of soda glass is that it is easily mass-produced and the better quality soda glass is hardwearing and relatively resistant to 'impact and thermal shock'.* The only British Standard for glassware is BS 3828 which ensures that full lead crystal must have 30 per cent lead oxide.

When purchasing glassware, the following design features should be considered. There is a wide variety of different types and sizes of glassware and a strong tradition that certain types of alcoholic drinks should be served in specific types of glass; for instance, it has been suggested that the origin of the green-stemmed Moselle wine glass was that formerly German wines were cloudy, which the green colour disguised,† and even though this is no longer so the tradition continues. However, the caterer should not tie up capital in items of glassware that are only to be used infrequently.

Fitness for purpose is probably the most important criteria for glassware. There are certain drinks that in order to be fully appreciated should be served in particular glasses (see Fig. 13.2 in the box below). Apart from these design features, it is more a matter of aesthetic taste that determines what type of glass should be used. For instance, spirits with a mixer may be served in a Paris goblet, a tumbler or old-fashioned glass, and similarly, bottled beers in Wellington, Worthington or 'slim jims'. However, it *is* necessary to purchase glasses marked with the Imperial stamp if serving draught beers drawn from unmetered pumps, although their design is immaterial and can include straight glass, dimple mugs or Guinness mugs.

The size of the various designs available varies widely too, but the most practicable sizes are:

Wine	5–6⅔ fl. oz.
Tumbler	8–10 fl oz.
Bottle beer	12 fl. oz.
Sherry or port	3–4 fl. oz.
Liqueur	2–3 fl. oz.

There is a long tradition of using glasses that are identical in size to the measure used, notably the Elgin glass which is used for sherry. The origin of this is probably that the shape appears to hold more than it actually does (see Fig. 13.3) but it is difficult to use without spillage, both from the waiter's and the customer's viewpoint.

---

* *Making Glass*, Glass Manufacturers' Federation, London: Glass Manufacturers' Federation.
† E. Good, *Tableware*, London: Design Centre.

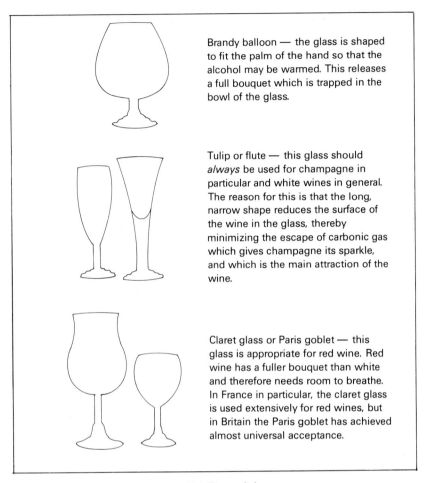

Brandy balloon — the glass is shaped to fit the palm of the hand so that the alcohol may be warmed. This releases a full bouquet which is trapped in the bowl of the glass.

Tulip or flute — this glass should *always* be used for champagne in particular and white wines in general. The reason for this is that the long, narrow shape reduces the surface of the wine in the glass, thereby minimizing the escape of carbonic gas which gives champagne its sparkle, and which is the main attraction of the wine.

Claret glass or Paris goblet — this glass is appropriate for red wine. Red wine has a fuller bouquet than white and therefore needs room to breathe. In France in particular, the claret glass is used extensively for red wines, but in Britain the Paris goblet has achieved almost universal acceptance.

Figure 13.2 *Types of glasses.*

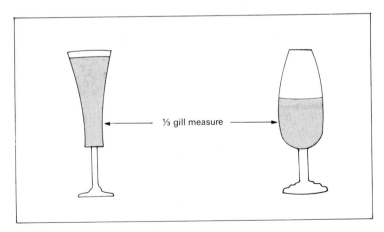

⅓ gill measure

Figure 13.3 *One-third gill measures in different glasses.*

In many respects the quality of the glassware can best be judged by its price but good quality glass that will be hard wearing should be perfectly clear, without any air bubbles trapped in the glass, and feel relatively heavy.

Cutlery

Essentially we are talking about knives, forks and spoons (Fig. 13.4). The two basic materials suitable for cutlery used in catering are either EPNS or stainless steel, and it is extremely unlikely that solid silver cutlery is in use except in the most exceptional circumstances. The major difference between the two materials is appearance and cost. It is invidious to suggest that silver-plate looks 'better' than stainless steel cutlery, as it depends upon the style of the operation in which they are being used, just as the cost factor will be relative to the scale and type of unit. Both types of cutlery need careful attention. The quality of EPNS depends on the thickness of the silver plating, which will wear through if not cleaned and handled properly. Stainless steel too has various grades, including 18/8 (18 per cent chromium, 8 per cent nickel) which is commonly used in the industry and 12/12 (12 per cent chromium, 12 per cent nickel), and can be purchased with a matt or shiny finish. However, equal care must be taken with this type of cutlery, for while it is rustproof, detergent, if not rinsed off, will dull the surface finish and substances like lemon juice and salt will pitt the cutlery's surface if left in contact with them.

The design features of cutlery suitable for restaurant use are as follows. It is possible to purchase cutlery with plastic, wood or horn handles, but these are very unsatisfactory for the catering industry as they are unlikely to stand up to machine washing and the high water temperatures. As in the case of crockery, there is a proliferation of

Figure 13.4 *EPNS cutlery (courtesy of Grant & Cork (Sheffield) Ltd).*

items available, but as David Mellor demonstrated in 1965, when commissioned by the Ministry of Public Building and Works to design a set for institutional catering, it is possible to reduce the number of pieces required down to just five. None the less, most units would have more than this. However, consideration ought to be given to such factors as purchasing main knives with a serrated edge, so that they can be used as steak knives; or even not purchasing fish knives and forks, as unlike silver, stainless steel does not hold the flavour of fish, so that fish could be eaten with a side knife and sweet fork.* Also a combined tea and coffee spoon is preferable, especially in busy establishments where staff may find it difficult to select the correct cover. Attempts to design ergonomically better sets of cutlery have been attempted but the basic shape of the knife, fork and spoon are timeless. As with crockery, selection should be based on suitability for purpose and value for capital invested, rather than on esoteric considerations. So look for simple design characteristics—spoons should have a deep bowl to avoid spillage, forks should have four prongs for ease of use, knives should be well balanced and so on.

Table linen

As we shall see with disposables, table linen is expensive to purchase and maintain. Stock requirements if using linen are quite high, since a minimum of six times the number of tables and place setting is required, with replacement taking place every five years, or 20 per cent of the stock being replaced every year. In general terms the factors to consider when choosing a table cloth and napkins are as follows. Appearance, colour and pattern should be integrated with the decor and style of the unit. The major disadvantages of coloured or patterned linens is that fading may occur with use so that cloths and napkins may no longer match, or colours may run if not washed at the necessary washing temperature.

Durability and resistance to wear are important and so are the ease and cost of cleaning, or in the case of disposables, ease and cost of replacement. The quality of the product and particularly in the case of linen, the edging of cloths should be remembered. Poor quality laundering and poor quality linen will result in cloths shrinking out of shape.

There is now available a wide range of fabrics including:

1. Linen. The traditional fabric for use in high-class restaurants. It is tough, long lasting and has a first-class appearance if it is properly laundered. Also stains may be removed more easily than from some other fabrics.
2. Cotton. It is easier to launder than linen and is available in a wider range of colours and designs, but it is not so hard-wearing.
3. Artificial fibres. Materials such as Dralon, Courtelle and Terylene are suitable for table cloths as they are crease-resistant, easily washed and are relatively cheap, but they cannot be used for napkins as they are generally non-absorbent.
4. Plastic-coated fabrics. The major advantage of such cloths are that they may be wiped clean, although those with a textured surface may need scrubbing. For napkins, the same material without a plastic coating can be used.

Tablecloths and napkins come in a variety of sizes, but are designed to have a drop of

---

* This may appear to be heresy but on the Continent in restaurants this is quite common.

between 0.2 m and 0.3 m on standard sized tables. It is increasingly difficult, however, to obtain circular cloths needed for round tables.

Disposables

The recent improvement in the quality, design and durability of disposable equipment has made its use much more common in outside catering, and with the advent of fast-food operations, disposables are also much more acceptable to the public. Almost anything that is required in a food service outlet is made in a throwaway form, usually in paper or plastic. This includes:

serviettes and napkins
place mats and coasters
slip cloths and banqueting roll
knives, forks and spoons
cups for beverages and 'glasses' for drinks
plates and dishes of all sizes.

The advantages of disposables are as follows:

1. Reduces the number of staff and amount of equipment needed for washing-up, thereby reducing costs.
2. Reduces the need for laundering facilities.
3. Greatly improves standards of hygiene.
4. Reduces the amount of capital investment in the long-term.
5. Eliminates losses due to breakages and pilferage.
6. Takes up less storage space and easier to transport.
7. May be used as a sales promotional aid, as manufacturers can now print whatever the caterer desires on most disposable equipment.

The major disadvantage of disposables is the litter that they may create. It is essential that the caterer and event organizers have arranged efficient refuse disposal teams and provided sufficient refuse bags and bins to ensure that visitors are not surrounded with litter. It must be pointed out that the use of disposables is relevant not only to the outside catering sector of the industry but also in takeaway outlets, transport catering, hospitals, fast-food operations and automatic vending, as the following case studies illustrate.

Case study 13.2   Use of disposables

(1) The Tower Hotel, when instigating EMI's 'Picnic Basket' theme into the coffee-shop operation, introduced a paper place mat. In terms of cost, each paper place mat cost 1.18 pence whereas to launder a linen variety cost 9 pence each.

(2) Jenner's department store in Edinburgh introduced white disposable table covers as over-cloths to linen in its restaurant in 1979. The restaurant manager is reported as saying, 'In the first month, taking in the cost of table covers, we saved £120. We have gone from washing 80 to 100 tablecloths a day to 10 or 20 a day. And we've had no adverse comments from customers.' (*Catering and Hotel Management*, April 1979).

Task 13.1

Investigate the cost of hiring plates, glasses and cutlery for a buffet function of 100 covers. Compare this with the cost of buying disposable items.

Service equipment

Essentially the difference between service equipment and tableware is that the former is used and handled by staff only, whereas the latter is either handled by the customers or placed on the table in front of them.

Service utensils

These include service spoon and fork, ladle, slice, and so on. It is incorrect to think that such equipment is used only in silver-service or gueridon restaurants, as self-service and tray-service systems also rely upon utensils. However, there is a slightly different approach in its use between the two types of operation. In cafeterias and institutions, the service utensils are used as a precise means of portion control as well as a means to serve the food. It is therefore important that the established size of ladle, scoop or spoon is used in order to help achieve the desired gross profit. In restaurants, the waiting staff have a certain degree of flexibility in their approach, so that while exact portion control is desirable, no waiter will insist that the customer has the exact portion if asked for a smaller portion by a customer. In this situation, the chef will attempt to achieve good portion control by issuing the correct portion of food items from the kitchen. The sweet trolley, for instance, is notoriously difficult to control but by dishing sweets into individual coupes, designing a gateau so that the portion size is clearly indicated and making individual sweet items, some degree of control can be achieved.

Points to consider when purchasing service utensils are:

1. Service utensils in use should be of similar, if not identical quality, to the tableware in use, i.e. if silver cutlery is in use, silver service equipment should be used.
2. Silver-service restaurants should have at least three service spoons and forks for every cover to ensure that staff always have equipment available for service. One of the basic standards of good silver service is that different food items are served with a different spoon and fork.
3. Ladles should have the correct capacity with deep, rather than shallow bowls.
4. Items of specialist equipment such as asparagus trays, grape scissors and so on, should be available so long as they are likely to be used on a regular basis.

Flats and dishes

Flats and dishes are required for service in units using family, silver or gueridon service. They are available in EPNS or stainless steel to match the tableware available.

Particular features of design include:

1. Rectangular flats and dishes are recommended as this shape stacks more easily and it is easier to arrange a number of equal portions on a rectangular dish rather than on an oval one.
2. Flats and dishes are available in sizes from 0.15 m to 0.6 m in length, increasing in

size by intervals of 0.05 m. For ease of use and for the sake of appearance, their width should be approximately 60 per cent of the length.

3.   Dishes should be about 0.035 m deep and have 'roll radius corners' which ensures high standard of hygiene and eases the service of items.
4.   Covers to dishes should be designed so that they may be used as an underflat for that dish, or as flats in their own right.
5.   Dishes divided into two compartments have the advantage that for single portions staff need only make half the number of journeys to the table. However, they do tend to allow staff to use only one service spoon and fork to serve both items.

Trays

As we have seen in Chapter 7, trays have been specifically designed for use in institutional catering, but whether for use in restaurants, in-flight catering, cafeterias or hospitals, trays should have similar features. They should be:

1.   Light in weight for ease of use and carrying.
2.   Strong so that when loaded there is no sagging or warping.
3.   Hygienic by use of easily cleaned materials and avoidance of unnecessary mouldings.
4.   Heat resistant.
5.   Non-slip (a salver for carrying glasses should not have to have a damp serviette placed on it to make its use safer).
6.   Stackable.

It is for this reason that many trays in use today are a plastic of some sort, which ensures that the above design features may be obtained at a relatively low cost.

Trolleys

There is a wide range of trolleys available for use in catering, but their two main functions are:

1.   To display food to the customer, e.g. sweet trolley, hors-d'œuvre trolley, carving trolley.
2.   To carry clean items of equipment or clear away dirty ones, particularly in cafeteria operations.

Task 13.2

Identify the salient design features of a trolley to be used in a food service operation.

13.5 MAINTENANCE AND CARE OF EQUIPMENT

In the catering industry, a major consideration and responsibility of management is the washing up during or after service of crockery and cutlery, as well as the general

PLASTICS

The use of plastics in tableware and service equipment has increased substantially in general terms, particularly for use at picnics or tableware for children. Its use in the industry has, however, developed only slowly, although the product itself offers a great deal to the caterer: it is tough, lightweight and colourful. The principal disadvantages of the material are that while they can withstand temperatures as high as that of boiling water, they will deform or melt if heated more directly, and their surface is easily scratched and therefore stained. The types of plastics used for tableware include the following.

Acrylics—mainly used for trays, this material may be highly polished or have a textured surface, with a wide range of colours available.

Polycarbonate—withstands temperatures up to 121°C and is particularly robust, but may be pitted or scarred by the alkali in certain detergents.

Polypropylene—also hard and tough and may be washed in temperatures up to 121°C.

Melamine—is capable of withstanding temperatures up to 121°C, and most closely resembles ceramics since it does not stain easily, is resistant to most chemicals and is lightweight and tough.

maintenance and care of all food service equipment. In most cases, the care of table linen is delegated to expert launderers, although such firms are difficult to find, hence the growth in the use of other fabrics, disposables and contract linen hire. But with regard to all other types of equipment, discussed previously, cleaning is done in house. The need for effective and efficient cleaning facilities and procedures is because:

1. In the catering industry, the caterer has a duty in law, as well as a moral obligation, to ensure that food items are served in a hygienic manner.
2. The appearance and polish of table settings and equipment is an important contributing factor to the customer's meal experience.
3. The capital investment in equipment is large, so that the effective working life must be maximized by ensuring proper use, care and attention is paid to washing and cleaning procedures.

The items that must be cared for are made basically from four materials—metal, ceramics, glass and wood.

Care of ceramics

Most china hotelware or earthenware in use today may be washed in dish-washing machines, although it is likely that any on-glaze decoration will eventually be worn away with repeated washing. These machines also depend on a detergent that produces little or no foam, but which is more corrosive than other types of detergent; for this reason it is recommended that wash cycle temperatures should not exceed 60°C. In those machines that have a self-drying cycle, a higher rinsing temperature is both essential and acceptable with the addition of a suitable rinse aid.

Crockery that is in constant use should be stored on shelving in the servery area, on shelving at a height of between 1 m and 1.6 m from the ground. There should be no more than 0.3 m between each shelf, to discourage equipment being stacked in piles too high. The width of the shelving should be sufficient to ensure that a main plate does not overhang the edge of the shelf, i.e. between 0.3 m to 0.35 m. Crockery should not be stored in hot plates or plate-warming cupboards or dispensers, but should be placed in them approximately one hour before service. This allows the staff to check each item to see that it is cleaned, polished and free from chips or cracks, leaves the hotplate empty so that it can be regularly cleaned by a kitchen hand and reduces the amount of energy consumption as the unit is only switched on just before and during the service. Crockery that is in storage should be placed in proper containers, with each item separated from that next to it by a cardboard or paper filler and each box clearly marked to identify what it contains.

Metal

Most EPNS or stainless-steel items can be washed by machine, although forks and cutlery in general may be more effectively washed by hand. As pointed out earlier, it is important with stainless steel to ensure that it has been thoroughly rinsed to prevent pitting, while self-drying is to be avoided, since it can lead to 'spotting'. Stainless steel will also be permanently discoloured if placed in a naked flame or at temperatures above 204°C (although it is extremely unlikely that a dishwasher could ever achieve this, kitchen staff should be discouraged from heating flats too much). With regard to silver plate, in addition to the need for washing, the equipment must also be regularly polished to prevent tarnishing. There are four main ways of polishing silver, each of which is appropriate for differing types of equipment.

Burnishing machine

This comprises a hexagonal or octagonal drum, two-thirds full with small ballbearings. It is used to clean in particular dishes and flats which are pushed into the ball bearings. The drum is then half-filled with water and a special detergent added, which has the function of lubricating and cleaning the metal. The drum is then closed and slowly rotated for about ten minutes, during which time the action of the ball bearings and detergent removes any tarnish. After removal from the drum, the equipment should be rinsed, dried and polished by hand. This method is unsuitable for cutlery as the prongs of forks are not effectively cleaned, while it may dull the cutting edge of knives.

Polivit

This method relies upon a chemical reaction. Aluminium plates with large holes through them are placed in a deep sink, with the silver items to be cleaned in contact with the plates. Soda and hot water are then added, which results in a reaction that removes the tarnish from the silver onto the aluminium sheets. As this is a relatively strong process, it is not suitable for particularly delicate items of equipment.

Silver dip

This method is used almost exclusively for cleaning the prongs of forks, which not only tarnish but also turn black if used for eating egg dishes. The silver dip is particularly strong and should be placed in a plastic or non-metallic bowl; the fork prongs need only be dipped in the liquid for 2 or 3 seconds before being rinsed in warm water and dried with a cloth.

Silver polish

This is the more time-consuming, labour intensive and costly means of cleaning silver than the others mentioned. However, there are certain items of silver plate such as carving trolleys, flambé lamps and such like that can only be cleaned by this method. The proprietary brand of polish is applied with a soft cloth, left for a few moments, then removed with a second cloth and buffed up to a polished finish. Such polish used to be available in the form of a powder, called plate powder, which was mixed with methylated spirits to form a paste, and applied as with the modern liquid polishes.

Glass

Glassware too can be washed by machine, either in a glasswasher using high pressure, revolving wash arms, or the glass-washing machines usually found in public houses comprising upright brushes rotating in a bowl of water. Automatic glasswashers can wash between 500 and 1000 glasses per hour depending on their type and have a wash cycle of between 2½ to 3½ minutes, so they are essential where there is a high throughput of glassware. Some have been designed to operate under the bar counter, but if turnover is such that a glasswasher is needed, it is probably best to locate it back of house. The brush type machines which are meant to be sited in the bar have their limitations since bar staff must handle each glass as it is washed and the base of the glass may not be effectively cleaned. Generally the best results are achieved by hand washing, although this of course is very labour intensive.

Glasses should be washed in warm water, with a detergent specifically designed for glassware and rinsed in clear warm water and then inverted to allow them to dry naturally, on a surface that allows the free circulation of air into the bowl of the glass. They may then be polished with a linen glass cloth to ensure a proper sparkle. Where glasses are in frequent use, it may be advisable to store them on shelves the right way up as the rim of the glass is the weakest part; however, to avoid dust and debris falling into stored glassware, it may be better to store them upside down. Glassware not in use should always be stored in compartmentalized storage containers or cardboard boxes. One common instance of bad practice is the use of glassware designed for the consumption of drinks being used for the service of food items such as prawn cocktail and grapefruit cocktails.

Wood

Items of equipment in wood include cheese boards, salad bowls and so on. They should never be machine washed, but always rinsed in tepid water and dried thoroughly. Oiling the wood with an edible oil also helps to improve the appearance of wood as well as to prevent cracking or splitting.

13.6 WASH-UP FACILITIES

Although this is perhaps the least glamorous aspect of catering, it is none the less very important and can be one of the major problem areas of the operation. In many respects, the problem stems from people's attitudes towards washing up, which for many years has been seen and treated as a very low status occupation. Attitudes are, however, changing, partly because managers are realizing that the wash-up facility is as important as any other part of the operation and partly because the technology of dishwashers has become more sophisticated so that staff today are 'operatives' rather than manual workers. Management must also recognize that wash-up staff are handling daily hundreds of items with a capital investment of between 50 p and £2 per item and operating machinery costing between £5000 and £50 000, so that ill-trained or incompetent employees could cost the operation a great deal of money.

As we saw in Fig. 1.2 it is simple enough to describe in theory where the wash-up facility should be located. In real terms, however, there are problems related to the flow of equipment and staff. In essence, wash-up facilities for waiter-service operations are different from other types of operation. In institutional, cafeteria or in-flight catering, the dirties are assembled on trolleys which can be taken to any part of the site to be washed, so that the clean items finish their cycle at the point at which they are to be stored or re-used for the next service.

In waiter-service operations, there is a real need to locate the wash up close to the point at which waiting staff exit from the restaurant to minimize the amount of carrying they have to do. This means that wash ups should be situated near the 'out-door', while clean equipment needs to be stored near the hot plate and 'in-door'. Most restaurants have double doors between restaurant and kitchen so that customers can neither see nor hear the activity in the food preparation or wash-up areas.

Dish washing machines come in three types:

1. Fixed jet with revolving rack machines (Fig. 13.5(a)) have fixed hot-water wash arms above and/or below the dirty items which are placed in a circular rack. This rack rotates during the wash and rinse cycles to ensure the items are thoroughly cleaned. An example of such a machine is the Zanussi LS50 which can wash 16 plates every two minutes or 80–120 items of cutlery.
2. Revolving wash arm machines (Fig. 13.5(b)) have water directed, usually from above and below, onto the items which are stacked in dish racks placed into the machine. To ensure an even wash and no 'dead spots', the wash jets are positioned assymetrically to ensure an even spray as they revolve. A typical machine is the Hobart WM2E which has similar performance figures to a revolving rack machine.
3. Conveyor belt machines have (Fig. 13.5(c)) fixed jets through which the dirties

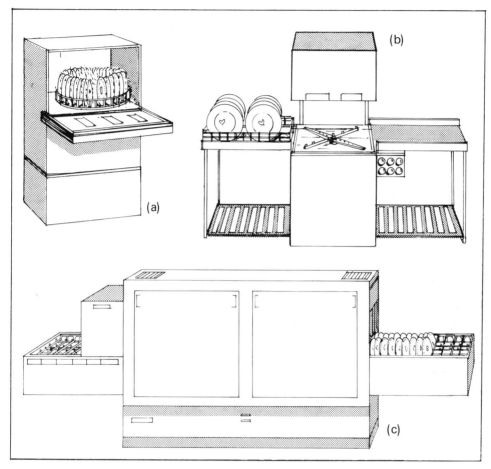

Figure 13.5 *Types of dishwasher* (**a**) *fixed jet with revolving rack;* (**b**) *revolving wash-arm machine;* (**c**) *conveyor-belt or flight wash-up machine.*

slowly pass stacked either in racks or on the conveyor belt itself. These machines often referred to as flight wash ups, are designed for a very large throughput of plates and are very large, for instance the Gastronom WPA PFWNT can wash over 6000 plates per hour, and the dishwasher is 2 m high, nearly 5 m long and 1.3 m wide.

13.7 THE STILL ROOM

This area, back-of-house in larger establishments derives its name from the still-set used to make coffee in bulk, which is the principal item of equipment to be found there. Essentially the function of the still-room attendant is to undertake all those jobs that are necessary for the operation of a restaurant, but need only relatively unskilled labour, such as making coffee and tea, preparing Melba toast and hot toast, making butter pats and so on. Thus other items of equipment to be found in a still-room includes a toaster, salamander, butter-pat making machine, refrigerator, and so on. In smaller restaurants, with less sophisticated styles of service, most of the functions of the still room are carried out by the waiting staff.

13.8 CONCLUSION

Food service equipment is a major capital and operating cost of the business. Very often the people employed to handle and clean this equipment are untrained and unskilled. Therefore it is essential that as part of their induction or training they are made aware of the cost of equipment. It is common practice in fact, especially in the larger hotels, to display prominently in the wash-up and storage areas the main items of crockery, along with their price, to reinforce daily this fact. In addition to keeping the running costs to a minimum, great care must be exercised in the selection of equipment to ensure value for money and a quality of product suited to the style of the establishment. By establishing the correct levels of stock for each item of equipment, capital investment can be minimized, but this must not be at the expense of operational efficiency.

Exercise

Select from manufacturers' ranges of crockery and tableware, equipment suitable for an executive dining room, seating a maximum of 30 covers. Establish the level of stock required for the operation and calculate the level of capital investment.

14 Staffing and Training

How to keep staff happy and happy customers

OBJECTIVES: to identify the labour market for food service personnel in Britain
. . . to understand how to find and select food service personnel . . . to describe an
induction programme for a food service operation . . . to outline the training of food
service personnel . . . identify the tools of good personnel management . . . to establish the staffing levels required for a variety of operations

*The Trusthouse Forte Group sincerely believes that its management and staff are its
greatest asset for without their efforts the company would not continue to expand and
prosper*

Look to Your Future with THF

14.1 INTRODUCTION

THE problem that appears to be the most urgent and recurring headache for the
caterer is that of staff. Despite the fact that in comparison to many occupations waiting at table is only a semi-skilled job, the industry has for many years found it difficult
to recruit and keep its waiting staff. This may well be due to the fact that very great
emphasis has been placed upon the education and training of chefs since the time of
Escoffier with far less emphasis on educating and training the people who are to serve
the food. For instance, most catering colleges run part-time, day-release courses for
chefs, but only a handful provide such a course for waiting staff. Likewise, organizations within the industry and education, such as City and Guilds, have been slow to
recognize the skill content involved in the service of food, particularly human contact
skills, as well as technical virtuosity. Many caterers faced with the difficulties of
finding the right people have 'solved' the problem by adopting various different poli-

cies, such as the service of *cuisine nouvelle*, i.e. high-class cuisine on a plate; the introduction of carvery operations; employing foreign staff and so on.

14.2 SOURCES OF STAFF

Food service personnel can be recruited from four separate labour markets.

1. Unqualified and inexperienced, e.g. school leaver.
2. Qualified and inexperienced, e.g. college leaver with some recognized qualifica-
    tion such as City and Guilds 705, 707/1 or 707/2.
3. Unqualified and experienced, e.g. a waiter who has never been to college.
4. Qualified and experienced, e.g. a college leaver who has worked in the industry.

The advantages of employing unqualified and inexperienced staff are as follows:

1. Their wage cost is likely to be lower than for qualified or experienced staff.
2. They can be trained to meet the specific requirements and standards of the opera-
    tion.
3. They may be selected for their fresh, enthusiastic attitude towards restaurant
    operations.

On the other hand, there are advantages in employing trained and qualified staff.

1. Their qualifications indicate their level of skill and amount of knowledge.
2. Their previous experience means that they may require less on-the-job training,
    thereby reducing training costs.

Whatever policy is adopted, there are a variety of ways to locate possible recruits.

1. Through recommendations of staff working for you, e.g. advertise the job on the
    notice board or in the staff journal or paper.
2. Through the media, i.e. advertise in the press; for unskilled staff in local newspap-
    ers, for more skilled and senior staff in national newspapers or the catering press.
3. Through professional bodies, e.g. the HCIMA publishes a 'News and Appoint-
    ments' bulletin twice a month.
4. Through the Department of Employment's Manpower Services Commission, i.e.
    the Jobcentre.
5. From other employment agencies, many of whom particularly in large cities spe-
    cialize in catering staff.
6. From colleges, by circulating details of job opportunities to the Hotel and Cater-
    ing departments.

Task 14.1

Imagine that you are the manager of a restaurant and banqueting suite, with full silver
service. Put in order of importance the means you would use in order to recruit: (a) a
commis waiter, (b) a head waiter, (c) casual banqueting staff.

Case study 14.1   Norfolk Capital Hotels

In a television programme for the Open University (Open University 1979 D222 Micro-economics) Norfolk Capital Hotels compared their markets for staff according to two criteria: skilled/unskilled staff; and geographical location of unit, namely London and Scarborough. They found that they had to approach the problem of getting staff in different ways.

1. Unskilled staff in the provinces. Here it was relatively easy to find applicants, particularly married women, especially if the job was structured to take into account their needs, for example by not starting until 8.30 or 9.00 a.m. and/or finishing at 4.00 p.m. They obtained staff by advertising in local papers, posters on notice-boards in hotels, staff dining rooms and leaflets to householders in the immediate vicinity of the hotel.
2. Unskilled staff in London. Here it was more difficult to find staff of the right quality. Applicants tended to be single, young and from a wide variety of ethnic origins, so Norfolk relied heavily on Jobcentres and staffing agencies for personnel.
3. Skilled staff in the provinces. Norfolk advertised on a regional basis in the local press at first and used the national catering press for higher grades of personnel. There were a relatively low number of skilled staff so long as salary scales remained competitive in the locality.
4. Skilled staff in London. Norfolk used specialist catering staff agencies, London evening papers, and if necessary the national catering press. There are a relatively high number of skilled staff available here.

14.3 STAFFING LEVELS AND PRODUCTIVITY

Throughout this book, we have identified the level of staffing required in a wide variety of units operating different styles of service, and this is summarized in Table 14.1.

Table 14.1 *Staffing in different types of operation.*

	Self-service operations	Tray operations	Waiter operations
Number of food service personnel	low	low	medium/high
Level of food service technical expertise	low	negligible	medium/high
Staff contact level with customers	low/medium	low	high
Time needed for training	medium	low	high
Rates of pay for service staff	medium	variable	high

Whatever service style is adopted, however, there is a very real need to minimize the labour cost of the restaurant, as this is a very substantial element of total operational costs. Labour costs are far more than just the regular wages of staff, they include overtime payments, National Insurance contributions, superannuation, employees' meals, uniform costs, administrative costs associated with payment of staff and personnel records, and so on. In order to reduce this cost, the food service operator must establish carefully the level of staffing required for day-to-day operation and monitor regularly these staffing levels. There are four stages involved in this process.

Determining productivity

It is standard practice in many industries to measure very accurately the productivity of the worker, but such procedures have not up till now been widely adopted in the food service industry. However, there is no reason why productivity levels could not be measured and then set for waiting staff. One way to do so, is to measure the sales per waiter over a given period of time. In restaurants where sales per head do not vary greatly from the average spend per head a more satisfactory measure is the number of covers served. Over a period of time, perhaps one week, the total number of covers served and the number of hours worked can be established. This establishes the average number of covers served per work-hour

$$\frac{\text{Total covers served}}{\text{Total hours worked}} = \text{Covers per work-hour}$$

This average can then be used as a basis for comparing the productivity of different waiting staff and productivity at different hours of the day. Thus, for instance, if the average number of covers served per work-hour is 12.3 and some staff achieved only 10 covers, these staff can be appraised to see if their performance can be improved, with the specific aim of achieving higher average productivity. Likewise, if waiting staff are achieving higher levels of productivity at certain times of the day than at other hours, this may be used to determine if there is overstaffing at off-peak periods. At all times, however, it must be remembered that the aim is to maximize productivity within the twin constraints of (1) maintaining job satisfaction and (2) maintaining standards of performance, i.e. providing the service that the customer expects.

Forecast demand

The second stage in achieving the correct staffing level for the operation is to forecast the amount of business that will be done in each meal period over one week. Demand is likely to vary both during the day and from day to day. By analysing past sales records or by implementing a policy to measure sales over a period of time a pattern will emerge (see Fig. 14.1). While it is not surprising to find peaks at lunch and dinner times and on weekdays, this analysis does help to establish the forecast of demand. These forecasts will never be completely accurate, as they will not take into account unexpected effects (such as bad weather) but they should become accurate to within 5 per cent of actual turnover with experience and practice.

Devising staffing rotas

Once the forecast of demand is arrived at for any given period, the number of staff needed can be determined by dividing the number of covers forecast by the average productivity

$$\frac{\text{Total covers forecast}}{\text{Average productivity}} = \text{Number of staff required}$$

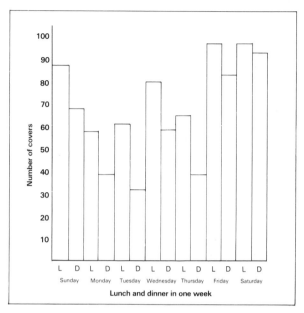

Figure 14.1 *Lunch and dinner sales over one week.*

This calculation will enable operators to make the best use of full-time staff and to employ part-time staff effectively and efficiently.

It has long been the practice in the catering industry for employees to work split shifts, although during the 1970s this practice had been declining. However, with the recession in the 1980s, it was re-introduced as the only way to cope with the typical twin peaks of demand at midday and in the evening. Many caterers have also recognized that every effort should be made to maximize the use of their premises, and units that in the past were not in the business of serving breakfasts are now attempting to develop this trade. Operations such as Happy Eater and Little Chef have shown that this can be done successfully.

A rota, then, should satisfy the staffing needs of the unit and also the employees. There will be times where these two aims are incompatible, but staff must recognize that unless there was a reason for employing them then they would have little to do. Job enrichment and job satisfaction are important but this should stem from active participation in a busy restaurant.

Task 14.2

Each waiter in the Castle Restaurant is expected to serve 15 covers an hour. Fig. 14.1 is a record of turnover in one week. Assuming that the staff work split shifts and a five-day week establish the staffing level required and develop a staffing rota that will meet this need.

Improving productivity

The question of improving productivity is not, however, simply one of staffing the operation correctly. There are many other options that management can take which will influence productivity. If in analysing the flow of business, it is evident that there are off-peak or slow periods, then action can be taken to increase sales at these times by specific sales promotion and marketing efforts. Reviewing the opening hours of the operation could eliminate 'wasted' hours at the beginning or end of the service period. Managers should analyse how reservations, if any, are made. For instance if a table is booked for 8.00 p.m. it is likely to be usable only once in the evening, whereas if it were only possible to reserve a table at 7.30 p.m. or 9.30 p.m., two sittings could be achieved. Overtime should be controlled by ensuring that staff will only be paid over-time if they are asked by management to work extra hours. A relatively simple work study observation can be made to ensure that time is well spent. Standardized lay-ups for sideboards are based on the concept of efficient working procedures, and other ideas, such as placing coffee machines in the room, use of sweet trolleys and so on, can all reduce the amount of unproductive time.

Case study 14.2   Mise-en-place

The preparation for service of the Tudor restaurant originally involved all the staff coming on duty at 10.30 a.m. The commis waiters were involved in those activities such as refilling cruet sets, polishing equipment, cleaning sideboards, preparing accompaniments, making butter and so on, while station waiters were responsible for laying up their own sideboards and stations. The reason for this was that it was believed that it would enhance job satisfaction if waiters were responsible for their own stations.

After reviewing the situation, the manager altered the procedure by allocating spe-cific tasks to all the staff. One waiter laid all the cloths, another did a specific job for each table, and so on for the entire room. Furthermore, all the equipment needed was placed on trolleys and brought into the restaurant so that less time was wasted in fetching and carrying equipment from the storage area. This procedure considerably speeded up the mise-en-place and while staff continued to start work at 10.30 a.m., the time saved was used constructively for staff discussion, on-the-job training and staff performance appraisal. The new procedures had the added advantages of creat-ing a better team spirit among all the brigade, ensuring uniformity of table lay-ups throughout the room, and enabling the manager to supervise operations more effec-tively, since staff were no longer going in and out of the room all the time.

14.4 STAFF TURNOVER

Labour turnover in the catering industry has always been very high. The Hotel and Catering Jobcentre in London estimates it is 20 per cent per quarter in the central London area, which means that in one year four out of five staff leave. The reasons for such high levels of mobility are numerous, and there will always be reasons for move-ment of staff that the caterer will be unable to combat, but there are three important areas over which control must be exercised.

1.   Selection of staff. If care is taken to recruit the right people for the right jobs, it should help to ensure high levels of job security.
2.   Staff induction. The HCITB believe firmly that many staff leave 'within the first few weeks or months of employment. Leaving staff to sink or swim does not help'.
3.   Motivation and morale. All employees need to be motivated and the role of the food service manager is to ensure that staff are happy. This can be achieved in many different ways, for staff are prompted by different needs, but it includes equitable treatment, fair pay, promotion prospects, personal praise and encouragement, staff performance appraisal and staff development programmes.

All these points are developed further, but the caterer should be aware of the disadvantages that high staff turnover has upon the unit.

1.   Low morale. A brigade or section which has a high turnover is very unlikely to have a happy, enthusiastic outlook.
2.   Untrained personnel. Every new member of staff must require some training in the operational standards expected, however well qualified they might be, during which time they are not as productive as regular members of staff.
3.   Recruitment costs. Replacing staff is an expensive business.

Case study 14.3   The Dickens Inn

In November 1981 it was necessary to recruit an assistant restaurant manager and a general assistant manager. An advertisement was placed in *Caterer & Hotelkeeper* for one week, requiring written replies. Twenty-two replies were received, four of which were followed up. The remainder were written to expressing regrets. One of the four potential candidates had just accepted another job. Interviews were arranged for the other three. One applicant did not show up for the interview, and two were seen. Out of the two, one was not suitable and the other was called back for a second interview. She was offered the position, which she subsequently turned down! In the meantime, an advertisement was placed in the *New Standard* for a general assistant manager, in the hope of a more local response. Twenty-five telephoned enquiries were received, three were sent application forms and four interviews were arranged. At the same time the vacancy had been registered with a catering management agency and two applications were put forward, both of whom were interviewed. Of the four interviewees from the *New Standard* advertisement, three were unsuccessful, and one was offered and accepted the position of assistant restaurant manager. Of the two applications from the agency, one was offered the job and is now general assistant manager.

   The cost of this is broken down below. This is a conservative estimate and does not include the cost of time spent with their managers during training.

	£
Advertisement in *Caterer & Hotelkeeper*	127.80
Advertisement in *New Standard*	105.00
Agency fees (8 per cent of salary)	472.00
Interviewing time (9 hours)	26.00
Reading and replying to letters	14.90
Time answering telephone	3.60
Stationery/stamps, etc.	9.20
Two days' induction each	126.20
	£885.20

Selection of staff

In many catering operations the selection of food service personnel is not the responsibility of food service management, but of the personnel department. None the less, food service managers need to be able to identify those qualities they are looking for in a member of staff, either because they may become involved in the selection process or so that they can communicate these to the personnel department.

The current emphasis in the industry is on the personal attributes and social skills of staff, rather than a high degree of technical skill. This is due to many factors but principally because caterers have become much more effective in training staff in technical skills due to the work of the HCITB and also because they have adopted food service systems that require lower technical skills. It is also recognized that the waiting staff have a very great influence upon customers' enjoyment of the meal.

The personal attributes of food service personnel can be broken down into those that any employer would wish for in staff, and those especially required by staff who must serve food and deal with customers.

General attributes

Honesty. Throughout the catering industry the opportunities for dishonesty are numerous, with regards to both handling cash and expensive materials.

Reliability. Food service units must operate by serving the needs of their customers and managers must be able to rely on their staff; in particular staff must be punctual.

Specific attributes

Courtesy. It is the hallmark of a good waiter to be courteous on all occasions. This old-fashioned attribute is as important today as always, although food service is much less formal than in the past.

Smart appearance. Food service staff must have high standards of personal hygiene and present themselves in a smart manner.

Speech. Although only top-class establishments in large centres expect staff to have knowledge of a second language, they should be able to speak clear and precise English.

Knowledge. Members of staff must not only have a sound knowledge of the food items and drinks available in the unit, but also know about the facilities in the hotel, locality and other units operated by the company.

Attitude. The professional waiter will have a professional attitude to work. This will include a sense of urgency, good memory for faces and preferences of regular clients, pleasant but not servile approach to customers and an ability to sell and promote sales.

Job analysis, job description and job specification

So far we have looked at staffing from the point of view of employing the right kind and right number of staff. The personnel function of the operation may well have developed to use three 'tools' which provide guidance in these staffing matters.

Job analysis

This, as its name suggests is an in-depth study of what a particular job involves, its relationship to other jobs, the personal qualities that the employee should have and the conditions under which the job will be carried out.

Job description

This states the particular tasks that an employee is expected to carry out. This enables everyone involved in the operation to identify their role and to ensure that jobs do not overlap and that work is allocated fairly. (See Fig. 14.2.)

Job specification

This is designed to help when interviewing applicants as it outlines in summary form many of the facts specified in the job analysis and job description. (See Fig. 14.3.)

In addition to the main tasks shown on the job description there may be other responsibilities that all staff may be expected to comply with. In the case of the Royal Horseguards Hotel these said staff were expected to maintain a high standard of personal hygiene with special attention to hands, fingernails, hair and uniform; to observe all company and statutory fire and safety regulations and to promote good safety habits; to be aware of all fire and emergency evacuation procedures; to observe all company rules and regulations; to participate in any training or career promotion development as recommended by management; and to promote good inter-staff relationships.

Task 14.3

Either prepare a job description for a head bar steward and a head floor waiter, *or* for a restaurant manager and a station waiter.

Induction of new staff

Most catering businesses now have an induction programme for new employees, but even those units where formal induction is carried out invariably allow for informal

Job description

Title:	Head waiter (man or woman)
Department:	Restaurant
Salary scale:	£5000 per annum
Scope and general purpose of job:	To be responsible for supervising the lay-up of food and beverage service and clearing down of the restaurant.
Responsible to:	Restaurant manager or assistant
Responsible for:	Station waiters
Working relationships:	Restaurant cashier Aboyeur
Main tasks:	The supervision of food service in the restaurant including:

    Full working and service knowledge of all items on the menu and wine list.

    Presentation of all restaurant equipment in a scrupulously clean and undamaged state prior to and during service.

    Greeting and seating customers courteously.

    Taking food orders and assisting the customers with their selection.

    Promotion of food and beverage sales.

    Maintenance of restaurant and service areas in a tidy state during service.

    Dealing with customers' complaints and if necessary reporting them to the restaurant manager.

    Ensuring that station waiters pass all checks to the cashier and that correct bills are presented to the customer.

    Control of waste.

Figure 14.2 *Job description for a head waiter.*

orientation to take place. The purpose of an induction programme is to make the employee feel welcome and part of a team, to identify the standards set in the operation to carry out any statutory, union or in-house administrative matters and to specify in detail the employee's role in the organization.

The HCITB lists four main headings under which information may be given to a new employee

1. The immediate job, e.g. job description, workplace, standard.
2. The people, e.g. supervisors, colleagues, subordinates, shop steward etc.
3. Conditions of employment, e.g. pay, laws, sickness, absence, staff facilities.
4. Other essential information, e.g., the firm or company, health and safety security, opportunities within the organization.

Job specification

Job title:	Head waiter (for restaurant) (man or woman)
Age range:	30–50
Qualifications:	Preferably City and Guilds 705 or 707/1, 707/2. Languages an asset.
Experience:	Worked as station waiter in silver-service restaurant. At least one year's experience of controlling a food service brigade (not necessarily in a restaurant). Recent experience in good quality à la carte restaurant serving at least 60 covers per service.
Personal qualities:	Smart appearance. Able to control and motivate staff. Stable employment record. Above average intelligence.
Personal circumstances:	Able to work till midnight if necessary. Male staff will have to live out.

Figure 14.3 *Job specification for a head waiter.*

Case study 14.4   Gardner-Merchant induction programme

An induction manual for all staff below management entry was produced by the London regional training officer for all Gardner-Merchant units in that region. This manual outlines the manager's role in the induction process as follows:

The induction process is broken down into two parts
1. Reception
2. Early training

The first step in planning the reception phase is to list all the information that the employee needs to know. A great deal of this information is contained in the company handbook 'Working with Gardner Merchant' and although this booklet is useful in giving general information it will be necessary to expand and include all the details relevant to your establishment and the job for which the new employee has been engaged. It would also be helpful to write out a check list showing what action you need to take prior to the new employee's arrival and the information that the employee needs to know and when they need to know it. Although some of the points listed may have been briefly discussed prior to the employee starting, it would be sensible to mention them again using your check list so ensuring that no item has been omitted. The following format would suffice.

Check list

Before arrival

1. Have you allowed free time to deal with the new employee?
2. Have you made arrangements to have them met at reception or has reception been informed and will they direct the employee to the catering department?
3. Have you got the staff handbook and brochure?
4. Have you got a suitable overall?
5. Have you planned the first day's duties?
6. Have you an application form?

On arrival

1. Personal introduction.
2. Offer tea/coffee; make welcome; enquire about travel difficulties, etc.
3. Collect necessary documentation—P45 complete staff application form if not completed at initial interview.
4. Discuss briefly—
    The company and company benefits (using company handbook and brochure).
5. The establishment
    (a) Numbers of staff.
    (b) Services provided.
    (c) Hours of work.
    (d) Meal breaks.
    (e) Pay day.
    (f) Union membership (if applicable).
                              Discuss in greater detail
6. The jobs she/he will be doing today and first week.
7. What do you expect of the person and by when.
8. Immediate and future training.
9. Safety precautions such as dangerous machines.
    (not to use until instruction has been given).
10. Working environment including slippery floors, protective clothing.
11. Other rules. No smoking and regulations which may apply to your particular establishment, e.g. restricted areas. Fire precaution procedures.
12. To whom she/he will be responsible (immediate supervisor).

Depending on the size of establishment, at this stage you could introduce the new employee to her/his immediate supervisor or person with whom she/he will be spending initial working period. This person can then complete the remainder of the informal induction stage which will include

On arrival

Location of changing rooms/toilets
Allocation of lockers
Changing into overalls/laundry procedure
Tour of restaurant and kitchen area
Introduction to other members of staff
First aid facilities
Emergency exits
Signing time book or clocking in
Break time.

Some of these points could be dealt with at any time during the first day, i.e. it may well be that some introductions would take place at lunch time, also visiting various parts of the restaurant might well be achieved whilst assisting with trolley round and so on.

Early training—part 1

This phase should take the form of a more formal training programme and will include on-the-job instruction in personal hygiene, food hygiene, equipment recognition, safety procedures and fire precautions, customer relationships, attitudes, team work, logical work methods, the role of the counterhand, food service assistant.

The scope of the subjects is limited and you should not confuse induction with basic skills, which can only be learnt over a period and must include considerable practical experience.

The programme should once again be 'drawn up' in the form of a check list which will become an individual training assessment and needs for that member of staff, and for this purpose, the training record card and induction check list provided is to be used. You should endeavour to complete the early training programme within 6–8 weeks of the newcomer's starting date.

When giving instruction, it is important to ensure that all the relevant information for a particular subject is included and for this purpose you should have prepared an information sheet listing all key points to be covered in each of the early training subjects.

14.5 STAFF TRAINING

When one considers that the HCITB originally ran a 10-day course to develop on-the-job instructors for the industry, in the short space available, the question of training can only briefly be dealt with here. This is also an area where other bodies outside the unit may become involved—the colleges with day-release courses, the HCITB, head office training managers and so on. Whatever method of training is used, however, there are clearly identifiable objectives for a training programme.

1. To maintain and improve the quality of service.
2. To increase productivity.
3. To enhance job satisfaction.
4. To reduce customers' complaints.
5. To minimize the incidence of accidents.

The basis of good training is the development of a training programme suited to the needs of the individual employee and scheduled over a specified period of time. This means that there will be three basic stages to the programme. (1) Initial appraisal of the new employee to determine training programme. (2) Training the employee to meet the required standards as set down in the job description. (3) Regular staff performance appraisal and re-training where necessary.

Determining the training programme

It is not being suggested that all new employees will have a completely new and different training programme developed specifically for them. As we have already seen, the company will employ people who meet fairly specific criteria and who will therefore have very similar training needs. Likewise the required end result of training will be almost identical, so that the training programme for any grade of staff is likely to be clear cut. However, it is important that the programme is flexible enough to cope with an individual's own rate of progress and to cope with any deficiencies that a particular employee may have. Thus, the training programme for an employee will be determined by previous experience, age and performance at the selection interview, which may include a written test. This programme will then be discussed with the employee during the induction period and regularly reviewed.

The waiter will receive on-the-job training and where possible a period of 15 minutes in the morning and afternoon should be set aside for specific-skill training sessions. The following tasks should be covered by the end of:

		Date	On-the-job instructor
Week 1	Operating the floor service lift.		
	Laying up early morning tea tray.		
	Serving early morning tea.		
	Laying up and checking breakfast trays.		
	Clearing all equipment and debris from rooms.		
Week 2	Serving breakfast on trays in bedrooms.		
	Serving snacks on trays.		
	Serving alcoholic drinks.		
	Making out bills.		
	Passing bills for transfer to billing office.		
	Taking cash, giving change.		
Week 3	Attending to calls for service.		
	Dealing with special requirements.		
	Communicating with other departments.		

Based on the HCITB lists of basic food service tasks.

Figure 14.4 *Training programme for a room-service waiter.*

Training

A good training programme is likely to use a variety of methods to achieve its objectives (see Fig. 14.4) these may include:

On-the-job instruction.
Self-instruction from company handbook or performance manuals.
Group training seminars.
Audio-visual aids.
Day-release element and so on.

Staff performance appraisal

In many respects it is very difficult to appraise staff while they are at work, especially if they feel threatened or are made nervous by such an appraisal. However, if staff are regularly appraised and full, frank discussion takes place, these problems may be resolved. There are basically two types of standard against which appraisal can take place.

Quantity

One station waiter might be expected to serve four tables of four customers at one sitting. This type of measurement is that used to establish productivity earlier. This does have the advantage that it is quite clearly measurable, but some consideration must also be given to the second standard.

Quality

The station waiter must employ the service techniques as laid down for the restaurant. To a certain extent, this measurement is a subjective one as even within establishments using the same service style there may be very different standards of performance. Neverthless, whatever the problem, staff performance must be regularly reviewed to ensure that standards are maintained; to identify any training or re-training needs; and to motivate staff by promoting them once they have achieved the required standard.

14.6 SETTING STANDARDS

This is one of the most difficult functions of the food service manager. In large organizations, these standards are set at senior management level and are laid down in company policy. For smaller operators, standards are often implicit, informal and a matter of personal opinion. Nevertheless, it is essential for the operation that there are very clear standards set in all aspects, for while standards are laid down by the caterer they are derived from the expectations of customers. As we have seen in Chapter 10 many factors affect customers' enjoyment of meals and it is the relative importance of these in different types of unit that will determine the required standards. Further guidelines with regard to this can also be derived from considering the critical success variables of the operation; for instance, in an up-market restaurant using full silver service or gueridons, the customer will expect a high degree of precision so that one of the standards set in such an operation may be always to serve from the left and clear from the right. This also has the advantage that staff will find it easier and safer to operate to this standard. However, in less formal surroundings, where plate service is used, there seems little point in setting a standard with regard to which side to serve from, especially since in such an operation seating is likely to be more intensive making it very difficult to serve all the tables from the same side.

One particular area of standard-setting that is particularly important is with regards to the appearance and personal hygiene of the staff. The following list from *Food Services* by W. O. Smith and R. Lynch (1979, New York: McGraw-Hill) is the 'grooming guidelines' that a group of restaurant managers have stipulated for their employees to follow:

[© 1979 McGraw-Hill, reproduced with permission].

1. Body care (a) Bathe with soap every day
              (b) Use deodorant
              (c) Do not use strong perfume or after-shave
2. Hands   (a) Wash often and keep clean
              (b) Wash after using toilet
              (c) Keep nails clean and well manicured (no long nails)
3. Feet   (a) Wear clean hose or socks daily
              (b) Use foot powder, if needed
              (c) Wear well-fitted shoes
4. Hair   (a) Keep it clean
              (b) Current styles OK if kept groomed
              (c) Observe health department guidelines (caps, nets, etc.)
5. Face   (a) Do not use heavy make-up (natural look preferred)
              (b) Brush teeth at least twice daily
              (c) Use mouthwash if needed
              (d) Facial hair must be trimmed and neat
6. Clothing   (a) Wear uniforms that are provided
              (b) Keep uniform laundered and wear a fresh uniform daily
              (c) Change uniform if it becomes soiled
7. Jewellery (a) Wear only watches and engagement or wedding rings; no necklaces
                   or bracelets

14.7 CONCLUSION

The food service manager has three priorities:

1. To ensure that staffing levels are kept as low as possible while achieving the required level of service standards.
2. To minimize staff turnover.
3. To maintain a friendly, courteous, and co-operative attitude amongst all staff.

The first and second of these objectives are clearly measurable and therefore the manager has clear procedures to follow in order to effect them. The third priority, however, is a very subjective and indeterminate matter.

The managers have some limits that may suggest their staff are meeting this objective—for instance, few customer complaints, little or no industrial disputes, low staff turnover and feedback and appraisal sessions. However, if there are problems in this area, there are no clear prescriptions for remedying the situation.

Exercise

Planning training courses

New food service assistants are being engaged for a restaurant offering a medium-class service including some, but not all, aspects of silver service.

The restaurant is open:

10.00–11.30 for coffee
12.00–14.30 for lunch
15.00–17.00 for afternoon tea

Staff take lunch between 11.00 and 12.00 in the staff dining room. Working hours are 09.00–17.00.

The manager is a qualified instructor and the head waiter is qualified to give 'on-the-job' instruction. Plan a programme of training for new FSAs aiming to get them productive as quickly as possible.

Task list

Filling condiments
Making mustard
Folding napkins
Preparing sideboards for service
Use of spoon and fork
Serving rolls
Use of service cloth
Carrying dishes, cutlery and other small equipment
Recognition of menu items and prices
Serving coffee
Serving afternoon tea
The role of the FSA
Appearance, posture, dress
Recognition of equipment
Using a tray
Carrying plates on a tray
Preparing and setting tables
Introductions, regulations and general information
Clearing tables, wiping down, changing ashtrays
Hygiene
Cleaning duties
Laying and removing tablecloths
Mechanical cleaning
Sensitivity—customer approach
The customer—communication and sales skills
Serving from a silver flat, plate, salver
Offering and placing accompaniments
Serving sweets and cheese
Billing and checking
Work cycle
Complaints procedure
Fire and safety precautions
Greeting and seating
Presenting menu and bill
Placing plates in front of customers
Placing other crockery and cutlery
Clearing plates, crumbing down

15 Financial Aspects

How to succeed in business

OBJECTIVES: to relate the importance of both cost and revenue control . . . to understand the principles of budgetary control . . . to outline the elements of food and beverage control . . . to identify alternative pricing strategies of the catering business . . . to identify the billing and checking systems used in restaurants . . . to explain the use of credit cards, travellers' cheques and Luncheon Vouchers . . . to describe sales analysis and explain its role in the food service operation.

General awareness by hotel managers that the profitable operation of hotels is intimately related to the availability and understanding of operational data is, of course, long standing.

Hotel and Catering E.D.C.

15.1 INTRODUCTION

THROUGHOUT this book, an underlying theme has been the role of the caterer in minimizing operating costs, maximizing revenue and identifying areas of capital investment. As with marketing and personnel, the financial running of an operation will depend on the scale of operation and size of the operating firm. In addition, the concept of financial control is closely interdependent with the food production element of the business. In this chapter, we consider those elements of control for which the food service manager would be responsible and some of the systems used to ensure that control is effective.

The food service industry is, to a certain extent, unique since it is both a manufacturing and retailing industry—not only does it take raw materials and make these into a finished product, it sells that product directly to the consumer. It is for this reason that both *cost control* (i.e. careful analysis of the costs involved in manufacture) and *revenue control* (i.e. the analysis of sales, pricing and profitability) are important. This uniqueness is not helped by the unpredictable and complex nature of operations. Additional problems are also created.

1. Unstable demand. Demand for the product can vary on a daily, weekly or seasonal basis.
2. Unidentifiable product. One of the important functions of caterers is to ensure that the quality of the product is consistent with the standards they have laid down and the expectations of customers. But it is very difficult to achieve this for the product consists of two elements—first the food and drink to be consumed and second the service provided—and both are subject to inevitable fluctuations, such as changes in personnel, seasonal variation in the quality of raw materials, the need to introduce different dishes on the menu to stimulate consumer interest, and so on.
3. Perishability of product. Both the raw materials and finished product of food service operations are perishable. There is therefore a very real need to ensure that the purchase of supplies and the production of meals is closely related to demand, as far as possible.
4. Cycle of operation. The perishability of the product and the nature of the business means that catering operates over a very short time period; supplies can be delivered in the morning, prepared in the afternoon and sold in the evening. This very quick turnover makes control very difficult and also necessitates frequent analysis and reporting in order to clarify the situation.
5. Sales and turnover. The industry relies upon many sales and relatively low receipts. The sales per head will vary widely from unit to unit, but even in expensive up-market restaurants there will be probably 30 or 40 transactions a day, while in a fast-food outlet, there will be thousands of transactions. Each of these sales, of course, must be controlled.
6. Sales mix. Apart from the need for consistent production and service, there is the problem that in many respects the customers 'assemble' the finished product themselves inasmuch as they choose a selection of dishes from the menu. This also increases the unpredictability of the operation and adds to the problems of effective control.

We shall therefore attempt to identify how these problems may be overcome but we have already seen two approaches to overcoming the problem of unstable demand. First, in Chapter 11, we identify the need to maximize demand at *all* times and to eliminate any slack periods of sales, i.e. revenue control. Second, in Chapter 14, in order to minimize over-staffing, demand was forecast on the basis of previous sales figures to ensure the right number of staff were on duty at any moment in time, i.e. cost control, while the problem of production we have also identified previously. One of the reasons for proper induction and systematic training of new staff, identified in Chapter 14, is to introduce consistent standards of production and service.

15.2 BUDGETARY CONTROL

A budget has been defined as a 'statement in monetary or quantitive terms, reflecting the policy of a business and determining business operations in respect of a particular trading period.* Kotas and Davis have identified several types of budget (see Fig. 15.1).

These budgets may be used to effect control with the following objectives in mind.

1. To set a target against which the actual performance of the business can be measured.
2. To make the best use of resources available.
3. To co-ordinate the activities of the management team and the various departments within the operation.
4. To regulate the spending of money within the confines of income.
5. To establish clear lines of responsibility.

Such control is used extensively in the industrial and institutional sectors, whereby the funds available for operating the facilities are prescribed by a budget, while in other sectors, budgets may also be devised to set target sales figures.

The most common budget headings under which a food service manager might operate are:

1. Food and beverage cost percentage. Catering establishments have traditionally worked on the basis of a gross profit percentage, so that food cost is expected to

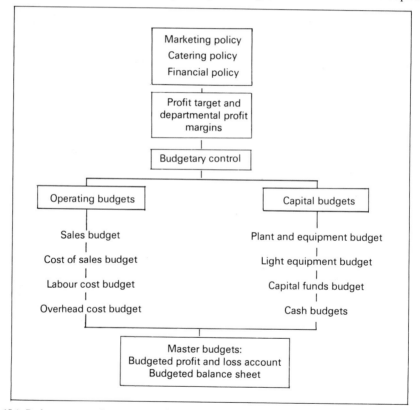

Figure 15.1 *Budgetary control as part of company policy. The catering manager is concerned with meeting operational and possibly capital budgets. (Reproduced with kind permission of the Blackie Publishing Group Ltd).*

---

* Kotas, R. & B. Davis (1981), *Food and Beverage Control*, Glasgow: International Textbook.

be kept at a set percentage of sales. A common figure was 40 per cent of sales, but recent increases in labour and overhead costs have found caterers increasing their mark-up and food cost is now commonly 30–35 per cent of sales.

2. Labour budget. Like the food cost budget, this budget is usually proportional to the sales figure, although staffing does not increase with sales volume exactly as food and drink cost does, since the extra staff employed may be recruited at lower rates of pay.

3. Overheads budget. The manager may well have several separate budget headings covering overheads such as rent/rates, fuel, energy, advertising, equipment and so on. These will be fixed budgets in the main although some will be flexible, particularly those for energy and fuel.

4. Sales budget. This budget is likely to be broken down into larger sales figures for all aspects of the operation. First into food and drink and second into different departments, such as restaurant, bar, lounge, coffee-shop and so on.

Such budgets are of course only effective if they are a fair and realistic estimate of sales and costs, so that great care must be exercised in setting the target figure. This may be achieved by an awareness of current trends in the national and local economy, discussion between those setting the budgets and those who are to meet the targets set and information supplied by sales analysis. The limitation of budgetary control is that it is of course only a guide to good performance—a measure against which the actual performance of the enterprise can be measured. It is not as such a system designed to effect physical control over the business activities on a day-to-day basis and in the rest of the chapter we look at methods and means of controlling more specifically the business environment.

Task 15.1

Whilst it is usual for a budget to be in monetary terms, it can also be in volume terms, for instance the number of covers to be served per month, the amount of heating oil to be consumed, etc. Table 15.1 shows the budgeted figure, the actual figure and the variance from budget in volume terms of cups for a hot-drink vending machine sited in a university. Comment upon the results.

Table 15.1 *Budget for a vending machine.*

	Jan	Feb	Mar	Apr	May	Jun	Jul	Aug	Sep	Oct	Nov	Dec
Budget	6000	7000	5000	3000	2500	2000	1000	1000	2000	5000	6500	5000
Actual	6200	7000	4500	4000	2400	2400	500	1000	1000	4500	6400	4500
Varience	+200	0	−500	+1000	−100	+400	−500	0	−1000	−500	−100	−500

15.3 FOOD AND BEVERAGE CONTROL

In order to achieve the necessary degree of control over the enterprise, and to meet budgets, the caterer must exercise close control over the purchase, storage, issuing and preparing of the raw materials of the business. In the catering industry, these raw materials can be divided into food and 'beverage'.

Although in many sectors of the industry, the food service manager will be responsible for all aspects of this control, we shall consider here only that part of the procedure that take place front-of-house. An important point needs to be made here; control should be thought of as a complete system. There is no point in achieving effective stores control or sales control if there is not effective control of the food preparation areas, or vice versa. However, we are not considering *all* aspects of control as this is a subject about which a whole book could be written. Instead we shall consider only ways and means of ensuring that food service staff are not wasteful, incompetent or dishonest, so that satisfactory levels of gross profit can be maintained.

The purpose of all control is to contribute to the financial well-being of the operation—in the commercial sector, this means achieving a satisfactory level of profit and return on investment, and in the public sector it means ensuring the provision of the desired level of service at the lowest possible cost. Control of food and beverages contributes to the total system by monitoring all stages of the process from receipt of raw materials through to the service of the finished product. In the case of food, food service personnel are mainly involved in the very last stage of the process, i.e. the service of the meal, but in the case of beverages, bar staff may have the added responsibility of storage and preparation in addition to serving the product.

Vulnerability of stock

Liquor stocks are particularly vulnerable because

1. Liquor is a high value item. A 40 oz. bottle of spirits costs around £10 and its sales value to the caterer can be over £25.
2. Although not a perishable product, like meat, fish or vegetables, it is a fragile product so that mishandling can result in costly breakages.
3. Although it is perhaps difficult to physically steal the product when bottled, it is easily consumed and its loss is therefore difficult to detect.
4. The product can be adulterated fairly easily in order to cover up any losses due to incompetence or theft, i.e. by watering down or replacing an expensive liquor with a cheaper one, so quality control is required.
5. It is broken down for sales purposes into smaller quantities, so that precision in measurement is required—in some cases by law (see Chapter 16).

Receiving and issuing goods

Food items are also vulnerable, but much of their effective control lies with the ordering, storage and preparation of food items, which is outside the scope of this book. However, the broad outline of control procedures is outlined below.

In order to control this area, each movement of stock must be recorded and documented. All orders for goods should be recorded in an order book, so that upon delivery the delivery note can be checked against the order. The storeman or woman, cellarkeeper or whoever is designated to check goods upon their delivery should ensure that the listed items are in fact brought onto the premises *and* that no stock is taken away except those items that should be removed, such as empty bottles and so on. As a result of the delivery, the goods inward book would be brought up to date and as each item is placed in its appropriate place on the shelf or bin, the bin card would be corrected to show the new balance. No goods are issued without a requisition from the department requiring the items, which has been signed by a designated person or persons. Such requisitions are usually in triplicate—one copy is retained by the department, and the other two are sent to the stores or cellar; if items are unavailable, the stores will correct the two copies they receive and send back one copy with the issued goods to the appropriate department, while they retain one copy. When the goods are received the original copy is adjusted to agree with the actual goods received, and the copy received back from stores is sent to the control office.

Stock control

Any system of stock control should achieve the following:

1. Ensure sufficient stock is held to meet demand.
2. Minimize the level of stock held in order to reduce capital investment in stocks and the likelihood of spoilage of goods with a limited shelf life.
3. Prevent and discover errors, fraud and theft.
4. Safeguard that goods are sold in perfect condition.
5. Record changes in sales volume in order to forecast future trends more accurately.
6. Enable the profit margin on sales to be calculated accurately.

This is achieved by using bin cards and requisitions as outlined above, by effective stock-taking procedures and standardized portion control. The procedure for stock-taking is to establish the opening stock, add to that purchases which have been received since the opening stock-take, and deduct from that the present stock. This establishes the actual amount of goods that have been sold, which can be used to calculate the estimated value of goods sold, either at cost or sales price. The latter value is usually adopted since it can quickly be compared with the actual sales receipts.

Task 15.2

The following stock-take figures for a dispense bar of a hotel for one month were as follows:

Item	Opening stock	Purchases	Closing stock
	£	£	£
Spirits	271	119	236
Fortified wines	189	220	203
Wines	456	736	398
Minerals	98	187	117
Beers	76	82	59

Calculate the cost of the beverages consumed.

If the gross profit percentages were spirits 60 per cent; fortified wines 65 per cent;

wines 55 per cent; minerals 75 per cent and beers 70 per cent, calculate the estimated sales figure.

If actual sales for that month were £3700, comment on the results.

Portion control

Effective portion control is essential. In those establishments serving plated meals or silver-service operations such control is effected by the kitchen personnel, but there are many styles of service, i.e. cafeteria, fast food, trolley service, bar sales, where the service personnel will actually be portioning the product. Correct portioning can be achieved by a variety of means, but a basic requirement is that staff should be trained to identify the correct portion size of the products on sale. However, in order to help and facilitate their portioning, three aids can be employed.

1. The food can be designed and presented so that it is pre-portioned or portioning is self-evident, for instance, a gateau can be decorated so that the repeated pattern results in 12 or 16 portions being cut from it, meat pies can be made individually, yogurt is sold in individual cartons and so on.
2. Equipment can be provided that serves the precise portion laid down, for instance a soup ladle with a capacity of 8 fl. oz, a scoop for ice cream, an optic to dispense a measure of a spirit and so on. Such equipment can be quite simple (a spoon or ladle) or quite sophisticated (a metered pump to dispense draught beer in quantities of half a pint).
3. The product can be served in a container that holds the correct amount of the item, for instance, a pint mug for draught beer; or less precisely, on a plate or dish that encourages portion control. For instance, 8.5 inch or 9 inch diameter plates are often used to give the appearance of a plateful in pub, carvery and cafeteria operations.

Sales control

Kotas and Davis (1981 op. cit.) believe that a restaurant checking system should achieve the following objectives:

1. Ensure that no food or beverage is issued to a revenue-producing department without documentary evidence.
2. Ensure that the unit receives cash or a credit voucher equal to the total of food and beverage issued.
3. Provide a record for control purposes.

There are two types of checking system.

Duplicate checking systems

This is usually in the form of a perforated top sheet and card backing (see Fig. 15.2). As the customer orders, each section of the top copy can be completed and priced by hand and/or put through a billing machine, then taken to the appropriate depart-

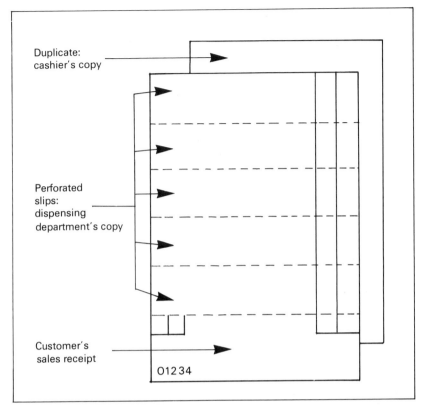

Duplicate:
cashier's copy

Perforated
slips:
dispensing
department's copy

Customer's
sales receipt

01234

Figure 15.2 *Duplicate checking system.*

ment—kitchen bar, still room. The duplicate can be retained by the waiter or left on the table with the customer. When the customer has completed the meal, the bill is totalled, and the customer is given the bottom part of the top copy as a receipt. The duplicate copy is retained for control purposes. Control is effected by ensuring that all perforated copies received by a dispensing department relate to a duplicate. As a quick check that all is correct, the total of checks received by the kitchen and so on should equal the total sales receipts for the service.

Triplicate checking system

This consists of three copies (see Fig. 15.3). The top copy is sent to the dispensing department, the flimsy is retained by the waiter and the duplicate sent to the cashier. The cashier makes up a separate bill from the duplicate copies received. As with the duplicate system, top copies from dispensing departments are married to duplicates from the cashier for control purposes, and the checks for each table married with the bill for that table to see that they agree. As a cashier is employed, the checks do not need to be priced.

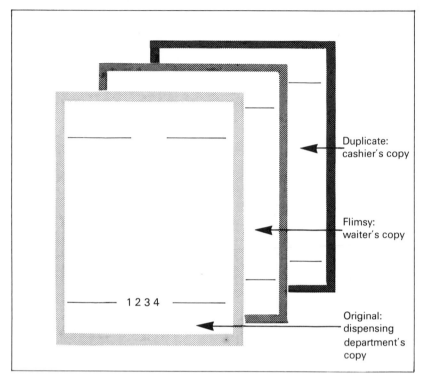

Figure 15.3 *Triplicate checking system.*

Task 15.3

Outline the advantages and disadvantages of the triplicate and duplicate checking systems.

15.4 SALES TRANSACTIONS

Control of sales receipts

Payment by the customer for goods received is the most vulnerable operation of all control procedures to error, theft or fraud. In order to facilitate handling receipts, a till should be provided that is not only a secure store for the different denominations of money, but also provides an indicator that can be seen by the operator, the supervisor and the customer; prevents its operation by anyone except those authorized to do so; stores either electronically or on a till roll all the transactions that have taken place; and identifies anyone opening the till drawer on a 'no sale' basis, either by recording the individual's key used to operate the machine or with an audio/visual signal that the till has been opened for a 'no sale'. At the end of any sales period, all cash, cheques and vouchers must be checked against the recorded sales. This may be done either by the cashier on a restaurant control sheet which records and analyses each sale, or by the till which will provide the same information. (See Fig. 15.4 below).

Table No.	Serial Nos. of Bills	Covers	FOOD £	p	WINES £	p	SUNDRIES £	p	TOTAL £	p	CASH		CREDIT CARD		OTHER	
4	008481	4	23	2o	4	69			27	89	27	89				
3	008482	2	11	41	3	98		60	15	99			15	99		
16	008483	6	35	94	11	42	1	84	49	2o			49	2o		
7	008484	4	27	48	9	37			36	85	36	85				
19	008485	3	15	60	3	27		40	19	27	19	27				
5	008486	2	9	43	5	81	1	16	16	40			16	40		
12	008487	2	10	83	2	61		60	14	04	14	04				

The Restaurant at the End of the Universe

Cashier R. Salmon   Date 19. 9. 1984

Figure 15.4 *Restaurant control sheet.*

Types of transactions

Customers may choose to pay bills in a variety of ways.

Cash

The advantage of cash is that apart from counterfeit currency, the caterer can be satisfied that payment has been made and it may be used immediately to pay for any operational expenses of the business. The major disadvantage of cash is that it is not easily traceable if it is lost or stolen.

Cheque

The advantage for customers paying by cheque is that they do not have to carry cash around with them. Now that all banks provide their customers with a cheque guarantee card, the caterer is assured of payment but a crossed cheque must be paid into a bank account before it is of value to the caterer and a third party is unable to cash it if it is stolen. Care must also be taken to comply with the regulations laid down by the banks concerning the writing of cheques and use of the cheque guarantee card.

Credit card

The advantage of a credit card such as Access or Barclaycard to users is that they do not carry cash and they receive up to 30 days' free credit, so long as they pay their monthly statements of transactions in full. Many restaurateurs do not accept credit cards because they have to pay a service charge to the banks of between 2 and 3 per cent. However, the trader is guaranteed payment and is protected against theft and fraud since the voucher has no use to a third party. Both vouchers are reimbursed immediately upon presentation to the bank. A poll by Gallup for *Caterer & Hotel-keeper* has estimated that 75 per cent of restaurants in Britain accept the two major credit cards. Barclaycard in 1980 was accepted by 13 000 hotels and restaurants.

Charge card

Charge-card holders must pay an enrolment fee and must settle in full upon receipt of their monthly statements but there is no pre-set spending limit as with credit cards. There are fewer charge-card holders but they tend to be senior business executives with a secure financial background, and are used especially by visiting business people and tourists to Britain. Fewer food service operations accept such cards as the commission is between 3–6 per cent but they have the same protection as a credit card. Diners Club and American Express vouchers are reimbursed on a weekly basis.

Luncheon Vouchers

These are given by firms, particularly those without their own catering facilities, to their employees as a 'perk' in order to enable them to get a reduction in the price of their midday meal. They come in a wide range of denominations and are received by the caterer and treated as cash, since if lost they may be redeemed by anyone.

15.5 PRICING

One cannot talk about controlling the enterprise without discussing how sales price is established. The nature of the industry, its breadth of scope and differences in scale of operation make it impossible to be specific, but broadly, there are three important factors affecting the pricing policy of an operation.

1. Compared with many industries, catering has a high degree of fixed costs for in addition to overheads of 20–30 per cent on average, the labour cost is only a semi-variable cost at best, in view of the difficulties in hiring and firing staff.
2. The industry is extremely competitive, and a wide range of meal experiences, appealing to all sectors of the population, are available.
3. Caterers derive their income from the disposable income of customers and must compete with other factors that may be viewed as 'luxuries'.

In view of these things, caterers have a high degree of price discrimination, for since their gross profit margin is quite high, there is a range of prices they can choose from. This allows them to discriminate on the basis of price by offering different prices to different sectors of the market, so that a hotel could be achieving 55 per cent gross profit on its carvery operation, 60 per cent in its à la carte restaurant, 65 per cent on its coffee shop and 75 per cent on function catering.

Broadly speaking there are three methods of pricing employed in the catering industry.

Informal pricing

Smaller operators in particular may not use a formal method to calculate their prices. Five informal strategies may influence the price that is established.

Intuition

Establishes price on some intuitive feeling for public demand in terms of what 'the traffic will bear'. Generally, little may be known about the expected volume of sales that a particular price may generate or the full cost of the service. This may result in failure to recover full costs or an unsatisfactory profit margin.

Competition

A simple method whereby a firm charges the same as its competitors for the same product or service. This may be satisfactory if the product or service is completely comparable, but it assumes that customers do not discriminate between meal experiences. Thus an operator may be able to charge more than a competitor without affecting sales volume. Also, it assumes that the costs of operation are the same as those of competitors, for if they are not, one price can result in a healthy profit margin for one firm, but a loss for another.

Follow the leader

Where there is a leader or dominant firm, whose price structure is followed by others in the market. So it is similar to 'competition' above and suffers from the same deficiencies.

Trial and error

Prices are established for a test period, during which sales are monitored very carefully. Prices are then adjusted up or down in order to maximize profits. While this has certain merits, it is an expensive and time-consuming exercise. It also assumes that customer reaction will occur in a sufficiently short period of time to arrive at a proper price and that once a price is determined, market conditions and customer tastes will remain constant.

Psychological

Prices are set according to a conscious expectation of what the customer wants to pay. In this respect, Anthea Rogers believes that 'industries competing for the discretionary element of consumer spending cannot ignore this aspect of pricing and moreover have found that there are considerable rewards to be reaped if the psychological connotations attached to pricing are fully exploited when deciding on the marketing strategy.'*

Several points should be borne in mind. Customers will be more concerned and more aware of the price being charged if the level of their discretionary spending power is low and they purchase the product frequently. Also, if comparison with com-

---

* 'Psychological aspects of pricing'—A. Rogers in *HCIMA Journal* January 1977.

petitors' facilities is easy, and prominence is given to price in the transaction, then price is a more significant element.

The implications of this depend upon which sector of the industry the caterer is working in. Nevertheless, some broad guidelines may be established. First in the 'popular' catering sector appealing to the lower and middle socioeconomic groups, pricing must be seen to give value for money—the market is competitive and the consumer only has a limited amount to spend. For many years, operators in the industry believed that by pricing the menu relatively cheaply and adding on a table charge, service charge and VAT, they could attract custom and achieve satisfactory profits. In fact, the Price Display Order now makes this difficult, but in any case consumers are not as naïve as this (The success of steakhouse chains such as Berni's, was founded on the fact that customers knew exactly what they would get for an all-inclusive price.) Second, prominence should only be given to the price in advertising and display material, if the pricing compares favourably with close competitors. Moreover, price is an effective promotional tool since the product being sold is a service which it is difficult for customers to evaluate objectively and they therefore tend to use price as an indicator of quality. Lastly, value for money is not judged on every item sold but on certain items; for instance, a public house is 'cheap' if the price of the particular drink a customer usually imbibes is cheap, irrespective of other prices. This is particularly important for those units which are selling dishes individually priced.

Cost percentage

The basic cost plus method, which is used extensively in the catering industry, is to take the cost of the raw material and add to this an amount to achieve a certain gross profit percentage on sales price, e.g. if a dish costs 40p, in order to achieve 60 per cent gross profit it must be sold for £1. There are two methods that may be used:

1. Prime ingredient cost. Only the cost of the prime ingredient is taken in order to establish price. It is used primarily for pricing alcoholic beverages because liquor cost is a large percentage if not all of ingredient cost.
2. Standard dish costing. All the costs of producing an item are taken into account to establish price.

The main advantage to the caterer of this pricing method is its simplicity. Experience has shown over many years that by achieving a certain gross profit, a satisfactory net profit will result, so it provides a safer method of calculating price than informal methods. However, there are disadvantages.

First, since no account of labour or overhead cost is built in to the calculation, a satisfactory net profit is *not* assured. Second, if we accept as we have done in Chapter 12 that the food service industry is market oriented, then a cost based pricing method is nonsensical, especially in view of Anthea Rogers' comments above. Third, the customer is purchasing not just the food, but service and atmosphere as well. It could be that a higher price is acceptable to the customer, especially in up-market units, than that established only on the cost price of the food. Lastly, the method is simple to use only if the same gross profit percentage is applied to all dishes. However, this has the effect that low cost items are priced cheaply, whereas high cost items are made even more expensive. This means that differential cost percentages have to be applied, for instance, starters at 80 per cent, meat dishes at 50 per cent, vegetables at 70 per cent, and so on. The caterer must then rely upon the sales mix achieving the desired overall gross profit percentages, but already a simple pricing method has become very much more complex.

Rate of return method

This is not used extensively in pricing in the food service industry, although it is used to establish tariffs for accommodation in hotels; for instance, the 'Hubbart formula' has been developed by the American Hotel and Motel Association for this. However, the method may have 'applications' in food service, particularly when opening a new unit since it may help to establish sales budget figures. Essentially, it is concerned with the rate of return on capital invested in the business. For instance, if a unit cost £300 000 to set up and was likely to cost £250 000 to operate in the first year, then sales would have to be set at £310 000 to achieve a net profit of 20 per cent return on capital invested. Once again, the technique is wholly profit centred and has no sympathy for the customer or market.

15.6 SALES ANALYSIS

The analysis of sales and trading is 'post-operation and control' (Kotas, R. & B. Davis (1981) op. cit.), that is to say, the information collected provides a résumé of past business activity, highlighting problems and enabling more effective forecasts and budgets to be made. The extent of this analysis will vary from unit to unit, as we have already seen in previous case studies, but the type of analysis that is possible includes the following.

Sales

An analysis of how sales vary over a given period, usually on a daily basis. (See Fig. 15.5).

Task 15.4

Identify two ways in which this analysis may be used by the operator.

Sales mix

This analyses sales and breaks them down into constituent parts. A standard breakdown is to divide total restaurant sales into food, drink and tobacco. However, with the introduction of sophisticated cash registers and till systems, it is now possible to analyse the sales of each menu item quickly. In a unit where such analysis takes place, this information enables the caterer to revise menus by taking off the least popular items and to see how individual dish sales may affect the average gross profit margin. (See Fig. 15.6).

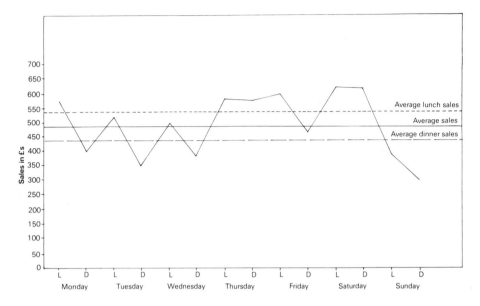

Figure 15.5 *Turnover for one week in a restaurant.*

Task 15.5

Describe the fluctuations in demand for the five products shown in Fig. 15.6 and speculate why this should be so.

Average spend

This figure is established by dividing total sales or food and drink sales by the number of customers served in any given period. This establishes how much the average customer spends in the unit which enables caterers to estimate customer reaction to their pricing policies. An analysis of the range of customer spending on either side of the average will also enable the caterer to establish if the restaurant is appealing to one, two or even more identifiable market segments. For instance, the average spend in a restaurant may be £8.50, but further analysis shows that approximately 40 per cent of customers spend £10 or more, while the remainder spend between £7.00 and £7.50. This situation reflects the two menus available, a table d'hôte priced at £6.50 which appeals to the majority of customers and an individually priced à la carte menu. Quite clearly, if the table d'hôte menu was dropped, the average spend would increase substantially but the number of customers would be reduced, while if only a table d'hôte menu was offered, the number of customers might well hold up quite well but the average spend would fall.

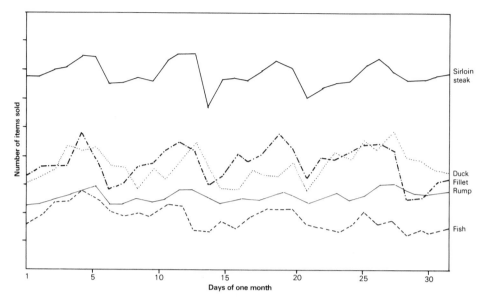

Figure 15.6 *Analysis of sales mix of a steak bar over one month.*

Sales per member of staff

In those units, such as fast-food operations and steakhouses, where sales can be identified with a particular member of staff using a till, or sales point, it is possible to establish the contribution of each member of staff. Thus a waiter whose total sales are consistently lower than those of his colleagues may be shirking responsibility or taking too long over the service, whilst on the positive side, such analysis can be used as an incentive to other staff to achieve similar targets. For instance, McDonald's have a policy of rewarding the till operator who achieves the highest sales during a given period.

Restaurant occupancy

As we have already seen, an analysis of the occupancy of the restaurant can provide information that identifies slack periods and productivity of staff. While it is possible to show occupancy as a percentage of capacity, the usual way of expressing this relationship is simply to divide actual occupancy by the seating capacity for a given service period or day so that an occupancy of one means that each seat was occupied once, or of two means that each seat was turned over twice.

15.7 CONCLUSION

In looking at the financial aspects of food service, we have identified systems that 'control' the past, present and future operations. By using the tools of sales analysis and the various measures of such analysis, we can identify the ways in which the business should be directed in order to maximize its opportunities: this is very much part of the market-oriented approach that was outlined in Chapter 11. Food and beverage control systems are designed to monitor the business's operation on a day-to-day basis to ensure that no malpractice caused an unnecessary increase in running costs or loss of sales potential. And finally, budgetary control looks to the future to predict how the business should be operated in order to achieve satisfactory trading results. We have also seen that a knowledge of financial matters can affect the marketing of the operation, either through the pricing policy adopted or through the willingness or otherwise of the operator to accept payment by means other than legal tender.

Exercise

The two food cost reports (Figs. 15.7 and 15.8) are for consecutive months. If you were the food and beverage manager of this hotel, what items on January's report would attract your attention and how would you go about investigating them?

MONTHLY CATERING REPORT

Month DECEMBER 1983

Name of Supplier	Meat		Poultry		Fish		Veg/Fruit		Dairy		Sundries		Total	
	£	p	£	p	£	p	£	p	£	p	£	p	£	p
Allied Bakeries											219	60	219	60
Alveston Kitchens	23	81											23	81
Birds Eye			43	21	19	16	45	80	21	00	98	32	227	49
Bookes Belmont											161	80	161	80
Dewhurst	457	11	89	30									546	41
Danish Bacon	183	40											183	40
Eden Vale									184	95			184	95
Greenacres							119	19					119	19
Holmes + Son											211	35	211	35
Igloo Ices									38	71			38	71
Johnson + Green							28	72			205	31	234	03
Kings	231	41	109	63									341	04
Matthews Turkeys			150	55									150	55
Price + Son											251	82	251	82
Ross Frozen Food			73	40			83	82					157	22
Southern Dairies									129	01			129	01
Tetley Catering											147	89	147	89
T.F.C. Foods							31	42			131	52	162	94
United Yeast											238	28	238	28
Walls	194	18											194	18
Youngs Seafood					158	91	68	20					227	11
Zachariah											497	31	497	31
Total	1089	71	466	09	178	07	377	15	373	67	2163	20	4648	09
Cost % purchases	23%		10.01%		3%		8.53%		8.46%		46%			

(All invoices for current work to be included, exclusive of VAT)

	Food		Liquor		Total	
	£	p	£	p	£	p
Income	18057	35	7517	82		
VAT	2355	30				
Net receipts	15702	05				
Cost	4648	09				
Profit	11053	96				
%	71%					
Wages	4985	40				
%	31%					
Net profit	6068	92				
%	40%					

	Receipts		Target		%
	£	p	£	p	
Breakfast	1158	72	1200	00	
Lunch	3318	41	3200	00	
Dinner	3121	45	3000	00	
Lounge	485	22	500	00	
Floors	993	57	1100	00	
Functions	6624	68	6000	00	
Total	15702	05	15000	00	
Net cost sales	4648	09	6000	00	
Over/under					

Comments

Signed Gordon Blue

Figure 15.7 *Monthly catering report—December 1983.*

MONTHLY CATERING REPORT   Month JANUARY 1984

Name of Supplier	Meat £	Meat p	Poultry £	Poultry p	Fish £	Fish p	Veg/Fruit £	Veg/Fruit p	Dairy £	Dairy p	Sundries £	Sundries p	Total £	Total p
Allied Bakeries											192	32	192	32
Alveston Kitchens	47	39											47	39
Associated Biscuits											57	00	57	00
Birds Eye Foods			41	20	28	31	55	18	45	06	81	06	250	81
Gosher Belmont											90	37	90	37
Chisholm							71	03					71	03
Dewhurst	389	04	21	09									410	13
Danish Bacon	181	34											181	34
Eden Vale									129	82			129	82
Greenacres							101	78					101	78
Holmes + Son											176	38	176	38
Igloo Ices									18	21			18	21
Johnson + Green							50	99					50	99
Kings	175	31			111	82							287	13
Masons					17	81							17	81
Price + Son											157	80	157	80
Ross Frozen Foods			93	42			95	29					188	71
Southern Dairies									89	17			89	17
Terley Catering											135	01	135	01
T.F.C. Foods			21	02			25	17			128	81	168	00
United Yeast											160	35	160	35
Wells	149	17											149	17
Youngs Seafood					39	41							39	41
Zachariah											401	62	401	62
Total	942	25	288	55	85	53	399	44	282	26	1547	72	3545	75
Cost % purchases	26.57%		8.13%		2.39%		11.26%		7.96%		43.64%			

(All invoices for current work to be included, exclusive of VAT)

	Food £	Food p	Liquor £	Liquor p	Total £	Total p
Income	12028	95	6418	79		
VAT	1568	99				
Net receipts	10459	96				
Cost	3545	75				
Profit	6914	21				
%	66.1%					
Wages	3834	90				
%	36.66%					
Net profit	3079	31				
%	29.44%					

	Receipts £	Receipts p	Target £	Target p	%
Breakfast	1039	21	1200	00	
Lunch	2741	56	3000	00	
Dinner	2504	17	3000	00	
Lounge	454	29	500	00	
Floors	874	14	1100	00	
Functions	2846	59	5500	00	
Total	10459	96	14300	00	
Net cost sales	3545	75	5720	00	
Over/under					

Comments

Signed Gordon Blue

Figure 15.8 *Monthly catering report—January 1984.*

16 Legal Aspects

What the caterer needs to know of the law

OBJECTIVES: to discuss those statutes and legal regulations that affect the operation of catering premises . . . to identify the statutory notices that must be displayed in catering premises . . . to outline the legal rights of the customer and the caterer.

Ignorantia iuris non excusat   *but*   De minimis non curat lex
Ignorance of the law is no defence   *The law is not concerned with trifles*

16.1 INTRODUCTION

THERE is no doubt that a book of this nature can deal but briefly with the legal aspects of operating a catering establishment. The law is a complex subject area and the caterer is well advised to take expert advice on any particular point that arises. None the less, in developing the role of the manager mention must be made of the legal obligations. The problem is that there is so much legislation that to pick out the main points can so easily give the impression that this is all that one needs to know. This is not so, the purpose of this chapter is to illuminate the important areas and make reference to the principal pieces of legislation. Some apply solely to one sector of industry, such as the Hotel Proprietors Act 1956; others concern principally the industry, such as the liquor licensing laws; but most legislation applies to businesses and industry in general, notably employment and health and safety legislation.

There is no simple way of categorizing legislation affecting the caterer but legislation affects (1) the product, (2) the premises and (3) people.

16.2 THE PRODUCT AND THE LAW

In a lawless state, a caterer could sell a product to a customer without any fear of civil suit or criminal charge; despite the proliferation of consumer protection legislation the principle of *caveat emptor* or 'buyer beware' still applies today. None the less the caterer must be careful to comply with laws relating to the following subjects.

The description of the product

Trades Description Act 1968

False and misleading statements about the standards of service, facilities and product, as well as making caterers or hoteliers liable to civil action make caterers and hoteliers subject to criminal prosecution under the Act. The defences that can be offered against a false trade description are that it was a pure mistake, the statement was based on information supplied by some other person or that it was the result of an act or default of some other person.

Price Marking (Food and Drink On Premises) Order 1979

The basic purpose of this Order is that customers should be made fully aware of what they may have to pay for food and drink *before* placing an order, or in the case of a restaurant, *before* entering the premises. The Order requires that all price displays be clear and legible, so that they may be easily read by an intending purchaser. It defines two sorts of establishment as follows:

1. 'Eating areas', e.g. restaurants, cafeterias, hotel coffee shops, snack bars where table service is provided. In such places, the display must be placed at or near the entrance so that customers can see and read it before entering.
2. 'Supply areas', e.g. pubs, wine bars, buffet bars, self-service cafeterias where the customer purchases food and/or drink from a counter prior to consumption. In these establishments the display must be located behind the counter or bar from which customers select their purchases and, if this cannot be seen by customers before entering the unit, a further display must be located at the entrance.

Some establishments are excluded. Those which ordinarily supply only members with food and/or drink, such as clubs, or cater privately for guests or residents such as boarding-houses, staff canteens, school and college restaurants are excluded.

The order also defines what information must be displayed:

1. Prices *must* be inclusive of VAT.
2. If there is a service charge (either an amount or percentage of the price) it *must* be shown as prominently as the prices of food and drink.
3. If there is a cover charge or minimum price, it *must* be shown prominently.
4. Menus, wine lists or bar lists with fewer than 30 items must show each item priced separately, unless it is a table d'hôte menu, but if there are more than 30 items listed, only 30 of them need to be priced, so long as in the case of an à la carte menu, at least five (if there are five) items in each course are priced.
5. The prices of no more than 6 table wines need be displayed.

The condition of the product

Food and Drugs Act 1955

Section 8(1) states that 'any person who (a) sells, or offers or exposes for sale, or has in his possession for the purpose of sale or of preparation for sale, or (b) deposits with, or consigns to, any person for the purpose of sale or of preparation for sale any food intended for, but unfit for human consumption shall be guilty of a (criminal) offence'. Maximum sentence is £100 fine and/or 3 months imprisonment.

Case study 16.1   Hobbs v. Winchester Corporation 1910 2KB 471

It is no defence for vendors to claim they are unaware that the food is unfit for consumption. In this case, the Court of Appeal determined that 'if a man chooses for profit to engage in a business which involves the offering for sale of that which may be deadly or injurious to health he must take that risk'.

   Section 2 of the Food and Drugs Act states that 'if a person sells to the prejudice of the purchaser any food which is not of the nature or not of the substance, or not of the quality of the food demanded by the purchaser, he shall be guilty of an offence'.

Sale of Goods Act (1979)

This Act applies to contracts for the sale of goods by description. In this respect, a contract is implicitly entered into by the caterer when he accepts the order of a customer for food or drink. Thus under the Act a *customer can refuse to pay or demand a replacement for goods* that either (a) do not correspond with the description of the goods, e.g. if a steak is described as tender and is tough (section 13(1)) *or* (b) if a displayed item is not what it seems, e.g. if a cream bun selected from a sweet trolley is found to contain artificial and not real cream (section 13(3)) [It makes no difference if the customer has partly or entirely consumed the purchase. Of course, the customer may also choose to report the caterer under the Trades Description Act.] *or* (c) prove to be inedible (section 14).

Food Hygiene (General) Regulations 1970

Among other things these regulations stipulate the temperature at which certain foods are to be kept on catering premises.

16.3 THE PREMISES AND THE LAW

There is wide ranging legislation affecting catering premises.

Food Hygiene (General) Regulations 1970

These regulations lay down requirements for the cleanliness of food premises.

Regulation 6 states that 'no food business shall be carried out at any unsavoury premises or place or at any premises or place the condition, situation or construction of which is such that food is exposed to the risk of contamination.'

Regulation 14 relates that no fresh air intake or any ventilation pipe included in the soil drainage system of food premises may be situated in a food room and any inlet to the system must be trapped.

Regulation 15 demands that a cistern supplying water to a food room must not also supply a sanitary convenience otherwise than through an efficient flushing cistern.

Regulation 16 refers to sanitary conveniences which must be kept clean, in efficient working order, well-ventilated and lit. Toilets may not be used as, or communicate directly with, food rooms.

Regulation 17 a constant supply of clean, wholesome water must be available for use on all premises.

Regulation 18 refers to wash-hand basins which must be provided near to where persons are working with food. They must be equipped with hot and cold water, soap or suitable detergent, nail brushes and clean towels or suitable hand-drying facilities. They must be kept clean and used solely for the purpose of personal cleanliness.

Regulation 21 concerns facilities for washing food and equipment. Such sinks must be provided with hot and cold water; except sinks used only for washing fish, fruit and vegetables; or ice-cream scoops and servers; or drinking vessels, which may be supplied with cold water only.

Regulation 22 demands that lighting of food rooms be suitable and sufficient.

Regulation 23 refers to ventilation which must also be suitable and sufficient.

Regulation 24 states that no food room can be used as a sleeping place.

There is no doubt that the description 'food business' could apply to all enterprises in the catering industry where food is *sold* for human consumption. The maximum penalty for breaking these regulations is £100 fine and/or 3 months imprisonment.

Food and Drugs (Control of Food Premises) Act 1976

Upon successful conviction under the regulations the local authority can apply for a 'closure order'. The order stipulates those measures that the convicted person must take to remove any danger to health. The operator must be given 14 days to comply with this order, before the order is put into practice, and is subject to a maximum fine of £400 if the closure order is contravened.

Likewise, the local authority, where action under the 1970 regulations is being undertaken in court, can apply for an emergency order to close the premises, if they believe there is an imminent danger to health. The operator must receive notice in writing of their intention to apply for such an order, to allow him or her time to rectify the situation. If when the case comes to court the local authority cannot prove there was imminent danger to health and the operator incurred loss due to the emergency order, then the local authority may be ordered to pay appropriate compensation.

Public Health Acts 1936 and 1961

The local authority can require the owner or occupier of premises considered unwholesome, filthy or verminous to clean and disinfect them, and if necessary repaint, repaper or redistemper the interior surfaces. Maximum fine if the person fails to comply with such a notice is £25 plus £2 for each day the offence continues after conviction. Furthermore 'the local authority may by notice require the owner or occupier of any inn, public house, beer-house, refreshment house or place of public entertainment to provide and maintain in a suitable position such number of sanitary conveniences for the use of persons frequenting the premises as may be reasonable' (section 89).

Prevention of Damage by Pests Act 1949

Under this Act and the Public Health Acts local authorities are empowered to enter and inspect infested premises; to order the destruction of infested food; to order the destruction or removal of vermin; to require the carrying out of structural alterations for preventing or remedying infestation; and to prohibit or restrict the sale or storage of food on infested premises. The Act also requires the operator to report any infestation to the Ministry of Agriculture, Fisheries and Food. Failure to report or comply with directions given by the inspectors is a criminal offence, with maximum fine of £200.

Offices, Shops and Railway Premises Act 1963

This Act applies to all office and administrative areas of hotel and catering premises, takeaway food shops and all cafeterias, public houses and restaurants which serve food and drink for immediate consumption by members of the public and includes adjacent kitchens, cellars, stores, etc. Many of the items dealt with under the Food Hygiene Regulations are also regulated under this Act. In addition under section 4 all premises, furniture, furnishings and fittings to which the Act applies must be kept in a clean state. Floors and staircases must be swept, vacuum-cleaned or washed down at least once a week, so that no dirt or refuse can accumulate.

   Section 5 requires that all employees have 40 square feet (3.7 square metres) of floor space and 400 cubic feet (3.45 cubic metres) of breathing space each. For the purpose of calculating floor area, account must be taken of fittings, equipment and furniture and in determining breathing space any space above 10 feet (3.04 metres) may not be included. The essence of the Act is to see that employees do not work in cramped or overcrowded conditions. It does not apply to public areas used by customers.

   Section 6 (2) requires that if staff are not involved in severe physical effort that the temperature of the room be a minimum of 20°C (68°F) after the first hour. The employer must provide a thermometer in a conspicuous place.

Sanitary Conveniences Regulations 1964

Where fewer than 6 people are regularly employed, one WC will suffice. In all other cases, separate sanitary accommodation must be provided for persons of both sexes, if both are employed.

Fire Precautions Act 1971

Under section 1 of this Act premises designated by order of the Home Secretary must have a fire certificate. Two such orders have been made: (a) The Fire Precautions (Hotels and Boarding Houses) Order 1972 refers to establishments with sleeping accommodation for more than 6 persons; and (b) The Fire Precautions (Factories, Offices, Shops and Railway Premises) Order 1976 applies if more than 20 persons are employed on the premises at any one time.

The fire certificate is issued by the 'fire authority' (which is usually the local authority) and specifies the following:

1. The particular use or uses of the premises.
2. Means of escape, width of doorways and gangways.
3. Fire resistance of doors.
4. Permitted surface finishes on walls, ceilings and partitions.
5. The fire alarm system.
6. Specifications for emergency lighting, heat and/or smoke detectors.
7. The number, type and location of fire-fighting equipment.
8. The provision of fire exit signs.
9. Requirements for training employees, especially new members of staff.
10. Conduct fire drills, testing alarms and maintenance of fire-fighting equipment.
11. Introduction and dissemination of fire evacuation procedures.

Once issued, to comply with the Act, the certificate (or copy of it) must be kept on the premises and a record must be kept of all fire practices, training of staff and maintenance of equipment.

16.4 PEOPLE AND THE LAW

In order to simplify the presentation of information, one must categorize caterers' legal obligations to people as follows:

to staff
to customers
to the world at large e.g. neighbours, tradespeople, suppliers etc.

Health and safety

At common law there exists a common duty of care, that is to say employers owe it to their employees to take reasonable care for their safety, and likewise the occupier of premises owes a duty to persons invited or permitted to be on the premises. Thus employees, guests, clients or tradespeople if injured on a caterer's premises due to the negligence of the caterer, may sue for damages. It is said to be negligence if

1. There is a breach of the common-law duty of care, e.g. premises (which might include the car park outside) are in a poor state of repair *or*
2. There is a breach of a duty imposed by statute, e.g. failing to guard a piece of machinery specified as dangerous under the Offices, Shops and Railway Premises Act.

RIGHT OF ENTRY INTO PREMISES

The following persons may enter catering premises under the stated circumstances.

1. Local authority

Inspectors may enter any building exceeding two storeys in height which is used as an inn, hotel, boarding house, or restaurant (which also has sleeping accommodation in the same premises) in order to inspect the adequacy of the means of escape from fire. Under the Health and Safety at Work Act 1974 and the Offices, Shops and Railway Premises Act 1963 an inspector may enter premises at any reasonable time for the purpose of carrying out inspection and enforcement of the law.

2. Police

May enter a late-night refreshment house, i.e. an all-night café open at any time between 10 p.m. and 5 a.m. and since January 1983 any public house. They are under no obligation to give their reasons for demanding entry, and can enter any premises if invited to do so, or if they have a search warrant naming the premises.

EXCLUSION OF PERSONS FROM PREMISES

The following circumstances allow a caterer or licensee to exclude persons from premises. Under the Licensed Premises (Exclusion of Certain Persons) Act 1980 a licensee can prohibit from his/her premises a person against whom a court has made an exclusion order. Under s. 174 of the Licensing Act 1964, a licensee has the right to refuse admission (or expel) any person who is drunken, violent, quarrelsome or disorderly. In order to expel such a person who refuses to leave, the assistance of a police constable must be sought.

OBLIGATION TO SERVE CUSTOMERS

An innkeeper under the Hotel Proprietors Act 1954 must provide food and drink to *any* traveller who appears willing and able to pay. The refreshment must be appropriate for the time of day, e.g. late at night, a sandwich and a glass of milk would be adequate.

RIGHT OF REFUSAL TO SERVE CUSTOMERS

Under the Hotel Proprietors Act 1954, innkeepers are relieved of their obligations if the customer is not in a fit state to be received or appears to be unable to pay. Under the Licensing Act 1964 it is an offence for the holder of a licence to sell intoxicating liquor to a drunken person or a person under the age of 18. Licence holders also have the right to refuse to serve anyone if they so wish.

Furthermore the caterer is subject to four pieces of legislation:

(1) Health and Safety at Work Act 1974

Under this Act an employer is criminally liable for the health, safety and welfare at work of employees and has a general duty to conduct their undertakings in such a way as to ensure that members of the general public are not needlessly exposed to risk to their health and safety. This makes negligence a criminal office as well as a civil duty.

(2) Occupiers' Liability Act 1957

This Act has codified the common duty of care, and applies to all bona fide 'visitors' to the premises. For instance, negligence may be the case if a customer is injured in a fall due to a loose carpet fitting or a guest suffers burns from faulty electrical wiring, a delivering trader slips on a wet floor. The only two exceptions to this are (1) 'that a person in the exercise of his calling, will appreciate and guard against any special risks ordinarily incident to it, so far as the occupier leaves him free to do so'. For instance, an electrician may be presumed to know to switch off the supply at the mains before rewiring. (2) That an occupier cannot be held responsible for injuries resulting from the faulty work of an independent contractor, so long as the occupier is satisfied that the contractor is competent—for instance if a person was injured by a window clean-er's bucket, the window cleaner would be liable if recognizably employed in a window cleaning organization, whereas, the occupier would be liable if the occupier had paid someone to do the job as a holiday job.

Generally speaking an occupier cannot be liable for any injury to a person who has not been invited onto the premises or who are in a part of the building clearly identified as 'out of bounds'. For instance, a notice on doors stating 'staff only' or 'keep out' may suffice. However, the Act continues that the owner or occupier 'must be prepared for children to be less careful than adults', so that a notice may not be enough. Thus in the case of *Penett v. McGuiness & Co Ltd*, it was ruled 'that even if children are trespassers, precautions must be taken if the activity is going on in a place where it could be anticipated that children might come'.

(3) Employers' Liability (Compulsory Insurance) Act 1969

Nowadays, an employer must insure against civil liability for damages arising out of personal injury sustained by employees (who are not members of her/his family) and she/he would be wise to do the same with regard to public liabilities, although she or

Statutory Notices and Recommended Notices
The caterer is obliged to display certain notices on premises. These include the following:

Please wash your hands

Under Regulation 16 of the Food Hygiene Regulations a notice such as this should be placed on the inside door of every toilet used by staff engaged in handling food (cooks, chefs, waiters, kitchen porters, still-room attendants, storekeepers, etc.)

NO SMOKING

Although not obligatory, the employer must take steps to prevent staff contravening Regulation 10(e) of the Food Hygiene Regulations.

See the Price Marking (Food and Drink on Premises) Order 1979.

Under the Weights and Measures Act 1963 a notice stating the measure used in serving gin, whisky, rum and vodka must be displayed in a conspicuous place, usually behind the bar. Likewise under the 1976 amendment to the Act, a notice concerning the quantities in which wine is sold (either 25 cl, 50 cl, 75 cl or 1 litre) must be displayed.

Schedule C

Under the Young Persons (Employment) Act 1938 an abstract of the relevant provisions, as outlined in Schedule C of the Young Persons (Employment) Order, must be displayed.

Under the Wages Councils Act all employers must display a copy of the wages order in a prominent position where all the workers affected can read it.

Figure 16.1 *Some notices and their legal implications.*

he is not required to do so. Under the Act '. . . every employer carrying on any business in Great Britain shall insure under one or more approved policies with an authorized insurer against liability for bodily injury or disease sustained by his employees and arising out of and in the course of their employment . . .' The policy document must be made available for inspection by the Health and Safety Executive.

Under the Shops Act 1950 the working hours and condition of employment of persons employed about the business of a shop are regulated. This includes catering business and public houses, so to avoid the restrictions on working hours that would be unworkable in the catering industry, caterers can adopt the so-called 'Catering Trade Scheme'. If they do so, the Shops Regulation 1913 must be displayed.

OFFICES SHOPS and RAILWAY PREMISES ACT

Under this Act a poster or booklet of the main points of the Act must be displayed in any premises to which the Act applies.

Hotel Proprietors Act 1956 allows the liability for loss or damage to guests' property to be restricted to £50 (or £100 for more than one article) if the appropriate notice is displayed.

Certificate of Insurance

The Employers' Liability (Compulsory Insurance) Act 1969 states that a copy of the certificate of insurance must be displayed so as to be easily read by employees.

The position of these signs will be laid down by the fire authority in the fire certificate for the premises.

Such a notice does not 'exclude or restrict a caterer's or publican's liability for death or personal injury resulting from negligence' under the Unfair Contract Terms Act 1977 (s.2 (1)).

Figure 16.1 *Some notices and their legal implications (continued).*

(4) Notification of Accidents and Dangerous Occurrences Regulations 1980

In the event of accidents, caterers are subject to these regulations and must notify and report any accident arising out of the manner in which their business is conducted which either results in:

1. The death of, or major injury (e.g. fracture, amputation, loss of sight or pro-
    longed hospitalization) to, *any* person; *or*
2. The case of an employee at work, in his or her being incapacitated with regard to
    work for more than three days, excluding rest days and the day of the accident.

In the event of (1), the local authority's Health and Safety Inspector must be informed
immediately, i.e. by telephone and a report using form F2508 must be sent within
seven days. In the event of either (1) or (2), a record must be kept, usually in an accident book. Details that must be recorded include:

Full name, address and occupation of injured person.
Date and time of the accident.
Place where the accident happened.
Cause and nature of the injury.
Name, address and occupation of the person giving notice, if other than the injured
person.

This must then be signed by the person noting the entry. The book must be kept for
three years from the date of the last entry.

Case study 16.2   Campbell v. Shelbourne Hotel (1939)

At 11.20 p.m. Campbell left his room to go to the toilet. Along an unlit passage, the
guest fell down some stairs. The Court of Appeal determined that it was reasonable at
that hour for corridors to be lit, if there was the possibility that a guest might use the
corridor.

Case study 16.3   Wood v. Moreland (1971)

In January 1968, Mr Wood broke his leg as he left the Caversham Bridge Hotel at 1
a.m. following a dinner dance. He slipped on the ice and frost on the forecourt but
there was no suggestion that he had contributed to the negligence, for instance by
drinking too much. However, the court determined that it was unreasonable to expect
the management of the hotel to make efforts to clear the forecourt under adverse
weather conditions at that hour of the morning.

Task 16.1

Discuss the following cases and determine if the *caterer* would be liable for damages:

1. The greengrocer is delivering supplies of fruit and vegetables and slips on a wet
    patch of floor in the corridor leading to the stores. She breaks her leg.
2. The window cleaner who regularly cleans the unit's windows is washing the first-
    floor windows when he drops his bucket onto the head of a guest, injuring him.
3. A band has been hired by the organizers of a function. They arrive and set up
    their own equipment but during their performance the bass guitarist receives an
    electric shock.
4. A waiter in the restaurant spills soup on a guest, which results in a nasty scald.

Law of contract

A contract may be defined as a 'legally binding agreement between two parties'. In most cases the contract between the customer and the restaurant is a verbal one, but is no less legally binding on both parties. The most essential concepts with regard to entering a contract are 'offer' and 'acceptance'. A contract is entered into when one party agrees to the terms of an offer made by the other party. This may be the case in two clearly identifiable situations:

1. Table reservations. In this instance, the customer is usually the 'offerer' because he or she is stating the precise terms upon which the contract is to be made, i.e. a table at a certain time for a certain number of people. If the reservation cannot be made at that time and the restaurant suggests an alternative time or date, then the restaurateur becomes the offerer. In either case, the other party need only agree to the offer for there to be a contract in existence. A breach of contract occurs if either party then fails to comply with the terms of the contract; for instance if there is no table available at the time stipulated, or the customer fails to arrive at the correct time. Of course it is extremly unlikely (in the majority of cases) that any action will be taken by either party in the event of a breach of contract. It is bad public relations for a restaurant to sue its customers under such circumstances, whilst the public in Britain do not generally use litigation. Essentially however, the restaurateur is only *legally* obliged to keep a table available for the stipulated number of people at the stipulated time. If people arrive even one minute late, it is they who are in breach of contract and the restaurateur is no longer obliged to have the table reserved.

2. Chance customers. Now that by law, full details of menus and prices must be made available for viewing before a customer enters the establishment, it seems likely that this is regarded as an offer. Upon entering a restaurant and ordering a meal, the customer is accepting this implicit offer. As before, a breach of contract occurs if either party fails to keep to the terms of that contract. In this respect, customers are legally entitled to refuse to pay the bill if they believe that the food and/or service have not been up to the standard expected. In such a case, so long as the customers provide the restaurateur with proof of identity and home address, they cannot be restrained or accused of attempted or actual fraud. A restaurateur wishing to recover the sum would have to sue the customers for breach of contract, i.e. failing to pay the bill, and presumably the customers would offer the defence that, since the restaurant was in breach of contract in the first place for failing to provide the product or service expected, then there was no longer any binding contract between them.

It should be noted that a contract cannot be made with a minor (someone under the age of 18) unless it is for 'goods and services suitable to the minor's needs, and his station in life'. In this respect therefore, one should realize that one may be unable to sue a minor for failure to pay the bill since it will depend upon whether the meal in question was regarded as a 'necessity' and whether the minor could afford to pay.

Finally there are two main reasons why the failure of one of the parties to fulfil the terms of the contract will *NOT* constitute a breach of contract:

(1) Misrepresentation

If one of the parties is induced to enter the contract by false statements, then they are not obliged to continue with the contract, or if they do continue, they may claim damages for the disappointment caused (see also the Trades Description Act).

(2) Frustration

If either of the parties is unable to meet the terms of the contract due to unforeseen circumstances, then no breach is said to have taken place; for instance, if illness prevented a customer coming to the restaurant, or if the restaurant was accidentally burnt down.

Discrimination

The 1970s saw the enactment of legislation with regard to discrimination against persons on grounds of sex or race, namely the Sex Discrimination Act 1975, and the Race Relations Act 1976. Both Acts are very similar in intent and identify three forms of discrimination.

(1) Direct discrimination

This occurs when a person is treated less favourably because of sex, colour, race, nationality or ethnic origin. Examples of this include refusing to interview female or black applicants for vacancies, paying staff less on the grounds of race or sex alone, or refusing to serve customers of a particular sex or race.

(2) Indirect discrimination

Occurs when a person is effectively denied access to employment or consumer services by the imposition of an unjustifiable condition or requirement which places him or her at a disadvantage. Examples include requiring qualifications only obtainable in the UK or specifying a particular age-band for a vacancy that could not justifiably be required (Price and Civil Service Commission).

(3) Victimization

Relates to a person being treated unfavourably by another person who is accused of infringing that person's rights. For example, harassing or sacking a woman who is agitating for improved conditions relative to her male colleagues.

Discrimination with regard to employment:

1. Recruitment. It is unlawful for an employer to publish a job advertisement which clearly discriminates, unless being of a particular sex is a 'genuine occupational qualification'.
2. Selection. Race or sex may not be the basis for selecting personnel.
3. Remuneration. Staff may not lawfully be paid different wages on the basis of ethnic background or sex.

4.   Promotion. Female employees denied opportunities for promotion, transfer or training may also have grounds for claiming discrimination.
5.   Dismissal. An employee dismissed on racial grounds may present a complaint to an industrial tribunal.

Discrimination with regard to the provision of goods, facilities and services.

1.   Refusal of provision. The operator of a restaurant, public house, etc. who refuses to admit any guest on the basis of ethnic origins or sex is committing an offence.
2.   Omission of provision. It is equally unlawful to provide a product or facility to ethnic customers markedly inferior to that available to the public in general.

A person contemplating bringing legal proceedings for alleged unlawful discrimination may apply for assistance to the Commission of Racial Equality or the Equal Opportunities Commission depending on the type of discrimination. In the event of discrimination being proved, damages are awarded to the injured party. (Discrimination in the event of unlawful dismissal would be dealt with by an industrial tribunal.)

Employment legislation

The last ten years have seen a tremendous growth in legislation with regard to the employment of staff and industrial relations. In broad terms, this can be subdivided into legislation affecting

1.   Employing staff
2.   Employment conditions
3.   Dismissal

Employing staff

Under the Employment Protection (Consolidation) Act 1978, an employer must provide all full-time employees with written particulars of terms of employment within 13 weeks of starting work. The particulars that must be referred to are these.

1.   Name of the employer and employee.
2.   Date on which employment began.
3.   Job title.
4.   Scale or rate of remuneration, or the method of calculating remuneration.
5.   When wages or salary are to be paid, e.g. weekly, monthly.
6.   Terms and conditions relating to hours of work.
7.   Holiday entitlement.
8.   Sickness terms and conditions, including sick pay.
9.   Pension and pension schemes.
10. Disciplinary rules and grievance procedure, including name of person to whom the employee can apply if dissatisfied.
11. Length of notice.

Employment conditions

Wages. Originally, under the now repealed Truck Acts 1831 to 1940 and more specifically the Payment of Wages Act 1960 which replaced them, all manual workers must be paid in cash, unless the worker has requested payment in some other form, i.e. credit transfer, postal order, cheque or money order. Most catering staff would be regarded as manual workers. Certain sectors of the industry are subject to Wages Council Orders which fix minimum rates of pay, holidays and holiday pay and other terms and conditions.

The three councils are the Unlicensed Place of Refreshment Wages Council, the Licensed Non-Residential Establishment Wages Council and the Licensed Residential Establishment and Licensed Restaurant Wages Council. An employer must not pay less than the minimum rate, allow fewer days' holiday or apply less favourable terms and conditions than are set out in the relevant wages orders, and may be fined if found guilty of an offence.

Time off work. Every employer has the right to expect his or her employees to be at work when required, and to come to work on time, and any employees who absent themselves from work without permission are in breach of contract and could be dismissed. However, an employer must be careful to comply with those procedures laid down in the written particulars of employment and also ensure that such dismissal is not 'unfair'. In addition, certain categories of employee have the right to take time off work

1. With full pay. Pregnant women attending ante-natal care; an employee who is looking for new employment having been given notice of dismissal by reason of redundancy; safety representatives performing their functions or receiving training in such matters; trade-union officials engaged in trade-union business.
2. Without full pay. Trade-union members taking part in trade-union activities; employees engaged in public duties, e.g. school governor or JP.

Dismissal

An employer must have a legitimate reason for dismissing an employee and must also show that she or he acted reasonably in all the circumstances relating to the dismissal. The Employment Protection (Consolidation) Act 1978 identifies seven justifiable reasons for dismissal.

1. Incompetence. This is acceptable grounds for dismissal, but in considering whether or not such dismissal is unfair, an industrial tribunal would consider the length of service of the employee, the provision of training and advice to the employee, the amount of discussion with the employee concerning his shortcomings, and whether or not the employee was offered alternative employment better suited to his capabilities.
2. Ill health. This is grounds for dismissal so long as the employee has exhausted his or her sick pay entitlement; the employer is aware of the nature of the illness and that no recovery is likely in the short-term; the employer has considered the age and length of service of the employee, the employee's status, and the effect the absence has upon the firm.
3. Lack of qualifications. If the employee is not as well-qualified as the employer was led to believe upon appointment, the employee may be dismissed.
4. Misconduct. To some extent, this will depend upon the disciplinary rules and

grievance procedures as laid down in the written particulars of employment. However, the only grounds for instant dismissal are gross misconduct. This would include conduct which would endanger members of the public, cause serious damage to the employer's reputation, fighting or physical assault or serious breach of safety rules. In most instances, however, employees would not be dismissed for a first breach of discipline.

5. Redundancy. So long as the principle of 'last in, first out' is applied and that the employer can prove that the job held by an employee is no longer carried out by another person engaged solely for that purpose, this is a legitimate reason for dismissal.

6. Illegality of continued employment. If by continuing to employ an employee, the employer would be acting illegally, then he or she may fairly dismiss an otherwise satisfactory employee. For instance, a person found to be under the age of 18 working behind the bar in licensed premises must be dismissed if no other suitable work is available.

7. Some other substantial reason. These include dismissal if an employee refuses to accept new working conditions necessitated by business reorganization, clashes of personality, pressure from dissatisfied clients or the need to preserve confidential information.

16.5 LICENSING LAW

Finally, there is one legal matter that clearly applies to all these factors—namely licensing laws—which are granted to premises, specify criteria with regard to the sale of the product and stipulate the people to whom it may be served.

The major piece of legislation concerning the sale or supply of intoxicating liquor is the Licensing Act 1964. Basically, the law deals with four factors:

1. What intoxicating liquor may be sold.
2. Under what circumstances sales take place.
3. When it can be sold.
4. Whom it can be sold to.

Liquor licensing is a locally administered system. The 1964 Act demands that the local licensing justices hold their annual general licensing session in the first fortnight of February, at which they usually review existing licenses and determine permitted hours, and also hold between four and eight sessions during the year, in order to consider applications, transfers and removal of licences. Notice of such meetings is given in the local newspaper and sent to all parties concerned, i.e. licensees, police, applicants and so on.

Types of licence

There are two main types of licence:

1. On-licence. This authorises the sale of intoxicating liquor for consumption either on or off the premises. It prescribes the sale of liquor of *all* descriptions or may

restrict sale to wine only; cider only; beer and cider only; beer, cider and wine only.
2. 'Off-licence'. This authorises sale for consumption off the premises only.

Within the category of 'on-licence', it may be applied to different types of premises:

1. Full on-licence. Usually granted for public houses and proprietary clubs. No restrictions placed upon sale other than those applicable to all licences.
2. Restaurant licence. Obviously granted to catering establishments 'structurally adapted and bona fide used' for providing customers with main meals. Thus intoxicating liquor can only be sold or supplied to persons taking table meals on the premises and as an ancillary to the consumption of food.
3. Residential licence. The type of licence held by hotels, i.e. premises bona fide used for the purpose of providing board (breakfast and one main meal at least) and lodging. Intoxicating liquor may only be supplied to residential guests or their private guests.
4. Residential and restaurant licences, a combination of (2) and (3) above.

The holder of an on-licence may apply for an occasional licence in order to serve intoxicating liquor on premises other than those to which the licence was granted, but if a restaurant or combined licence, the occasional licence will be restricted in the same way as the original licence, and an occasional licence will not be granted to the holder of a residential licence.

Club licensing

There are two types of clubs defined under the 1964 Act, proprietary and registered clubs.

Proprietary clubs are clubs owned and operated as a business for profit by one person or group of people. Such clubs must apply for an 'on-licence' in the usual way, but included in the licence may be conditions concerning membership, club rules and the sale of liquor to non-members.

Registered clubs are clubs owned and operated by the members of the club, such as trade union clubs, rugby clubs and so on. Inasmuch as members, in buying drinks, are contributing to club funds rather than purchasing them in a commercial sense, such clubs do not require a licence but they must hold a registration certificate issued by a Magistrates' Court.

Permitted hours

England and Wales

The permitted hours in licensed premises are:

Metropolitan hours	Weekdays	11.30 a.m. to 11.00 p.m. with a 2½ hour break in the afternoon.
	Sundays*	12.00 noon to 10.30 p.m. with a 5 hour break beginning at 2.00 p.m.

---

* Licensed premises must apply for permission to open on Sundays. Residents of licensed hotels may be supplied intoxicating liquor at any time on any day.

Provincial hours   Weekdays   11.30 a.m. to 10.30 p.m. with a 2 hour break in
                                             the afternoon.
                           Sundays*   as for Metropolitan hours

On Christmas Day and Good Friday, Sunday opening hours must operate. Any licensing district can decide to adopt Metropolitan hours, if they wish, on any weekday. For instance, many large boroughs adopt Metropolitan hours on Fridays and Saturdays.

The licensing magistrates may also modify these permitted hours, so long as the total number of hours do not exceed 9 in the provinces and 9½ in metropolitan areas, and the afternoon break is not less than 2 hours. For instance, some premises may open at 11.00 a.m. and take a 2½ hour break in the afternoon.

Scotland

                         Weekdays   11.30 a.m. to 2.30 p.m.
                                          5.00 p.m. to 11.00 p.m.
                         Sundays*   12.30 p.m. to 2.30 p.m.
                                          6.30 p.m. to 11.00 p.m.

Drinking-up time

Although drink may not be sold outside permitted hours, a person may consume intoxicating liquor:

1. For up to ten minutes after the end of permitted hours; or
2. For 30 minutes after the end of permitted hours if taking a table meal.

Extensions to permitted hours

Depending on the circumstances, these permitted hours may be changed. A restaurant certificate (or supper hour certificate) may be granted for those parts of premises where customers are taking table meals and intoxicating liquor is supplied for consumption with the meal. Intoxicating liquor can be supplied up to 3.00 p.m. (in districts where general licensing hours end before 3.00 p.m.); and/or for one hour after normal evening closing time. An extended hours order may be granted for those premises which are structurally adapted for the purpose of serving meals; used for serving table meals where musical or other entertainment is also provided; or are already in possession of a restaurant certificate. Intoxicating liquor can be supplied until 1.00 a.m. so long as meals and entertainment are provided. A special hours certificate may be granted for those premises which comply with those conditions required to obtain an extended hours order, and have a music and dancing licence. Intoxicating liquor can be supplied then until 2.00 a.m. every weekday (or on a particular weekday) in the provinces; or until 3.00 a.m. in the London metropolitan area; so long as the sale of liquor is ancillary to the service of meals and the customers are there for the entertainment and dancing.

---

* Licensed premises must apply for permission to open on Sundays. Residents of licensed hotels may be supplied intoxicating liquor at any time on any day.

Exemption from permitted hours

General order of exemption. This order permits hours to be added onto normal permitted hours to provide a particular service to persons who may be unable to resort to licensed premises during those normal hours. Such orders are usually granted to premises near public markets. For instance, the pubs near New Covent Garden and Smithfield are open between 2.00 a.m. and 6.00 a.m.

Special order of exemption. This adds hours as for a general order but only for a specific occasion, such as for New Year's Eve celebrations, a dinner dance, and so on.

Restrictions on sale of alcohol

A licensee is committing an offence if he or she knowingly sells, or permits to be sold, intoxicating liquor to a person under 18. The only exception to this is that a person aged 16 or over may purchase beer, cider or perry in a part of the premises usually set aside for meals. Furthermore, no persons under the age of 14 are allowed in the bar of licensed premises unless they are passing through the bar to get to some other part of the building (or is the child of the licensee).

Alcohol must also be served in specific measures:

Beer

Draught beer must either be sold in ½ pint or 1 pint capacity* glasses stamped with the Imperial seal or through metered pumps that dispense exact measures of ½ pint.

Wine

Wine sold in carafes must be sold in quantities of 250 ml, 500 ml, 750 ml, or 1 litre and the licensee is required to state what size carafes are being used.

Spirits

Whisky, gin, rum and vodka must be sold in quantities of one-fourth, one-fifth or one-sixth of a gill or multiples thereof. Whichever of these measures is adopted, the licensee must display a notice to the effect in a prominent position.

16.6 CONCLUSION

It seems likely if present trends continue, that caterers will be subject to further restrictions and legislation with regard to the way in which they may operate. It is not possible for them to be experts on the subject, but it is their legal duty to comply with the

---

* The law also permits sale in quantities of ⅓ pint, although this is never put into practice.

law. The fact that in many instances, through ignorance or circumvention, many catering operations do not meet all the requirements does not mean that compliance is
unnecessary or unimportant. If for no other reason, caterers must be aware that public
relations are the bedrock of their success, so that any criminal or civil proceedings can
quickly and severely undermine the effect of good public relations, not only with customers, but with suppliers, the media and the local community in general. In addition
to which, the system of justice is such that law breakers are penalized, usually by a fine
(or damages) or imprisonment, so that there is no benefit to be gained from not com-
plying with the law.

Exercise

Identify the 'penalty' for the following: unfair dismissal; serving drinks after time;
racial discrimination; failing to maintain the temperature of an office at 20°C (68°F);
and failing to display a menu outside one's premises.

Index